ALSO BY CARL JEROME

The Good Health Microwave Book

The Complete Chicken

Recipes for the Cuisinart Food Processor
(with James Beard)

COOKING FOR A NEW EARTH

More Than 150

Irresistible Recipes to Promote

Wholesome Eating and Healthy Living

CARL JEROME

Henry Holt and Company

New York

To my nieces, Boomer and Bunni

Henry Holt and Company, Inc.
Publishers since 1866
115 West 18th Street
New York, New York 10011

Henry Holt® is a registered
trademark of Henry Holt and Company, Inc.

Published in Canada by Fitzhenry & Whiteside Ltd.,
195 Allstate Parkway, Markham, Ontario L3R 4T8.

Library of Congress Cataloging-in-Publication Data

Jerome, Carl.
Cooking for a new earth: More Than 150 Irresistible Recipes to
Promote Wholesome Eating and Healthy Living / Carl Jerome. —1st ed.
p.   cm.
Includes index.
1. Cookery (Natural foods)   2. Diet.   I. Title.
TX741.J48   1993
641.5'637—dc20   *92-8345*
                                                    CIP

ISBN 0-8050-1996-0
ISBN 0-8050-1995-2 (An Owl Book: pbk.)

Henry Holt books are available for special promotions
and premiums. For details contact: Director, Special Markets.

First published in hardcover in 1993 by
Henry Holt and Company, Inc.

First Owl Book Edition—1994

Designed by Katy Riegel

Printed in the United States of America
All first editions are printed on acid-free paper. ∞

1   3   5   7   9   10   8   6   4   2
1   3   5   7   9   10   8   6   4   2
(pbk.)

Contents

Contents

Acknowledgments

Thanks to Nicholas Valenziano, and my friend and agent, Sam Mitnick, for making this book possible.

For their support and ideas, my thanks to Ann Banville, John Bolton, Marian Burros, Linda Calafiore, Wayne and Maggie Callaway, Elizabeth Crossman, Marion Cunningham, Terry Dale, James Eaton, Mark Facklam, Robert Galano, David Goldstein, Ellen Haas, Jill Kasle, Karen MacNeil, Allen Rosenfeld, Michael Such, Nabuyuki Takakura, Jerry Wager, Catherine Whitney, and Jeff Wilson.

1

American Food, 1967–1992: From Counterculture to Mainstream

Although the generation that fought for civil rights, protested the war in Vietnam, tripped at Woodstock, and marched in Atlanta is now saddled with mortgages and bulging waistlines, this generation never lost sight of the values of its youth as it assimilated into the mainstream culture.

The youth of the 1960s—there were 76 million members of this group, more than any other previous generation in U.S. history—had grown up in a world radically different from that of their parents. As they became old enough and educated enough to articulate a response to their environment, America was confronted with more than a generation gap, more than an identity crisis. For by the early 1960s, the hip generation had become a counterculture. They were not dropouts, like the beatniks before them; they were activists, whose values and beliefs would eventually meld into, and ultimately redefine, the broader culture.

America's post–World War II development into a megatechnological society required that individuals turn off their emotions and shut down their senses. Television sitcoms and their commercials promoted this shutdown, while television news, ironically, promoted a global and interpersonal sensitivity that made it impossible for the youth of the 1960s to become emotively shut down, either to themselves or to the world around them.

Confronted with this contradiction, the youth of this generation demanded change. It wasn't necessary to define where this change would lead, for fundamental to these people was the belief that there was more to a right way of doing things than a set of rules to define what was to be done. When they failed to effect the broad social changes they had demanded through civil rights sit-ins and antiwar marches, they stopped trying to change the world, and instead demanded a change in themselves. What they sought was a personal change in consciousness, a new "self," in which one would be aware of oneself as a perceptive, concerned, and sensual being. They yearned for a society where blood and soil, earth and air, mankind and the environment, were one.

This need for a simpler life did not seem possible within the traditional culture, and so the counterculturists turned to group houses and communes, and to food. For it was in small-scale communal living and healthy eating that they believed they would find their new Utopia.

These pioneers established group houses and communes in an attempt to recapture tribal (family) values; they developed food co-ops in a search for safer, healthier foods; and they experimented with drugs and meditation in their search for peace and holism. They started the ecology movement on one level to provide themselves with healthy food, and on another to protest the destruction of the planet, both here and in Southeast Asia.

Although by the mid-1970s most of the group houses and communes had disintegrated, the members of the counterculture had settled upon the one element in their lives over which they had absolute control, the only element that was at the same time personal and global. They focused on food. In a sick world, they believed that they could be healthy if they ate properly. And eating right was more than just eating food that was good for them; for to this group, food could not be separated from the ecology of the planet. Food was the wave on which they would ride to a simpler life, return to more basic values.

In the early nineteenth century, most of America was family-oriented and farm-centered. Meals were a direct result of family effort. By the late nineteenth century, in large part as a result of the expansion of the railroads, the distance between field and table had grown radically, and new foods, like grapefruits and pineapples, were becoming available. Americans—fascinated by these new, expensive, perishable foods, to which they felt no connection—tried to take control of these new foods by canning and preserving them, stopping deterioration and extending shelf life. The burgeoning food processing industry at the turn of the century soon had cans of every conceivable fruit and vegetable on market shelves. Industrialization had started to displace the family farm. America had begun its technocratic, schizophrenic relationship with food, and Americans would soon be transformed into uniform, nonsensory machines whose gastronomic and nutritional needs could be met by standardized, prepackaged foods.

In order to successfully standardize the food inside cans and packages to make it dependable, the modern food producing industry, as it grew in this century, and most especially after 1940, homogenized the taste of its products (no longer were they even called foods), and introduced packaging designed to prevent the consumer from using his or her senses in making food choices. In the past, one could squeeze the sides, press on the bottom edge, tug at the leaves, and smell a fresh pineapple to determine if it was ripe, but all one could do with canned pineapple was to pick the can based on the visual appeal of its label.

The appeal of technocratic food is to the head. Rich food, gourmet food, fast food, convenience food, that's the food of the technocracy, and its appeal is to the secondary characteristics of food, not to the primary senses of touch, taste, and smell that are essential in finding real pleasure in eating. "Rich foods" and "gourmet foods," two of the worst felons, promote the use of expensive ingredients, appealing less to the senses than to economics and upward mobility. Indeed, the success of the modern food industry was dependent on convincing consumers not to acknowledge their senses or the flow of the seasons. This was precisely what the counterculture objected to.

The food industry's strategy was twofold. It had to prevail over nature to create the standardized, ever-ready foodstuffs it required (enter large-scale, chemical-dependent agribusiness) and at the same time, it had to standardize consumer expectations and definitions of food to make these products acceptable.

Already indifferent to conventional values, which were symbolically represented by processed food, members of the counterculture established a motley network of anti-establishment food co-ops where pesticide-free and unrefined foods were available, foods that appealed to the basic senses and that recognized seasonal and regional limitations. Although the counterculturists were somewhat unclear about what they did want, they were very clear about what they did not want; they did not want Wonder Bread. America was a country that bleached its food, and they set out to change that.

Convenience foods, wrapped in plastic or cellophane, cans, and cardboard boxes, devoid of aromas and taste, were the symbols of technology at the expense of the spirit. This was food as fuel. It viewed the body as a machine that was to be fueled up for work, and refueled when empty. This was food without taste, food that exploited the environment.

Not only was this food unacceptable, but the entire system that had brought it to market was unacceptable. Healthy bodies would be built by a return to the values of the earth, to the purity and simplicity of the garden, to nuts and seeds, not by white bread. Thus food, which had become central to the counterculture in the 1970s, was linked to ecology, and the exploitation of the environment.

Just as they had experimented with drugs and sex, this generation experimented with food. Anything processed (thus symbolizing a society in decay) was rejected. Experimentation was the byword. Breads were whole grain and homemade. Seeds—how much closer could you get to nature than seeds?—were scattered over everything from breakfast cereals to desserts. Cheese replaced meat.

By changing the way they ate, this generation believed they could change themselves into sensual, sensitive individuals, and that process, it was hoped, would change the world. Counterculture food, as cooked and served at California group houses in Berkeley and the Haight Ashbury, and at communes from Oregon to Woodstock, tried to be respectful of both the health of the body and the health of the planet. Anything complex, anything one couldn't pronounce, and especially anything chemical, was to be avoided.

For this generation, processed foods symbolized a sick society; natural foods symbolized health in the new Utopia. The rule of thumb was to eat "lower on the food chain." The closer to the original source of the food, the less likely it was to be contaminated. Best of all was growing your own food, next best were "natural" foods sold in counterculture co-ops or health food stores.

As they left the mainstream, counterculturists established agrarian communes (3.5 million members of this generation experimented with communal life), food co-ops, and hip restaurants, to provide themselves with a new, safe, healthy food supply. Most members of the movement, however, never made it to communes. Their food values were shaped by those who had, by media coverage of them, and by a small handful of counterculture cookbooks. Those who assimilated into the broader culture tried to balance their ideals with their need to enter the mainstream and take jobs, and to balance their eating with the practical demands of everyday life. Those that had gardens tried to grow some of their own food, but even this proved futile for most. By the mid to late 1970s, all that seemed to be left of their back-to-nature efforts was the tiny satisfaction of sprouting their own mung beans and culturing their own yogurt, and a few cookbooks that embodied their values.

The chief difference between traditional cookbooks and counterculture cookbooks of the 1970s was that the latter were, in a quite literal sense, life-style books. They advocated a new way of living, with food as the vehicle. They were not simple procedural manuals for kitchen operation.

Frances Moore Lappé's *Diet for a Small Planet*, published in 1971, was a major cookbook that embodied the holistic principles of the movement: health, vegetarianism, and ecology. Lappé stressed the ecological and environmental value of vegetarianism by explaining that it took sixteen pounds of cereals and grains, fed to an animal, to produce one pound of meat. Because sixteen pounds of cereals and grains were enough for thirty-two meals, whereas one pound of meat would barely make two meals, Lappé reasoned that eating meat was unsound, and that it was promoting a wasteful use of our food supply and encouraging world famine. Through her advocacy of vegetarianism, Lappé hoped to save the planet. Simplistic as her reasoning was, *Diet for a Small Planet* had an enormous impact on the counterculture in the early 1970s.

In 1972, just a year later, Anna Thomas wrote *Vegetarian Epicure*, a homey-looking book with a nostalgic bent. Though decidedly less important than Lappé's book, *Vegetarian Epicure* contained in its introduction one of the underlying principles of counterculture vegetarianism: "Good food is a celebration of life, and it seems absurd to me that in celebrating life we should take life. . . . Certainly we don't have to kill to nourish ourselves."

In 1976, with the publication of *Laurel's Kitchen*, the counterculture had its most complete and meaningful treatise on food. The return to the purity of the garden and the simple life based on simple values was powerfully and emotively embodied in the extensive introduction to this book. Laurel Robertson (with co-authors Carol Flinders and Bronwen Godfrey) begins by declaring her allegiance to Lappé's principle, but then extends that into a philosophy that includes everything from radical feminism to child rearing. She ties wasting food (even half-eaten

5

apples) in the kitchen to the destruction of the planet. She promotes meditation and Eastern philosophy as a way of finding spiritual peace in the face of the heavy demands of modern life. And she advocates an abandonment of modern appliances in favor of the traditional hands-on method of doing things.

Laurel's Kitchen was full of recipes like Soy Burgers, made with soy pulp, brown rice, cheese, and ground seeds bound with whole wheat flour and eggs, and Neat Balls made with bulgur, soy pulp, and cottage cheese bound with whole wheat bread crumbs. The authors were vegetarians, but they were still protein- or meat-centered in their thinking, rather than carbohydrate- and fiber-centered as vegetarians ideally would have been. This apparent contradiction was acceptable because its advocates, by the mid-1970s, had grown to see vegetarianism as a process, not a strict code of meatless eating. Many had eliminated red meat from their diets, but ate fish and chicken, and still considered themselves vegetarians. This was a generation who refused to be caught in a Catch-22.

Laurel's Kitchen propagandized a belief system, it was preaching to the converted, and it quickly became a counterculture culinary bible and a best-seller. And as densely packed nutritionally as the recipes in *Laurel's Kitchen* may have been, not many people, even in the counterculture, were going to find Neat Balls appealing or satisfying for very long.

But there were other spiritual siblings who did understand taste. Alice Waters was one of them, and ultimately she became the flag carrier for much of the movement as it entered the mainstream. She would add the dimension of good taste to counterculture food. The food served in her restaurant in Berkeley, Chez Panisse, embodied the values of this generation. It was homey in atmosphere and simple, natural, and fresh. Eventually, Chez Panisse would either grow or supervise the growing of most of the food it used. Its menu was experimental and seasonal. In the kitchen, like Laurel Robertson, Waters believed in doing as much as possible by hand. There was something satisfying and loving about making a dough by hand that simply couldn't be achieved with electric mixers and dough hooks.

As Waters had discovered when she opened Chez Panisse, it was one thing not to want to eat processed foods, or foods coated with chemicals. But that didn't tell you what to eat. Ultimately, Waters's palate and aesthetic discernment would guide this generation as it developed its culinary sensibilities.

By the mid-1970s, counterculture advocates had discovered that denial and ideals were not enough to maintain a life-style. Group houses, communes, and food co-ops had failed to provide lasting satisfaction. While this generation was accepting its failures and shortcomings and becoming part of the mainstream, mainstream agribusiness and the food producers quickly learned to capitalize on this new market by exploiting its values as Warren Belasco points out in *Appetite for Change: How the Counterculture Took on the Food Industry*. This rationale for explaining how this generation viewed food formed the basis for many of the ideas in this introduction.

THE REPACKAGING OF THE COUNTERCULTURE'S FOOD CONCEPTS

"Organic" as "Fresh"

Repackaging "organic" as "fresh" was one response by the food industry. Fresh produce sections expanded rapidly in supermarkets in the 1970s. Food was displayed more attractively, and more fresh foods were offered in an attempt to appeal to this now upscale market and to deflect buyers' attention away from their more serious concerns about agribusiness and pesticides. The illusion of freshness was so great that the cry for "organic" was overshadowed.

"Natural Foods"

The food industry also responded to the "natural" foods concept of the counterculture. "Natural" had been a loosely conceived state of mind in the counterculture. Now, in the hands of food manufacturers, "natural" was used to repackage old foods and to give them a new commercial appeal. Everywhere the hip generation turned in the 1970s, there would be molecularly reformulated or chemically contrived foods boldly labeled "natural."

The food industry's most obvious response to the idea of natural food was in the breakfast arena. Breakfast cereals were fortified and enriched with chemical vitamins, and were marketed for their seemingly "natural" nutrient value. To make these products seem simpler and closer to the earth, and so more natural, the food industry shifted its marketing emphasis. Rather than pitching the cereals for their sweetness (sugar content), cereals were marketed for their shape and texture, and for particular elements of their content. What, after all, could be more natural than a flake of corn or a speck of oat bran, or more natural than the crunchy wholesomeness of nuts and grains?

Other elements in the food establishment also responded to the new need for "natural." In restaurants, design changes were made to accommodate the new sensibility. Oak tables, hanging plants, and shingled walls reminiscent of bungalows were used to add an illusion of naturalness, of simpler times. Cookbook authors responded to this new sensibility by adding life-style elements and reminiscences of older, simple days of cooking to their books. Mainstream cookbooks became more personal and reflective, though they stopped far short of advocating anything like a new life-style.

"Health Foods" as "Light Foods"

By the 1980s, as the public lost its interest in the dangers of chemicals and became concerned with its waistlines, "health foods" became "diet foods," and "diet foods" rapidly became "light foods."

"Light" could mean almost anything. "Light" could be reduced in calories, or reduced in fat, or reduced in salt, or reduced in sugar, or reduced in alcohol. And because "light" was not technically a nutritional claim, government regulations did not require the food industry to define what was light about a product on the label.

One of the ironic contradictions in the light foods movement was that light led to gluttony. Now that previously unhealthy snacks and sodas were light and healthy, it seemed, you could eat them with abandon, and Americans did, downing bag after bag of this new "light" food. If a few light potato chips were healthy, what could be unhealthy about eating lots of them?

While the food industry was having a field day with "light," as Belasco points out, it discovered that ethnic or regional foods were perceived by the now mostly assimilated counterculture as somehow older and simpler, and thus healthier. Ethnic and regional foods implied real people, real places, and old-fashioned, honest values. While it was true that older cooking styles were generally higher in fiber and complex carbohydrates, and lower in meats and fats, the new ethnic and regional specialties that appeared in supermarket freezers and on the menus of fast food restaurants were not. These foods were carefully homogenized and packaged so that they were easy to understand, easy to swallow, and convenient. Forget the salted plums and miso of macrobiotic days; enter pizza and pasta, tacos and enchiladas.

The apparent contradiction between the desire for light on the one hand and for heavy ethnic/regional on the other hand was not as obvious as one might think, for both were perceived, albeit for very different reasons, as healthy.

The regional and ethnic shift in eating led to the rapid proliferation of regional and nostalgic American restaurants, serving up everything from local esoterica, such as geoduck fritters (in the Pacific Northwest) to utter nostalgia, such as meatloaf and lumpy mashed potatoes, and from spa cuisine on the East Coast to the highly decorative *nouvelle* or California cuisine on the West Coast. Many of these new restaurants were owned or operated by members of the counterculture, and restaurant food was becoming fresher and distinctly more colorful (a remnant of the drug experience?).

In their search for freshness, the new chefs of the 1980s looked to nearby farms for produce, and began featuring seasonal foods from local farmers. This trend, along with a heightened consumer interest in regional foods, led to farmers' markets appearing throughout the country. They had become the mainstream answer to the counterculture's now mostly defunct network of food co-ops.

Although attention seemingly had been deflected away from "organic" food, the farm crisis of the 1980s, along with the increasing interest of counterculture chefs in local, seasonal foods, led to a major reevaluation of traditional agriculture. The USDA, state departments of agriculture, and curriculums at most state universities recognized a need to return to "organic" food production, and some politicians and economists went so far as to suggest small-scale organic farming as a solution to the farm crisis in the Midwest and Texas.

By the mid-1980s, the counterculture's loosely formed idea of a politically correct food supply had become a part of mainstream agricultural thinking. Its ideas about natural foods had been distorted and perverted, but that seemed somewhat unimportant, because during the late 1980s a new element entered its thinking, and "health" changed from "light" into "nutrition."

"Light" as "Nutrition"

Nutritional science had little to offer the counterculture between 1967 and 1977. During the 1960s and 1970s, it had enmeshed itself in research on the relationship of diet to chronic diseases in preparation for the establishment of national dietary guidelines.

In 1977, the Senate Select Subcommittee on Dietary Goals for Americans, chaired by George McGovern, published a report recommending a high carbohydrate diet with restrictions on fat, salt, eggs, high-fat dairy products, and sugar. Barely off the presses, the report came under massive attack from the "food establishment," which at the time was reaping large profits from their new lines of sodium-saturated, lipid-laden "natural" and "light" products.

Counterculturists looked upon the McGovern report with favor, because it seemed to provide a real definition of "healthy" eating, something previously missing; that lack had made it all too easy for health consciousness to be exploited by the food establishment. But they also regarded the report with some skepticism.

One reason for the skepticism was the food-as-fuel man-as-machine attitude toward health inherent in the report. To be healthy, the report implied, all you had to do was to balance your fuel intake better. But to counterculture thinking, health was more than just the proper maintenance of the body-machine. Health was a state of being, and *being* healthy, in this counterculture's holistic way of thinking, meant, at the very least, being healthy spiritually as well as physically. Another reason for skepticism about the McGovern report was that the source (the government) was distrusted, even if the information was very likely valid.

In 1980, just three years after the McGovern report, the consensus of scientific opinion about the relationship of diet to health was so overwhelming that the first edition of the *Dietary Guidelines for Americans* (a watered-down reiteration of the McGovern committee findings), was published jointly by the Departments of Agriculture and Health and Human Services.

Finally, in December of 1989 the National Research Council/National Academy of Sciences issued its report, *Diet and Health, Implications for Reducing Chronic Disease.* That 1,400-page report methodically sifted through more than thirty years of nutritional research to conclude irrefutably that we should be eating a diet rich in cereals, grains, vegetables, and fruits, and low in fat and salt.

CONFUSION SLOWS CHANGE

Why, one might ask, given all that we have heard and read about health and nutrition, have most Americans been slow to change?

Eating is a daily event laden with complex and often contradictory social and emotional meanings. You are, after all, what you eat. Emotions, as well as ethnic, regional, and socioeconomic backgrounds, play a role in determining food choices, and these work both for and against making healthy choices.

Flaunting hard-guts bravado, for example, some people enjoy appearing indifferent to health dangers. Less conspicuously rebellious, and perhaps more pervasive, is the feeling that healthy food tastes bad. In addition, many people still separate food from nutrition—food should taste good, while nutrition is good for you but isn't much fun. For good taste, Americans have been conditioned to favor consistency, crisp (fatty) textures, salt, and sugar. Nutrition, however, is associated with foul-tasting pills and with foods with the texture of wet cardboard.

Compounding the problem is considerable confusion about what is good for you. To the average American, who only vaguely understands health and nutrition, it seems that just about everything causes cancer or heart disease. Even worse, it seems that the experts are constantly changing their minds—so why bother at all?

Take cholesterol, for example. First we were told that we needed to keep our cholesterol within certain safe limits. Next we were told that those "safe limits" were no longer safe, and that they were going to be changed, even though there was considerable debate over how great the change should be. Next we were told that there was good cholesterol and bad cholesterol. Then we were told that cholesterol wasn't as bad as saturated fat because saturated fat had a greater cholesterol-raising effect than cholesterol itself. Next we learned that eating fatty cold-water fish would help lower our cholesterol. Then we discovered that eating those fish was dangerous because they had been contaminated with mercury.

No nutritional recommendation, it seemed, had a shelf life of more than a few months. So you're doomed if you do, and doomed if you don't.

Actually, the experts have been more consistent than it appears, and they have been totally consistent about the prime directive of modern nutrition: Significantly reduce total fat intake. The apparent inconsistencies come from the things nutritionists are either just beginning to understand thoroughly, such as cholesterol, or from things nutritionists don't know much about yet, such as all the chemicals that have recently found their way into our food.

GENDER AND CLASS VARIABLES

Other factors also enter the healthy choice picture. On the whole, men tend to be less health-conscious than women. Moreover, in many working-class and ethnic subcultures, women subordinate their own nutritional concerns to the tastes of their husbands and children.

In addition, as sociologists have pointed out, the poor are less likely to defer gratification than the affluent—less likely to eat a bean soup instead of sirloin steak—because of their more pessimistic appraisal of the future. And people from lower socioeconomic backgrounds tend to prefer foods that show they're better off, such as refined sugar (long a symbol of the "sweet" life), fats (as in "fat cat" and "fat of the land"), and large portions of meat.

The most obvious class variable is price. Healthy food is generally more expensive than the supermarket variety, and so is less accessible to those with lower incomes. But the reasons for this higher cost are not so obvious. Why, after all, should a locally grown organic tomato cost more than a tomato raised in chemically treated soil, sprayed with fungicides, wrapped in protective plastic and cellophane, and shipped in from Mexico?

Part of the answer is that healthy food supplies have not kept up with growing demand. More important, however, is the fact that our supposedly inexpensive standard food does not begin to reflect the full social, medical, and ecological costs of its production: the damage to the soil, groundwater, and farm workers; the damage to rural culture as family farmers and supportive small towns lose out to corporate growers with no local ties; and the drain on the federal budget from massive price supports. Without government irrigation subsidies, a pint of California strawberries might cost $12. Granted, the USDA is rethinking its policies that encourage use of fertilizers and pesticides, and the government is rethinking its water subsidies. But in the meantime, American standard foods seem cheaper because none of the hidden costs are reflected in the shelf price.

In support of this class/price differential, surveys show that the affluent, more than the lower socioeconomic classes, do read food labels, worry about pesticides, buy exercise machines, count calories, order fish instead of steaks, smoke less, and buy natural foods. To be sure, not every upper-middle-class American is a "healthy gourmet," but most of them seem at least partly aware of health trends and appear to be trying to adapt.

TODAY'S HEALTHY GOURMET

Today's healthy gourmet is trying to eat by the lean and green formula. Small portions limit calories—the principle that has made frozen diet entrées such a growth industry for food producers. To keep cardiologists happy, today's healthy gourmet uses olive oil, yogurt, and lime juice to replace butter, cream, and salt. Expensive free-range chickens and "designer" beef, which have less fat, antibiotics, and hormones than their standard cultural counterparts—and which may be produced under better conditions—replace traditional meats. Expensive local produce, which is seasonal, regional, and often organically grown, replaces supermarket produce. In short, today's healthy gourmet food tries to be light, not just on the body but also on the environment.

What this new healthy gourmet food lacks in bulk it makes up in aesthetic density: a concentrated clash of textures, flavors, and styles. This is adventurous culinary jet-setting, with dishes leaping continents in a single bound. This is not authentic ethnic or regional fare, with its steamy street vendors, greasy finger foods, and one-pot camaraderie. Nor is it populist fare, as in the steak and cheese subs of Philadelphia lunch counters. Rather, this is a quieter and cooler new fare. What makes this new food "gourmet" is its sense of having distanced itself from populist foods, as well as its self-consciousness and tastefulness. Unfortunately, it is often self-conscious and all too aware of its own political correctness.

13

To some extent, this expensive new gourmet food has helped to reduce the uncertainty and confusion about which foods are good for us. Ultimately, however, with its dizzying and disjointed array of historical, geographical, and cultural references, this new food only exacerbates the current confusion about health, because it is so elaborate and expensive.

Be that as it may, the counterculture's early idea of forming a healthy world through healthy food has largely become the national norm. After twenty-five years of conflict and confusion, of skirmishes and antagonisms among health professionals, food manufacturers, politicians, and consumers, good home cooking has come to mean something very close to the organic, politically correct cuisine of the 1960s counterculture.

Counterculture food concepts have gone from outcast to mainstream.

A COMPARISON OF U.S. AND JAPANESE DIETARY GUIDELINES

Just as the counterculture of the 1960s looked toward the East for an infusion of spirituality, it again seems appropriate to look toward the East for guidance in developing a new set of culinary attitudes for the 1990s, a set of attitudes that include our spiritual, nutritional, and environmental needs. A comparison of the dietary guidelines for Americans with the Japanese dietary guidelines for health promotion (see the chart on page 15) shows how the relationship of man to his environment affects his attitude toward food and eating.

The American dietary guidelines are an example of scientific thought based on a purely mechanistic view of man. Inherent in these guidelines is modern science's reductionistic belief that the human body is simply a machine, and that if properly fueled it will operate efficiently. Unfortunately, despite the fact that these recommendations are nutritionally sound, they are ultimately unsatisfying and unsatisfactory because they address only the symptom, not the cause of the problem. Although the medical community has reacted to the fact indifferently, medical science has known for nearly thirty years that most chronic diseases are a response of the body to an unhealthy physical as well as spiritual (emotional) environment. It would seem therefore that any set of culinary or dietary guidelines

American Dietary Guidelines*	Japanese Dietary Guidelines*
Eat a variety of foods	Eat a variety of foods to assure a well-balanced diet
Choose a diet with plenty of vegetables, fruits, and grain products	Eat thirty or more different kinds of food per day from the six food groups Balance main and side dishes around the staple food (rice, grains, and noodles)
Maintain healthy weight	Match caloric intake with daily physical activity
Choose a diet low in fat, saturated fat, and cholesterol (Less than 30 percent total calories from fat)	Be aware that the quality and quantity of fats consumed are important 1) Avoid too much fat 2) Use vegetable oils, rather than animal fat (Daily intake for adults should be 20 percent to 25 percent of total energy from fat)
Use salt and sodium in moderation (No more than 1.1 to 3.3 grams per day)	Avoid too much salt 1) Aim for a salt intake of less than 10 grams per day 2) Resourceful cooking cuts down on excessive salt intake
Use sugars in moderation	
If you drink alcoholic beverages, do so in moderation	
	Make all activities pertaining to food and eating pleasurable ones 1) *Use the mealtime as an occasion for family communication* 2) *Treasure family taste and home cooking*

* The order of the guidelines has been changed to make comparisons easier. The six food groups referred to in the second Japanese guideline are (1) sources of protein, (2) sources of calcium, (3) sources of carotene, (4) sources of vitamin C, (5) sources of carbohydrate, and (6) sources of calories [fats]. Italics are the author's.

must address our psychological and spiritual health, and our environment, as well as the nutritional specifics of our diet.

The Japanese guidelines are similar to the American guidelines in that they provide a definition of a balanced diet. But the final Japanese guideline, "Make all activities pertaining to food and eating pleasurable," casts the guidelines in an entirely different light by adding a spiritual overlay to food and eating. This overlay reflects the underlying foundation of much of Japanese culture, Shintoism, a philosophy that promotes joy, gratitude, and a connectedness of man to his planet.

In other words, in order to eat healthily, from the Japanese or Shinto perspective, you must make everything connected with food and eating—the growing, the purchasing, the preparation, the table, the company with whom you eat, and the food itself—into a joyous spiritual event that is respectful of and thankful to nature, of which man is a part. Thus healthy eating cannot be separated from a healthy life-style, and eating a balanced diet is only one small part of a healthy life-style.

This Shinto view provides the Japanese with a spiritual connection to food, to the earth, and to the planet, a connection that the American dietary guidelines lack.

To the Japanese, the social aspects of eating are just as important as the kinds of foods eaten, so this last Japanese guideline promotes meals as a time for family communication, and for an appreciation of home cooking. It also suggests that reliance on convenience foods diminishes family togetherness and personal growth, and thus results in meals that are less healthy.

2

Culinary Guidelines
for a New Earth

As today's healthy gourmets are developing new attitudes toward themselves, their planet, and their food, some of which are reflected in the ever-increasing number of what have come to be known as "politically correct" restaurants and markets, a pattern of attitudes seems to be emerging that includes getting closer to the food we eat, celebrating each meal, thinking seasonally, respecting the environment, buying fewer processed and convenience foods, eating a balanced, high-carbohydrate diet, and eating less fat and salt, and becoming more sensual, sensitive human being. All of this together, it is now believed, will make us healthy, spiritually and physically.

The purpose of these guidelines is not to tell you what to eat and what not to eat, but to provide a map for healthy eating and a healthy life for your spiritual and physical well-being, and for the spiritual and physical well-being of the planet.

The first two guidelines are concerned with the spiritual aspects of food. Together they form a spiritually healthy view of eating and a respect for nature. The next six guidelines are essentially concerned with balancing your diet. These six suggestions are meant to guide you into a style for eating well, a style of eating that will balance your diet for you, without your ever having to think about calories or nutrients. Intrinsic in them is the idea of eating a great variety of foods. Eating lots of different foods banishes boredom from your meals and makes it a real pleasure to sit down at the table. When you consider these six guidelines together, not only do you find a diet that is high in carbohydrates and low in fat, but you discover a diet that is alive with colors and full of luscious flavors with varied textures. The final two guidelines are primarily concerned with ecology and the environment, with the relationship of our food to our environment.

In the broadest sense, in the Shinto sense, though, all ten guidelines reflect a single attitude toward health, an attitude in which being healthy means being a healthy part of nature. Getting closer to your food, for example, will lead you to cook sensitively and resourcefully, and that will lead you to celebrate each meal. Eating lots of different foods will lead you to think seasonally. Thinking seasonally will lead you to respect the environment. Respecting the environment will lead you into buying fewer processed and convenience foods, which will lead you into being a more sensual, sensitive human being. And all of this together will make you healthy, spiritually and physically.

GUIDELINES

1. Get closer to the food you eat.

While it isn't possible for most Americans to get closer to the soil, in the sense of returning to an agrarian life, it is possible to get closer to the soil by getting closer to the food you eat. As citizens of the technocracy, we have been conditioned to shut down our senses when buying and preparing food. With a little effort, though, you can turn those senses back on by learning to see, touch, feel, smell, and taste food. Be open to the sensuality of food; let food talk to you. Listen to what the food has to say. The best way to begin turning yourself back into a sensual, perceptive being is to use your hands in the kitchen.

Alice Waters was once asked by a journalist what she enjoyed most about cooking. Waters replied, "Washing lettuce," and then explained that as she rinsed each leaf, felt it, shook it, watched the water bead on it, the lettuce would tell her what kind of a salad it wanted to be part of, how it wanted to be dressed, and how it should be arranged on a plate.

Waters wasn't implying that she actually talked to vegetables, and that the vegetables talked back to her. Rather she felt closer to food from having handled it, caringly and sensitively, and that closeness dictated how she would prepare the food.

By handling food you can sense the seasons, the soil, and even a bit about the growing season, so take those few extra minutes to wash or clean and prepare your food from scratch. In the process, you will not only improve the quality of your life, but you will develop a deeper understanding of and commitment to the environment.

You can learn an enormous amount, for example, just by cleaning a pint of strawberries. Removing them from the container will tell you about the weather during the last week the berries were on the vine. If they are clean and brightly colored, their last week will have been sunny. On the other hand, if they are small, irregular in shape, unusually soft, and spotted with dirt, their last few days on the vine were cool and rainy. As the rain pounded into the little puddles that formed around the vines on the ground, it splashed mud onto the berries. Thus the dirt isn't a sign of bad production; it's a statement about the weather, or in a broader sense, the environment. Faced with several consecutive years of drought and periodic water shortages, we should be pleased when we occasionally find strawberries with a little dirt on them.

Removing strawberries from the container will tell you about their texture. If they are firm and intact, with no squashed spots from rubbing against the container, and they are evenly colored, though not deep red, for example, you know instantly they were picked underripe. And if the seeds are large and obvious, then the berries are telling you about their textural shortcomings. On the other hand, if the berries are small, tender, and oozing slightly in spots from having been pressed against the side of the container, you will know that the berries were picked ripe. Their lusciousness will demand that you pop at least one into your mouth before you finish washing them.

In addition, removing the berries from the container tells you how to wash them. The large, firm berries have let you know that they are quite durable, and wouldn't mind a shower under running cold tap water. On the other hand, the ripe berries are too fragile for a shower, and would prefer a quick bath, a quick rinse in a sink of cool water.

As you unpack the berries and begin to clean them, you will notice their fragrance. Large, hard, underripe berries will have barely any fragrance. But the ripe berries will fill the kitchen with their sweet, fruity aroma. Those with little aroma are telling you they have little flavor; those with a proud, fill-the-room fragrance, on the other hand, are letting you know how great they will taste.

Strawberries have a lot to say, if you take the time to listen. The underripe berries are telling you that they need help. They have textural shortcomings. They lack oomph. They are asking, perhaps even screaming, for a sauce. If they are large and beautifully shaped, then they are asking for flattery, perhaps in the form of a raspberry essence that could be spooned over them to enhance their color, add fragrance to them, and lightly sweeten them. If they are so-so in appearance, then they are asking for a small dollop of whipped cream or ice cream to mask their imperfections.

On the other hand, if they are tender and ripe, luscious in appearance and feel, small and somewhat irregular in shape, then they are saying that they want to be clustered, arranged close together on a small plate, touching, perhaps even stacked, and then they want to be left alone. No sauce, no ice cream, no sprinkling of sugar.

So the closer you get to your food, the closer you will get to your own sensuality, and the more you will respect yourself, what you eat, the soil in which it was grown, the weather that determined its characteristics, and the planet as a whole.

Washing strawberries isn't a chore. As we learned from the counterculture, it is a chance to communicate, spiritually, perhaps even meditatively, with the strawberries and yourself. It's one of the wonderful little satisfactions of not being a technocratic robot.

2. Make every meal a celebration.

Making each meal into a small celebration, making everything connected with food and eating a joyous event, will enhance your sensuality, relieve the stress of everyday life, and give you a renewed sense of yourself as a complete, perceptive, healthy person.

What better way can there be to celebrate life than to start the day with a wonderful breakfast, full of sensually stimulating foods—warm homemade breads, ripe bowls of fresh fruits and berries, flaky, mixed-grain cereals that remind you of your relationship to the earth, and glasses of freshly squeezed juice. The earthiness of the breads, the lushness of the fruit or berries, the crisp textures and nutty flavors of cereals, and the sweet, slightly acidic flavor of the juice will make you aware of yourself and your world, and will give you a joyous sense of your own spirituality. A good breakfast can turn the most ordinary workday into a life-affirming event.

Equally if not more important than the immediate good feelings you will gain from having a stimulating breakfast full of fine, fresh foods, is the sense of self-esteem you will develop, and that you will carry with you throughout the day.

Part of making any meal into a celebration is setting the table festively. Use linen rather than paper napkins. Set the table attractively. Serve the milk in a pitcher, not its carton; the jams and jellies in attractive crocks, ramekins, or containers (with a small spoon for serving), not in their commercial jars. Use a bread plate, and a butter knife. As Marion Cunningham writes in the introduction to the thirteenth edition of *The Fannie Farmer Cookbook*, "If your table looks like a hash-house counter, you encourage people to eat accordingly."

While setting an attractive table is important, it cannot make breakfast into a celebration if you eat the same boxed cereal or toasted English muffin, monotonously and repetitiously day after day. Ultimately it is the food, and your sensual perception of it, that makes a meal into a celebration. Let the seasons and the weather guide you into an exciting breakfast each day. Don't buy hard, acidic strawberries in March; have lusciously ripe pears instead. Don't buy boxed raisin bran cereal; make a loaf of whole wheat currant bread instead.

In order to make each meal into a small celebration, you will have to set aside more time for cooking and thinking about food than most Americans have been trained to do by the convenience foods industry, whose mission has been to reduce food to "instant eats," and to remove the joys of a good meal from our lives. And you will have to reorganize your mornings so the whole family can sit down to breakfast together.

While most American families shovel down breakfast hurriedly and without conversation, making breakfast into a celebration means sitting down with the family and learning anew to share life together. This is the kind of simpler, more meaningful communal life that the counterculture of the 1960s was seeking, and that the Japanese dietary guidelines are advocating. This is the way you can make yourself and your family into sensual, perceptive, spiritually, and physically aware beings.

When people tell me that they just don't have the time to cook and eat this way, I always wonder what they are saving that time for—so they can have an extra half hour in front of the television?

Although it is impossible for most American families to eat lunch together, lunch can still be a small celebration. If you are at the office, don't order a waxed-paper-wrapped sandwich from the deli and eat it at your desk. Instead, get into the habit of bringing your own lunch, and of going to the employee cafeteria, with a few co-workers, to eat and talk. And once or twice a week, go out for lunch, again with colleagues or friends. If you are at home, even if you are alone, set the table and have a quiet, relaxed meal—the errands and other daily chores can wait. This is a time for you to enjoy yourself.

School lunches, as we know from recent press exposés of their scandalously high fat and sodium content, are anything but life-affirming, and they are laden with the spoils of the food technocracy—surplus high-fat, sodium-saturated foods, usually frozen and reheated on steam tables. Although there is often peer group pressure on children to eat in school cafeterias, if you encourage your children to participate in the whole process of choosing, buying, and preparing foods, they will increasingly ask to take those foods to school with them and will be taking the first steps toward a lifetime of better eating.

Making dinner into a celebration means setting the table and serving a family meal, sometimes with friends or relatives as casual guests, talking about the food on the table, events of the day, plans for tomorrow, and about the world around us and our place in that world.

Mack Facklam, executive chef of the Cooking and Hospitality Institute of Chicago, says that a good rule of thumb for making every meal into a celebration is "Never eat standing, out of a box, or off a paper plate."

3. Eat two slices of bread with every meal.

If eating two slices of bread with every meal sounds like a lot of bread each day; you're right, it is. Remember, though, that this is a guideline, not a commandment; it is a goal to strive for, not an absolute. The reason for trying to eat two slices of bread with each meal is to ensure that you have the right amount of complex carbohydrates in your diet, but the ultimate effect of this guideline is to bring you closer to the food you eat, and thus to the earth.

When you begin eating this much bread every day, if you are like me, you'll discover that you want an ever-increasing number of different kinds of breads, with different flavors and textures, and you'll begin searching for new bakeries. Eventually, though, you'll discover that you want to supplement the breads you buy with homemade breads. And making your own bread is the single most satisfying thing you can do in the kitchen. Making breads from scratch will fill your home with a warm, inviting aroma that will kindle conversation and stimulate your appetite, and will leave you magically enthralled with life.

If you have never made a loaf of bread, one of the great sensual delights of the kitchen beckons you now. The directions for Your First Loaf of Bread (page 237) will take you by the hand and slowly walk you through your first wondrous experience as a breadmaker. After you have mastered the techniques, you can move on to more flavorful, nuttier, chewier breads with one or more whole grains.

Bear in mind, though, that eating too much fat is still your major dietary concern, so you will need to find alternatives to the butter, margarine, cream cheese, and mayonnaise you are used to spreading on breads.

At breakfast, serve the bread with several types of jams, jellies, preserves, and fruit butters. Occasionally you may want to serve a light cream cheese, or a homemade yogurt cheese. At lunch, use mustard or ketchup instead of mayonnaise on your sandwich. And at dinner, moisten the bread with the natural juices from your food, or spread the bread with one of the savory spreads from chapters 3 or 11.

Also, experiment with toasting the bread. A great slice of bread, with its cracked crust, chewy texture, and whole grain flavor, needs nothing else.

Part of celebrating each meal is making shopping into an adventure. Few of us think we have time to make all of our breads, so explore the bakeries, gourmet shops, health food stores, and food co-ops in your area in your search for a variety of fine flavored and textured loaves. Frequently you will find loaves with enticing flavors and textures that just aren't possible to duplicate at home, given the limitations of our ovens. And since breads freeze well, for up to a month, always buy extra, seal them in plastic bags or wrap them in freezer paper, and freeze them so you always have a stock of great breads on hand.

4. Eat two servings of cereals or grains a day.

Cereals and grains add a warm earthy flavor and feeling to a meal. They have a wide variety of flavors, textures, and aromas. Historically, however, Americans have limited their eating to little more than wheat, long-grain white rice, and an occasional bowl of oatmeal.

Long-grain white rice is only one of the many kinds of rice available. There are short-grain rices, which are sticky in texture and quite mild in flavor, medium-grain rices, which are creamy when cooked and slightly more flavorful than the short-grain varieties, and there are white and brown varieties of both. In the long-grain rice group, consider traditional Carolina-style rice as well as the aromatic rices, such as basmati rice, popcorn rice, and texmati rice, which have a heady, popcornlike aroma and a sweet taste. Like the short- and medium-grain rices, long-grain rice is available as white rice (with the bran removed), or as brown rice (with the bran still in place). There is also a deep purple-colored rice from the Philippines, called violet rice, which has a flowery fragrance. And finally, there is wild rice, with the boldest, nuttiest, toastiest flavor of any rice although it is in truth not a rice but a grain. Eating a variety of rices, many of which are available in health food stores from organic producers, will add exciting new flavors and textures to your meals.

Beyond rice, there are other cereals and grains that should be a part of your eating. Amaranth, once popular with the Aztecs, is an esoteric grain with a grassy flavor and a soft consistency. Barley, which is tender and earthy, can be used as a winter side dish or to flavor soups or breads. Bulgur (cracked wheat), which is soft in flavor and texture, makes excellent summer salads. Buckwheat groats (kasha) are tender and a little chewy, and are excellent mixed with small pastas; they may be the perfect grain for winter meals. Cornmeal can be made into a breakfast cereal, corn bran can be added to breads and muffins, and when cooked and cooled, slabs of cornmeal (called polenta) can be served as a side dish for supper or dinner, or can be served with a little maple syrup for breakfast. Most Americans are familiar with yellow and white cornmeal, made from yellow and white corn, respectively, but there is also blue cornmeal, made from blue corn, which has a rounder, bolder corn flavor and an exotic purple-blue color. Couscous, often categorized as a grain, is actually a pasta (bits of wheat cooked in water, then dehydrated). It makes excellent salads and a fluffy side dish that can replace rice. Millet is a mildly flavored grain, excellent for stuffings and casseroles. Quinoa, another esoteric grain, is like amaranth. Its bead shape with a mild, grassy flavor makes it an ideal addition to soups and salads. And, of course, there are oats, cream of wheat, and cream of rice, all of which make fine hot breakfast cereals. In addition, if you shop in a health food store or food co-op, you will find a variety of cereals and grains, everything from corn and wheat to oats, in dry flakes for making your own cold breakfast cereals.

5. Eat three or four different vegetables a day, one of which should be red or orange in color.

The nutritional value of vegetables has been neatly color-coded by nature. Each color just happens to represent a particular set of nutrients, such as vitamins and minerals, and nonnutrients, such as fiber. Dark green vegetables, for example, are high in calcium, iron, and potassium, and red and orange vegetables are high in vitamins A and C and beta carotene. Even though the nutritional value of vegetables does not correlate absolutely with color, it comes close enough so that, over long periods, color can be used as a basic guide.

In the long-term view, what is important is that you eat lots of different vegetables from the different color groups each day.

Vegetables fall into four basic color groups: green, dark green, red or orange, and other-colored.

Try to eat two or three different green vegetables each day, such as asparagus, broccoli, brussels sprouts, green cabbage, celery, green beans, green peppers, okra, peas, and snow peas, and a dark green vegetable, such as spinach, chard, kale, or collards, as often as possible. In addition, choose one red or orange vegetable each day, such as acorn squash, butternut squash, carrots, orange, yellow, or red peppers, pumpkin, red cabbage, sweet potatoes, tomatoes, yams, and any of the other winter squashes. And finally, each day try to eat one other-colored vegetable, such as dried beans, cauliflower, crookneck squash, eggplant, leeks, dried lentils, mushrooms, parsnips, potatoes, onions, turnips, and zucchini.

While supermarket produce sections have expanded dramatically since the early 1970s, when the counterculture began its assimilation into the mainstream, there are still major limitations to fresh supermarket produce. Most of it is still produced with a heavy dependence on chemicals, and the variety is still limited. For more variety and organic produce, shop at health food stores, gourmet shops, and farmers' markets (at most farmers' markets today you'll find at least one organic farmer) as much as possible. At farmers' markets, often you can talk to the farmers whose produce you are buying. They'll be able to tell you how the weather has affected the flavor and texture and when different varieties will become available, bringing you closer to the food you are buying. Because farmers do live close to the soil, their perspectives on food and eating are always worth exploring as you shop.

6. Eat two fruits a day, one of which should be a citrus fruit.

Adding lots of fruit to your daily menus will lead you more frequently to eat fruit for dessert, and so without thinking about it you will be eating fewer desserts that are high in fat.

Fruits, like vegetables, are an excellent source of nutrients and nonnutrients. Citrus fruits are particularly important, as they are very high in vitamin C, which has been shown to be a special need for most Americans.

What is important is that you include a large variety of different fruits in your day-to-day eating. Fruits that are particularly healthful, according to health officials and nutritionists, include apricots, berries, cantaloupes, cherries, mangoes, papayas, peaches, pineapples, plums, prunes, and watermelon. Citrus fruits include grapefruits, lemons, limes, oranges, and tangerines.

As much as possible, buy locally produced, seasonal fruits, and let go of the technocratic training that has led you to expect blemish-free, perfectly colored and shaped fruits. Often fruits with the best flavor are slightly misshapen and varied in color. The skins on great-flavored oranges, for example, are often slightly green or yellow.

7. Eat modest amounts of animal protein (fish, poultry without the skin, game, and lean red meats).

Use animal protein as a condiment to meals.

Lappé's belief that we could stop world famine by eliminating meats from our diet was naive, and in later editions of *Diet for a Small Planet*, she gently withdrew from that position. But her suggestion that eating less meat was healthier, and was a way of living lighter, was correct.

Reducing the amount of animal protein you eat three or four ounces a day is one of the most important culinary actions most Americans can take to live a longer, healthier life. Unfortunately, though, we live in a meat-centered culture that values meat so highly that we are constantly bombarded, directly and indirectly, with the message "Eat meat."

Eating meat has always been a sign of affluence, and historically, as countries get richer, they display their success by eating ever-increasing amounts of meat. America is a stunning and frightening example of this pattern.

The shift to vegetarianism by the counterculture in the late 1960s was a symbol of a new healthier way of eating, a symbol of a simpler way of life, but only now, after two decades of research into the relationship of diet to health, is it clear why eating less animal protein is nutritionally essential.

Animal protein accounts for about 30 percent of the fat in the American diet, and for about 40 percent of the saturated fat and cholesterol. So cutting down to just one serving of meat a day significantly reduces the amount of fat, saturated fat, and cholesterol in your diet.

In order to follow this guideline successfully, you must stop thinking of meat as the main event in a meal, and start thinking of meat as a condiment to a meal full of vegetables, cereals, and grains, or as only one small ingredient to be used in combination with other foods, such as a vegetable stir-fry with chicken or a hearty barley soup with lamb. This point is made emphatically in the Japanese dietary guidelines when they say, "Balance main and side dishes around the staple food." To the Japanese, the staple foods, which are the central focus of a meal, are grains, such as rice, bread, and noodles; the side dishes are vegetables; and the main dish, which is a minor part of the meal, is composed of fish, meat, and soybean products.

When ordering meats in a restaurant, where the standard portions are six ounces for fish, six to eight ounces for chicken, and eight to twelve ounces for red meats, either share an entrée with someone at the table or take home half the serving.

8. Prepare foods in ways that require little or no added fat or salt.

This is the "cook light" guideline, both aesthetically and nutritionally.

When Curnonsky, the famous French food writer of the 1950s, said "Food should taste of itself," he was articulating a standard for eating that was unattainable in the highly sophisticated system of French haute cuisine on which he was commenting. In part this was because of the complexity that dominated French cooking at the time. But it was in greater part because of the extraordinary excesses of fat and salt that were added to traditional French food, masking their natural flavors and textures and overpowering their subtleties.

The recipes in this book, and this guideline in particular, point toward a new, light style of cooking that respects and emphasizes natural flavors instead of masking them with fat and salt. To make up for the flavor lost when fats and salt are reduced, the light recipes use more acids (such as citrus juices and vinegars), more fresh herbs, and more spices. Just removing the salt and fat is not enough, as it leaves many foods flat-tasting and ultimately unsatisfying.

Once you become accustomed to cooking and eating light, you will discover a whole new world of simple, pure flavors and aromas that don't exist in the traditional, "heavy" way of cooking. Foods prepared without excesses of fat and salt are simple and honest. Their flavors are straightforward, their subtleties can be tasted, and they have textural integrities that were previously unrecognizable.

Cooking in this manner brings to fruition Curnonsky's aesthetic belief that food should taste of itself.

Learn to consider added fats as a condiment to be used judiciously and sparingly. Nonetheless, when you do add fat to food, either at the table or in cooking, pay attention to the quality of the fat, as the Japanese dietary guidelines suggest, and choose a fat that is beautifully flavored and ideally suited to your needs, such as a fine virgin or extra virgin olive oil, or an excellent unsalted butter. Whenever possible, use vegetable fats rather than animal fats.

You never need to add salt to your food. There is enough sodium in the foods you eat each day to more than meet your body's needs.

The easiest way to reduce sodium, a part of salt linked to high blood pressure and some forms of cancer, is to use as little salt as possible in your cooking, and not to add salt to foods at the table. In addition, reduce your consumption of salty prepared or processed foods, such as pickles, potato chips, and salt-cured meats.

When you do use salt, use a fine-quality sea salt with a complex, round flavor, rather than iodized table salt, with its additives, preservatives, and sharp, almost acrid flavor.

It is worth noting here that the Japanese eat considerably more salt than Americans. Indeed, the goal of the Japanese dietary guidelines is to reduce salt consumption to 10 grams a day, roughly four times as much as is recommended for Americans.

NOTE: Many of the recipes in this book call for a vegetable oil spray. Now that the propellants in these sprays are ecologically safe (they no longer contain fluorocarbons, the culprit in ozone depletion), I use them because they significantly reduce the amount of added fat in a recipe. A recipe that would require 2 teaspoons oil for sautéing can be reduced to ¼ teaspoon by using a spray.

9. Whenever possible, choose foods that have a minimum of or no chemical additives.

Pesticides, fungicides, and herbicides are just a few of the 15,000 nonnutritive chemicals added directly and indirectly to the foods we eat. While some of these chemicals may be necessary at times, the ultimate effect of adding some 15,000 chemicals to our food is that we are contaminating our environment as well as ourselves.

At this time, it is not possible to determine how great a risk these chemicals pose for us, though we know that most of them are toxins; nor is it possible to eliminate all of these chemicals from our food and our food production. Nonetheless, we should minimize our consumption of chemical additives by relying less on processed foods, by washing and peeling our produce, and by supporting sustainable or even alternative agriculture.

10. Think seasonally when planning meals and buying foods.

Whenever possible, out of respect for the environment, buy fresh, seasonal, locally grown foods from an organic farmer or a sustainable or alternative agriculture grower. If most Americans did this, we would quickly move our food supply onto safer ground, both for ourselves and our environment.

Thinking seasonally will enliven your meals and add variety to your menus. But you must learn to be flexible in planning meals and menus, and to make necessary adjustments while you shop. It is amazing how quickly asparagus can go out of season, for example. On the other hand, there is rarely a time when broccoli cannot be substituted for asparagus if you think flexibly as you shop.

Conclusion

If you follow these ten guidelines, you will significantly improve the quality of your life—you will be living a cleaner, healthier life, physically and spiritually, in a cleaner, healthier environment; you will feel better and you will live a longer, happier life. And, to paraphrase Mark Twain, why bother getting to ninety if you haven't enjoyed the trip along the way?

The New Vocabulary

To successfully make these changes in yourself, you must change the vocabulary with which you speak about food, because the words you use to describe foods determine how you value them. Words used to describe foods in the traditional view lead you to value foods for their "haute" preparation styles, their complexity, and their richness, so you need new words to lead you to value simply prepared family-style foods.

In the old view, in the traditional cultural view, words like *rich, creamy, crisp,* and *glistening* are used to describe the qualities in foods that were admired. These are words that convey, subtlety or overtly, the sophisticated preparation styles and high fat content of those foods.

In the new view, a new set of words is used to describe foods, words like *clean, pure, simple, fragrant, perfumed,* and *moist,* all of which describe a simpler, more natural approach to cooking and food.

In the introductions to the recipes in this book, you will see how the new vocabulary, with its clarity and integrity, brings you closer to the food you prepare.

PLANNING MEALS AND MENUS

When planning a typical company meal following the Culinary Guidelines for a New Earth, first you choose the vegetables, breads, cereals, and grains, distributing them among the entrée, soup, or appetizer. Then you choose the fruit for dessert. And finally, you choose a meat garnish to accompany the entrée. This is almost a complete reversal from the traditional cultural view and requires you to think of food differently. The major efforts in the kitchen are addressed to the vegetables, grains, and bread, all of which will need to be flavored and balanced. One of the vegetables might become a soup, another might be given a sauce or even become a sauce, and the grain will need to be flavored—perhaps with some fresh herbs and a little lemon zest, or with some tomatoes, or you might choose to combine two grains to add textural interest to your meal, such as lentils and rice.

In the old view, the meat and vegetables were rubbed with fat and seasoned with salt, and the meal was done. Now you have three or four different foods, which often will be on the same plate. So the dynamic of the plate has changed. Balancing all these flavors and textures will require more thought than in the past, where everything was reduced to a common denominator. For example, you probably wouldn't serve stewed okra on the same plate with ratatouille—both being vegetable stews, they are too similar in texture. Similarly, you wouldn't serve two steamed vegetables, or two hot and spicy dishes, such as Szechuan-style green beans and curried carrots.

The balance in this new way of cooking comes from a distribution of color, texture, flavor, and cooking technique. The recipes chosen for each of the three or four items on the plate need to be compatible yet remain individual. You have the culinary equivalents to plaids, tweeds, and patterns to deal with. In the old view, all you had were simple colored cottons.

There is an alternative to having to prepare three or four different recipes for a meal, and that is to combine everything into a one-dish meal, such as a pasta or a stir-fry. Chapter 7 is devoted to such one-dish recipes.

As you will see when you peruse the serving suggestions in this book, these healthy new meals are full of vibrant flavors, abundant with textures, and bold with color. In essence, the cooking is respectful of the foods it prepares. And because, for

31

aesthetic and health reasons, the foods are prepared with little or no fat or salt, there are more acidic flavors, more spices, and more herbs and textures on the plate than ever before, which makes this new style of cooking more lively and exciting than traditional cuisine.

Every meal needs a focus. In this new way of cooking, the focus is usually on the preparation, the visual impact, or the complexity of one of the items in the menu, and that food will often stand alone as a separate course. The focus might be placed on the soup. The soup could be a glorious, fuchsia-colored beet and buttermilk soup, slightly sweet, slightly tart, and perhaps whimsically garnished with spears of chives and chive blossoms. Ladled into a stark white soup plate, the soup would dazzle with its dramatic impact. If the focus is on the soup, then the entrée should be a less dramatic mix of sprightly flavored vegetables and grains. And the dessert should be light and simple, like fresh fruit or a poached pear or peach.

Family Meals

In this new way of eating, you will need to prepare a greater variety of different foods, so the secret to successful family meals is always to cook more than you plan to serve. Double recipes whenever possible and place half in containers in the freezer. With a freezer full of delicious breads, grains, and vegetables, you will be able to pull together a meal in minutes without having to rely on processed or convenience foods.

Not only is cooking more than you plan to eat a convenient, time-saving technique, but it is ecologically sound as well. For example, it takes about three hours to cook two quarts of soup; but it only takes three-and-one-half hours to make four to six quarts of soup, so "overcooking" saves energy.

Seasonal Shopping

In the traditional cultural view of food from the 1950s, you decided what your family would eat for a week, sometimes a month at a time. (Remember the weekly and monthly menus in women's magazines and home economics classes?) If the peas you had decided to serve on Thursday were out of season, you just walked over to the frozen food case. And if there weren't any frozen peas, there would certainly be some canned peas on the shelf. This was food without nature, food without seasons, and sometimes, food without taste.

In addition, in the old view of food, the main event of the meal was the meat. You selected the meat, wrapped in plastic and foam, by its size and price. As with the peas, you were allowed no sensory connection with the meat, nor did the meat display or imply any connection to a steer.

Now seasonal vegetables and fruits and cereals and grains are the most important part of a meal. The vegetables and fruits will constitute about two-thirds of your shopping list. Whenever possible, you'll want to explore places other than the supermarket for your shopping. Farmers' markets, food co-ops and whole food, natural food, and health food stores often have a larger selection of seasonal, local, pesticide-free vegetables and fruits than supermarkets, and gourmet shops often have a better selection of herbs and locally grown produce.

Most of the cereals and grains on your shopping list will be available in a large, upscale supermarket, though health food stores, ethnic markets, and gourmet shops will offer the greatest selection of grains, especially organically grown grains.

SPECIAL CONSIDERATIONS
Fake Fats

There are several types of fake fats. One is molecularly reformulated egg protein that deceives your taste buds into thinking you are eating fat. Another is a nonabsorbable fat (it passes through you without being absorbed in the gut) made from sucrose, a type of sugar.

Fake fats offer none of the taste advantages nor any of the nutritional advantages of real fat, and the nonabsorbable type of fake fat may actually interfere with the absorption of some nutrients, such as vitamin E. But even if both were completely safe, there would be no place for them in our cooking.

The primary objection to fake fats is that they position fats inappropriately in our eating, encouraging us to eat fats freely and frequently. And because they do this by offering only a shadow of the flavor and texture of real fats, they are ultimately unsatisfying, so they lead us back to eating more real fat than is healthy.

Sweeteners and Sugars

Currently, 10 percent of the calories in an average American's diet come from added sugars. The goal is to reduce that amount significantly, which will be easier to achieve than you might imagine because eating many vegetables, cereals, and grains, and eating them in three full meals a day (you really cannot make mealtime into a celebration if you are one of those people who eat constantly throughout the day), will naturally lead you to desire fewer sweets.

Although the counterculture in the late 1960s and early 1970s believed that honey was good for you and that refined white sugar was the enemy, we now know that all sugars are alike. Sugars include table sugar (sucrose), brown sugar, raw sugar, glucose (dextrose), fructose, maltose, lactose, honey, syrup, corn sweetener, high-fructose corn syrup, molasses, and fruit juice concentrate.

There are no health advantages to using artificial sweeteners, and there are some risks, though slight for most people, associated with their use. In addition, long-term use of artificial sweeteners leads to inappropriately positioning sweet foods as important.

Currently, an average American consumes about 20 pounds of artificial sugars each year. That is expected to increase as more and more different types of artificial sweeteners become available for commercial use in the 1990s.

There is no place for artificial sweeteners in our food and cooking.

Washing and Peeling Nonorganic Foods

An assortment of coatings, from shellac to paraffin, are sprayed onto most non-organic produce to improve its appearance and extend its shelf life. The coatings on these fruits and vegetables, which sometimes include the addition of fungicides, seal in the pesticides and other chemicals used to produce them and are usually impossible to wash off. Nutritional authorities, such as Bonnie Lieberman of the Center for Science in the Public Interest, recommend peeling all nonorganic produce, even though it removes many of the nutrients in these foods. Ideally, in recipes that call for grated citrus fruit zest, use only organic fruits.

SUSTAINABLE AND ALTERNATIVE AGRICULTURE AND THE ENVIRONMENT

The counterculture's belief in the sanctity of a vital, living planet as a source of life has led directly to today's sustainable agriculture movement, which can provide us with a greater variety of fine flavored foods (often at a lower cost) than is possible with traditional agriculture, and can provide us with safer foods—foods that are produced with a minimum of or no chemical contaminants, and are less destructive to the environment than foods produced by traditional large-scale agriculture.

Topsoil is the thin surface layer of the earth. Although the composition of the topsoil varies from place to place, it is basically a mix of mineral-rich sand, clay, gravel, and stone, and the organic remains of decomposed vegetable and animal matter, with air and water. This organic, living part of the planet is the major concern of today's sustainable agriculture movement.

In traditional monocrop mega-agriculture, the same crop is grown season after season, year after year in the same soil. As a result, the soil is depleted of certain nutrients, and chronic problems with insects and weeds occur. Once soft, fertile, and alive, most of America's topsoil has become brittle, hard, and nutrient-depleted. In order to keep the soil producing, traditional agriculture relies heavily on chemical fertilizers, pesticides, herbicides, and fungicides to manage the land. These chemicals not only find their way into our food and into the animals fed on crops grown this way, causing major health problems (especially cancer), but many of the chemicals remain in the soil, eventually contaminating our water supply. In addition, because the topsoil has become hard and brittle, erosion and desertification occur, each year shrinking the amount of fertile land available for agriculture.

In sustainable agriculture, a development of the original "organic" movement of Robert Rodale in the 1950s and 1960s, soil, and in a broader sense, the environment, is viewed as a living organism that should be naturally nourished so it will continue to provide us with a safe and abundant food supply. Sustainable agriculture uses multicrop plantings, crop rotation, and other more natural soil management techniques, such as the use of organic fertilizers (manure, composted vegetable matter, and the like), with no chemical fertilizers or pesticides. Pest

35

COOKING FOR A NEW EARTH

management is accomplished through the use of predatory insects and other natural, noncontaminating techniques. Together these effect a balanced and healthy biosystem and stop erosion. In addition, because sustainable agriculture is decentralized, a greater variety of locally produced and often better-tasting foods becomes available at a lower cost.

Although the distinction is being blurred, alternative agriculture is the compromise position between traditional, chemical-dependent monocrop agriculture and sustainable agriculture. Alternative agriculture is broad-scale, basically monocrop agriculture, which attempts to manage the soil with fewer and less indiscriminately used chemicals.

Alternative agriculture is a small step in the right direction, whereas sustainable agriculture is the right direction.

Organic farming was the norm in this country until about 1940, when large-scale industrial food producers shifted America into chemical-dependent agriculture. But a growing awareness of the need for a healthy environment, for a healthy, living biosystem, as well as the overwhelming recognition of the health risks that result from chemical-intensive agriculture, have fortunately led to today's renaissance in organic farming.

3

Breakfast

FRUIT

Compote of Dried Peaches and Apricots with Ginger
Stewed Prunes with Lemon
Fresh Pear Compote

FRUIT SALADS

JUICES

Lemonade
Grapefruit or Orange Juice with Grenadine
Fresh Carrot Juice
Freshly Extracted Pineapple Juice

OTHER FRESHLY EXTRACTED FRUIT JUICES

PANCAKES

Fabulously Light Whole Wheat Pancakes
Buckwheat Pancakes with Fresh Blueberry Sauce
Cornmeal Pancakes with Peaches
Mixed-Grain Pancakes

HOT CEREALS

Breakfast Risotto with Dried Cherries
Brown Basmati Rice with Cinnamon Sugar
Great Oatmeal
Bread Pudding with Currants

PRESERVES AND FRUIT BUTTERS

Blueberry Preserves
Peach Butter
Pear Butter
Apple Butter

SMOOTHIES

Strawberry-Banana-Orange Smoothy
Kiwi Smoothy
Orange Creamsicle Smoothy

Introduction

Breakfast is the bugle call with which we should begin each day. It helps to wake us by revving up our metabolism, it makes us more alert, it is a cognitive booster, allowing us to think better and more clearly throughout the day, and, if it includes a quarter of the day's calories, as a good breakfast should, it will minimize or eliminate the desire to snack in the afternoon.

Unfortunately, for far too many Americans, the large, healthful, traditional farmhouse breakfasts of our grandparents' generation have given way to a quick cup of coffee at home and a plastic-wrapped doughnut thrown into a bag at the snack shop on our run for the office elevator.

A healthy breakfast, in both the spiritual and nutritional senses, requires us to add another half hour or so to our wake-up ritual, enough time to prepare—and sit down to eat—a full meal. The satisfactions of starting the day with a few minutes of culinary celebration, with the quiet pleasures of eating this first meal of the day, more than justify the little extra time it takes each morning. With tempers and moods soothed by a night's sleep, breakfast also provides us with the calm necessary for the family to bond together spiritually.

The best breakfasts are high in carbohydrates, nutrients, and fiber, and low in fat and salt. They should include some fruit or fruit juice; cereal or pancakes; and warm bread or toast. What better way to start a day than with a bowl of ripe fresh fruits, or a glass of freshly squeezed juice, and the nutty flavor and tender textures of pancakes or the sweet grain flavors of a hot cereal, accompanied by thick slices of homemade bread.

In this chapter, there are recipes for preparing fresh and dried fruits, fruit juices, and fresh fruit drinks; there are recipes for everything from feathery light buttermilk pancakes to more deeply flavored buckwheat pancakes, as well as some new ideas for breakfast cereals, including a breakfast risotto with dried cherries. And because most breakfasts should include a slice or two of bread, there are recipes for fresh fruit preserves and fruit butters to replace the butter needlessly slathered on even the best of homemade breads.

These are meant to point toward a new way of eating at breakfast that is light on both the body and the environment. And they imply that breakfast must again become a family celebration with which to start each day.

Fruit

Fresh and dried fruits, with their sweet, inviting aromas, variety of colors, and gentle to intense flavors, should play an increasingly important role in breakfast. Fruit can be used as the main dish for a quick breakfast, as a side dish, in the form of juice, as an accent, like a topping for pancakes, or as a spread for bread, either as a jam or jelly or a fruit butter.

Now there are more different fruits available than ever before. Fruits like kiwis that were "exotic" in the early 1970s when the counterculture began its exploration of food are now commonplace. We should not only explore nontraditional varieties of fruits like banana apples, pale yellow-skinned apples with a juicy texture and a ripe banana fragrance, which I have seen at roadside stands and farmers' markets in New York and Michigan, but we should try fruits with which we are not familiar, like cherimoyas, lichees, and gooseberries.

Fruits provide important nutrients, especially citrus fruits and orange-colored fruits.

COMPOTE OF DRIED PEACHES AND
APRICOTS WITH GINGER

Makes about 2 quarts, about 12 servings

With their rich, sweet, and tart flavor and gingery spiciness, a small bowl of these poached peaches and apricots will liven up even the coldest winter morning. These dried fruits are very high in fiber, and, as their orange color implies, provide important nutrients such as beta carotene, potassium, and vitamin A.

Use fresh ginger for a simple flavor that supports the character of the dried fruits. Use crystallized ginger for an assertive ginger flavor that is competitive with the intense flavors of the peaches and apricots. For a more complex flavor, add the grated zest of a large orange to the compote just after it comes off the burner and before it is cooled.

Serve as a first course, as part of a big breakfast or brunch. Or for a quick breakfast, accompany a bowl of this compote with a couple of slices of toasted whole wheat bread.

4 cups hot tap water
2 cups sugar
6 quarter-sized slices peeled fresh gingerroot, or 1 tablespoon finely
    chopped crystallized ginger
12 ounces dried apricots
12 ounces dried peaches
¹/₄ cup golden raisins

In a medium-sized saucepan, bring the water and sugar to a boil, stirring occasionally to dissolve the sugar. Add the remaining ingredients. There should be enough liquid to cover the dried fruits. If not, add a little more water. Return to a boil, then adjust the heat and simmer until the peaches and apricots are puffed and tender, about 25 minutes.

Cool, then refrigerate in a covered jar until needed.

Poached dried fruits can be stored in the refrigerator for 4 to 6 weeks.

STEWED PRUNES WITH LEMON

Makes 1½ quarts, about 10 servings

As a child, I frequently ate stewed prunes as an after-school snack. Now that I no longer snack in the afternoon, I eat them for breakfast. For me, these are comfort food with the added advantage of being high in fiber and potassium.

If they are available, use small, thin-skinned lemons rather than the large, thicker-skinned variety that can be tough and chewy, even after cooking. It is important to slice the lemons very thin to ensure that they become tender.

When serving, spoon the prunes into small bowls with a little of the cooking liquid, and add at least 1 slice of lemon to each serving.

4 cups hot tap water
1⅓ cups sugar
2 small lemons, ends trimmed away, any brand names stamped on the skin peeled off, cut into very thin (⅛-inch) slices, and seeded
24 ounces dried prunes
A 3-inch cinnamon stick, broken in half

In a medium-sized saucepan, bring the water and sugar to a boil, stirring occasionally to dissolve the sugar. Add the remaining ingredients. There should be enough liquid to cover the prunes. If not, add a little more water. Return to a boil, then adjust the heat and simmer until prunes are puffed and very soft, about 25 minutes.

Cool, then refrigerate in a covered jar until needed.

Stewed prunes can be stored in the refrigerator for 4 to 6 weeks.

FRESH PEAR COMPOTE

Makes 4 to 6 servings

These pears are coaxed into tenderness in a very light syrup gently flavored with lemon, orange, and cinnamon.

Comice pears, which are sweet, with a complex flavor and a fine texture, are ideal for this recipe. However, Anjou pears, which are less finely textured, and Bosc pears, which are more tender and have a rich, almost buttery flavor, can be used if Comice are not available. Anjous and Boscs are smaller than Comice pears, so use 6 or 7 instead of 4.

For breakfast, serve the pears either warm straight from the saucepan, refrigerator cold, or quickly warmed in the microwave, with a thick slice or 2 of homemade bread. For dinner, serve as a light dessert, either cold or warm.

2 cups hot tap water
1/2 cup sugar
A 2- to 3-inch cinnamon stick, broken into several pieces
Juice of 1/2 lemon
Grated zest of a whole lemon
Grated zest of 1/2 orange
4 large ripe but still somewhat firm Comice pears

In a large saucepan, combine the sugar and water and place over high heat. Add the cinnamon and bring to a boil, stirring occasionally to dissolve the sugar. Add the lemon juice and the zests, and remove from the heat.

While the syrup is heating, halve, core, peel, and cut the pears, one at a time, into 1/2- to 3/4-inch dice. The easiest way to do this is with a double-bladed vegetable peeler, a melon baller, and a paring knife: Cut the pears in half lengthwise, scoop out the cores with the melon baller or a sharp-edged spoon, cut out the fibrous stem in a narrow wedge with the paring knife, peel with the vegetable peeler, and finally, place flat on a cutting board and cut into small cubes. As each pear is cubed, toss it into the syrup.

Set the pot over high heat again and bring back to a boil. Cover, remove from the heat, and set aside for about 30 minutes. The pears will finish cooking as the syrup cools.

Serve lukewarm, or transfer to a container, cover, and refrigerate.

These pears can be stored in the refrigerator for about a week.

Fruit Salads

Fruit salads are particularly welcome at breakfasts and brunches, where a light, colorful, naturally sweet dish makes the perfect first course. But because we should be eating more fruit each day, you may want to serve such a mixture of fruits as dessert after lunch or dinner as a light finish to the meal.

The most casual fruit salads are a combination of whatever fruits are on hand quickly cut up and tossed into a bowl for a quick family meal or for a school lunch box.

More formal fruit salads are made with a carefully selected combination of 6 or more fruits, each carefully cleaned and cut to just the right size to bring out its best flavor, and often with each marinated separately in a liqueur or flavored water. The arrangement on a large platter is designed and meant for presentation, either at the table or on a buffet. Whether casual or formal, the fruits used should be in season.

Fruit salads don't lend themselves to rigid recipes, so rather than trying to force them into a formal recipe format, here are some ideas and combinations to spark your imagination.

• Strawberries and lichees, in about equal amounts, with a few raspberries.

• Ripe pears, cut into chunks or sliced, rubbed with a little lemon juice to prevent discoloration, then tossed or topped with a few sweet blackberries and sprinkled with a little finely chopped fresh or candied ginger or chopped pistachio nuts.

• A golden fruit salad made of about equal amounts of sliced mangoes, papayas, apricots, and peaches, perhaps lightly tossed with a few drops of Grand Marnier, or ever so slightly dusted with Chinese five-spice powder, or briefly marinated in a little orange flower water.

• Dark sweet cherries and pineapple, drizzled with a sauce made from puréed strawberries, lightly sweetened with a little sugar and flavored with a big squirt of lemon juice.

• Diced cherimoya, sliced Japanese snow apples, and either pomegranate seeds or a few small, sweet blueberries.

• Peeled and sliced oranges, ever so slightly dusted with very finely chopped sweetened, dried coconut, and topped with a few sliced strawberries.

• Sliced bananas, sprinkled lightly with lemon juice to prevent discoloring, mixed with blueberries, and dusted with dark brown sugar.

• Kiwis and pears topped with raspberries.

• Grapefruit sections tossed with pomegranate seeds or coarsely chopped dried cranberries.

• Strawberries and pineapple, decoratively drizzled with grenadine and topped with a few raspberries.

Juices

LEMONADE

Makes 3 large glasses

A glass of lemonade, whether with breakfast or drunk later in the day, is an excellent way to get your citrus fruit once a day. For pink lemonade, stir 1 tablespoon of grenadine into the lemonade.

Juice of 3 large lemons
$2^{1}/_{2}$ cups water
$^{1}/_{4}$ cup sugar

Combine and stir until sugar dissolves. Serve refrigerator cold or over ice.

GRAPEFRUIT OR ORANGE JUICE
WITH GRENADINE

Most grapefruits in the marketplace are picked well before they have had a chance to sweeten on the tree, and, when juiced, are much too acidic for me, especially early in the morning. But with a little grenadine stirred into grapefruit or orange juice, this fine source of vitamin C makes a welcome eye-opener. Into the juice of 1 large grapefruit, stir 1 or 2 teaspoons of grenadine.

FRESH CARROT JUICE

Makes 16 ounces, 3 small breakfast servings

By the early 1970s, a juice extractor was an important symbol of counterculture culinary membership, and it was often the source of dark, bitter concoctions made by extracting everything from asparagus to zucchini into the same glass. Over the years, the juice extractor faded away into the back of a cabinet, to appear once or twice a year when a nostalgic yearning for carrot juice was felt. Now we are seeing a resurgence of extracted juices. Feeding a piece of fresh ginger about an inch long into the extractor with the carrots will give the juice a mild ginger flavor, and will add balance to the naturally quite sweet flavor of the carrot juice.

Serve for breakfast or as part of an after-school snack.

2 pounds carrots, refrigerator cold, trimmed and scrubbed
3 small lemon wedges

Feed the carrots through a juice extractor. Pour into juice glasses. Serve with a wedge of lemon on the side.

FRESHLY EXTRACTED
PINEAPPLE JUICE

Makes about 3 cups

Freshly extracted pineapple juice has a light yet creamy texture and a sweet, round flavor with only a hint of acidity. It will generate more questions and excitement, when served to guests at breakfast, than anything else you serve. Most will declare that this tastes nothing like pineapple juice, meaning that canned pineapple juice tastes nothing like pineapple juice. You can also add a 1-inch chunk of gingerroot to the pineapple.

Ripe pineapples are more yellow than green or brown in appearance, especially at the bottom of the fruit, and feel soft but not mushy when pressed firmly between your fingers.

2 medium-sized ripe pineapples
About 2 teaspoons sugar, if necessary

Cut the leaves off the top and a slice off the bottom of the pineapples. With a large, sharp knife, thickly cut off the peel, removing most of the "eyes."

Cut the pineapples in half lengthwise, and cut out the center cores. Discard the cores and cut the pineapples into wedges that will fit into the feed tube of the juice extractor.

Feed the pineapple wedges into the extractor. Taste the juice; if the pineapples were not tree-ripened, it may be necessary to stir a little sugar into the juice to give it a lightly sweetened flavor. Refrigerate until cold. Stir and serve.

Other Freshly Extracted Fruit Juices

Even using the ripest fruits available, it is sometimes necessary to stir a little sugar into freshly extracted juices to give them a gently sweetened flavor. A half-teaspoon per cup is usually all that is necessary. Here are a few of my favorites. All should be chilled in a covered glass pitcher, and stirred just before serving.

Fresh Mango Juice

Peel the mangoes and remove the flesh from the large, clinging pit before extracting. A large mango will yield about 1 generous cup of juice. A ¼-inch-thick slice of fresh ginger can be extracted with the mango.

Fresh Mango and Papaya Juice

Peel, seed, and cut the papayas into wedges. Extract 2 medium-sized papayas for each large mango to make 2 cups of juice.

Fresh Orange and Carrot Juice

Extract 3 juice oranges, thickly peeled so all the skin and white pith is removed, and 1 pound of carrots to yield about 2½ cups.

Fresh Apple Cider

Extracted apples produce a drink with the color, taste, and texture of apple cider, not processed apple juice. Wash the apples, then remove the stems and core (don't peel) before extracting. My favorite apple for making cider is the Jonathan, which has a beautifully balanced flavor—fruity without being too sweet or too tart. A pound of apples yields a generous cup of cider. For a quick, hot spiced fresh apple cider, shake a little Chinese five-spice powder over a cup of cider and microwave for 2 or 3 minutes on high (100%).

Fresh Pear Cider

Prepare and serve as you would apple cider (above). My favorite pears for cider are Comice and Bosc.

Pancakes

FABULOUSLY LIGHT
WHOLE WHEAT PANCAKES

Makes 4 servings, twelve 6-inch pancakes

This is a delicately balanced recipe that produces pancakes with a fine, feathery light texture. Whole wheat adds warmth to the character of the pancakes as well as a gentle, nutty taste, and buttermilk gives the pancakes a graceful, balanced flavor.

Serve these topped with sliced bananas, thin wedges of very ripe, juicy peaches, or diced ripe Bosc pears, depending on the season and the quality of the fruit. Accompany the pancakes with some warm maple syrup. I don't think these pancakes need butter, but if you just can't eat pancakes without butter, brush each pancake very lightly with sweet, unsalted melted butter as you stack them on plates.

2 eggs
1½ cup nonfat buttermilk
¾ cup all-purpose flour
¼ cup whole wheat flour
1 teaspoon baking powder
½ teaspoon baking soda
2 teaspoons sugar
Vegetable oil spray

Preheat the oven to 300 degrees F.

Separate the eggs, slipping the yolks into a large mixing bowl and the whites into a medium-sized bowl. Set the whites aside.

With a whisk, blend the buttermilk into the yolks. Add the flours, baking powder, and soda and beat just until a smooth batter forms. Overbeating here will cause the pancakes to be tough.

With an electric beater or a clean whisk, beat the egg whites until frothy and doubled in volume, then add the sugar and continue beating until the whites are soft and shiny and just barely hold a stiff peak when the beater is lifted out of them. Scoop the whites onto the buttermilk batter and, with a large rubber spatula, gently fold together just until blended. Do not overmix and deflate.

Spray a nonstick frying pan lightly with vegetable oil spray and set over medium heat. When it is hot, ladle ⅓ to ½ cup of the batter into the pan to make a 6-inch pancake. When the top of the pancake becomes pitted all over with holes (it will still be moist in appearance), flip over with a spatula and cook very briefly on the second side, just long enough to very lightly brown the underside. Slip onto a plate and keep warm in the oven while the remaining pancakes are being cooked. Wipe the pan clean and spray it lightly with vegetable oil spray before cooking the next pancake.

Whole Wheat Blueberry or Raspberry Pancakes

After ladling the batter into the pan, wait until holes appear on about half of the surface of the pancake, then gently drop 6 to 8 fresh blueberries or raspberries onto the pancake. When the rest of the surface becomes holey, indicating that the pancake is cooked on the underside, flip the pancake carefully to prevent it from breaking, cook for 20 to 30 seconds longer, then carefully slip it out of the pan.

BUCKWHEAT PANCAKES WITH
FRESH BLUEBERRY SAUCE

Makes 4 servings, twelve 6-inch pancakes

These are soft, puffy pancakes with a light, cushiony texture. The buckwheat aroma and flavor are surprisingly mild. Buckwheat flour is available in some premium markets and health food stores.

Serve with blueberry sauce or a light maple syrup, topped with thinly sliced bananas, if you wish.

2 cups skim milk
3 eggs, separated
1 teaspoon sugar
1 tablespoon melted butter
1 tablespoon vegetable oil
1½ cups buckwheat flour
½ cup all-purpose flour
1½ teaspoons baking powder
Vegetable oil spray

Preheat the oven to 300 degrees F.

Whisk together the milk, egg yolks, sugar, butter, and oil until well blended. Add the buckwheat flour, all-purpose flour, and baking powder and whisk just until a smooth batter is formed. Beat the egg whites in a separate bowl until they hold a soft peak.

Pour the batter over the whites and fold together until just blended, with no streaks of whites. At first, the batter will resist incorporating the egg whites, but with a little persistence, the whites will blend into the batter.

Spray a large nonstick frying pan with vegetable oil spray and set over medium-low heat. When it is hot, ladle $1/3$ cup of the batter into the pan to make a 6-inch pancake. When the top of the pancake becomes pitted all over with holes, flip it with a spatula and cook very briefly on the second side, just long enough to very lightly brown the underside. Slip onto a plate and keep warm in the oven while the remaining pancakes are being cooked. Wipe the pan clean before cooking the next pancake.

Buckwheat pancakes color much more rapidly than white flour pancakes or corn pancakes, so be careful not to burn them.

Fresh Blueberry Sauce

Makes 2 cups

This quick, very fresh-tasting blueberry sauce can be served with pancakes or fruit salads.

1 quart small, fresh, ripe blueberries
2 tablespoons water
2 tablespoons sugar
Juice of $1/4$ lemon (optional)

In a medium-sized saucepan, combine the berries, water, and sugar. Place over medium heat. As the berries heat, they will exude some of their juices. Stir occasionally, and cook for about 2 minutes after the sauce reaches a boil. The sauce should have a deep blue color, and there should be just enough liquid to moisten the berries. Do not cook too long or the berries will give off too much of their moisture, and the sauce will become soupy.

A squirt of lemon juice can be stirred in to balance the sweetness, if you wish.

CORNMEAL PANCAKES
WITH PEACHES

Makes 16 pancakes, about 5 servings

These light, traditional pancakes with a rich corn flavor have thin slices of peaches or nectarines hidden on their undersides. When peaches and nectarines are out of season, top with thin mango wedges or spread with Peach or Apple Butter (recipes pages 69 and 73).

Serve with a light maple syrup.

1¹/₄ cups cornmeal
¹/₂ cup all-purpose flour
³/₄ teaspoon baking soda
2 cups buttermilk
3 extra large eggs
Vegetable oil spray
2 peaches or nectarines, thinly sliced

Preheat the oven to 300 degrees F.

In a large bowl, blend together the cornmeal, flour, and baking soda. Separately, beat the buttermilk and eggs until blended, then pour over the dry ingredients. Whisk together to form a smooth batter.

Place a large nonstick sauté pan over medium heat. When it is hot, mist lightly with vegetable oil spray and ladle ¹/₃ cup of the batter into the pan to make a 6-inch pancake. When the top of the pancake becomes pitted all over with holes, flip it with a spatula and cook very briefly on the second side, just long enough to very lightly brown the underside. Slip onto a platter and keep warm in the oven while the remaining pancakes are being cooked. Wipe the pan clean before cooking the next pancake.

Stack the pancakes on serving plates, top with the sliced fruit, and serve.

MIXED-GRAIN PANCAKES

Makes 4 servings

The batter for these pancakes lies to you. It has a very heady grain aroma and a strong flavor. The pancakes, however, are tender, light, and delicate.

A little maple syrup is all these need for a family meal, though some Fresh Blueberry Sauce (recipe page 55) or some chunks of ripe peaches could be used as a topping.

For a spicy variation, stir 1 1/2 teaspoons of ground cinnamon into the batter. This version is fine with thinly sliced ripe bananas and maple syrup.

1 cup rolled oats (not instant)
1/2 cup all-purpose flour
1/2 cup whole wheat flour
1/2 cup buckwheat flour
1 tablespoon baking powder
1 tablespoon sugar
3 cups nonfat or lowfat buttermilk
2 eggs
Vegetable oil spray

Preheat the oven to 300 degrees F.

In a large bowl, mix together the oats, all-purpose flour, whole wheat flour, buckwheat flour, baking powder, and sugar. In a separate bowl, beat together the buttermilk and eggs until well blended. Pour over the flours and stir until a thick, well-blended batter forms. Cover and set aside for 10 minutes.

Place a large sauté pan over medium-low to low heat. When it is hot, mist with vegetable oil spray. Stir the batter, then scoop some into a 1/3-cup measure and pour onto the heated pan. Bake until some bubbles appear on the top surface, which will still be quite wet in appearance, then carefully flip with a thin spatula. Cook briefly on the underside. Slip onto a plate and keep warm in the oven while the remaining pancakes are cooked. Wipe the pan clean before cooking the next pancake.

These pancakes cook more slowly and brown more quickly than most, so watch carefully.

Hot Cereals

BREAKFAST RISOTTO WITH
DRIED CHERRIES

A Microwave Recipe

Makes 3 servings

We eat cream of rice, puffed rice, and rice bran cereals, so why not a risotto—sweetened and flavored with fruit to move it from dinner to breakfast?

Using the microwave, this recipe takes only a minute to prepare, and it will all but cook itself while you shower or make coffee.

There are dried sour and sweet (Bing) cherries available in gourmet shops and some supermarkets. Although I prefer the sweet Bings for this recipe, either can be used.

This is a special breakfast. Even if you are eating it alone, it deserves to be spooned into a beautiful bowl and to be eaten slowly. The elegant texture of the rice and the gentle sweet flavors added to it make this a fine dish for serving at a small brunch party.

1 cup Arborio or any similar medium-grain rice (see headnote,
   page 198)
2^1/$_3$ cups water
^{1}/$_3$ cup skim milk
1 or 2 tablespoons sugar or honey
2 or 3 tablespoons dried cherries

Combine the rice and water in a large bowl and seal airtight with plastic wrap. Place the bowl on a plate (to catch any liquid that froths up and spills during the cooking), and microwave on high (100%) for 18 minutes. All of the water should

59

have been absorbed and the rice should be just barely tender; if not, microwave for another 1 or 2 minutes.

The risotto and the bowl will be extremely hot. Carefully uncover, stir in the milk, sugar or honey to taste, and the fruit. Add a little more milk if you want a thinner consistency.

Spoon into bowls and serve.

NOTE: Two to 4 tablespoons of almost any dried fruit can be substituted for the cherries in this risotto. Try dried blueberries, dried cranberries, currants, or coarsely chopped dried peaches, dried apricots, dried mission figs, or pitted prunes.

BROWN BASMATI RICE WITH
CINNAMON SUGAR

Makes 3 to 6 servings

Warm, fragrant grains of brown basmati rice with a little milk and a sprinkling of cinnamon sugar are as comforting and invigorating a way to start a cold day as I know. Don't let the straightforwardness and simplicity of this recipe fool you. The flavors and textures are rich and complex. And, even with a little sugar to sweeten the rice, this cereal is a dietitian's delight.

I usually cook 2 cups of rice and keep the leftovers for dinner or another breakfast later in the week.

Brown basmati rice is available in some Middle Eastern and Asian markets and many health food stores and supermarkets.

This is family fare. Serve with toast spread with a fruit butter, and a glass of juice or a cup of coffee.

**1 or 2 cups brown basmati rice (1 cup for 3 servings, 2 cups for 6
 servings)**
Water
$1/2$ cup sugar mixed with 1 teaspoon ground cinnamon
$3/4$ to $1 1/2$ cups skim milk

Cook the rice, either traditionally or in the microwave.

Traditional method: Bring 2 quarts of water to a boil in a large pot. Stir in the rice, reduce the heat, and simmer until just barely tender, about 35 minutes.

Microwave method: For 3 servings, combine 1 cup of rice with 2 cups of water in a microwave-safe bowl. Cover tightly and microwave on high (100%) for 20 minutes. Carefully uncover. All of the water should be absorbed and the rice should be tender. If not, cover again and microwave for another 1 or 2 minutes, until done.

For 6 servings, combine 2 cups of rice with 4 cups of water, and microwave for 30 minutes.

To serve: Drain the rice if prepared traditionally. Place 1 cup of rice in a cereal bowl, stir in about ¼ cup milk, and sprinkle with cinnamon sugar (2 or so teaspoons per serving) to taste.

GREAT OATMEAL

Makes 4 servings

Steel-cut oats, with their natural, full-bodied, nutty flavor, give this bowl of cereal a variety of textures and dimensions. When a little light cream, brown sugar, cinnamon, other spices, vanilla, and raisins are added, the cereal becomes a really terrific breakfast dish.

There are 3 kinds of oats: steel-cut, simply oat kernels that have been cut in half with a steel blade; rolled, kernels that have been rolled flat; and instant, rolled oats that have been cooked and then dehydrated. Steel-cut oats, which are the least processed, have the best flavor and texture. Sometimes called Irish oats, they are available in premium supermarkets and health food stores.

3½ cups hot tap water
1 cup steel-cut (Irish) oats
¼ cup half-and-half
3 tablespoons brown sugar
½ teaspoon ground cinnamon
⅛ teaspoon ground ginger
⅛ teaspoon ground allspice
1 teaspoon vanilla extract
¼ cup currants

In a heavy-bottomed saucepan, bring the water to a boil. Add the oats, reduce the heat, and simmer, stirring occasionally, until oatmeal is thick and tender, about 35 minutes. During the last 10 minutes of cooking, stir frequently to prevent the oatmeal from scorching.

Stir in the remaining ingredients, taste, and adjust the flavors. Serve immediately.

Alternative procedure: If you cook the oats and water in the top of a double boiler set over simmering water, which will take an extra 10 minutes, there is virtually no need for stirring.

BREAD PUDDING WITH CURRANTS

Makes 4 servings

Light, tender, subtly flavored, and comforting, this cinnamon whole wheat bread pudding, which can be thrown together in about 10 minutes, is a complete breakfast in itself, power-packed with fiber, a vast array of nutrients, and calcium. When I served this for brunch, a friend said mockingly, "I love having sugar on my eggs in the morning."

Serve this with juice or a Fresh Pear Compote (page 43) or topped with Fresh Blueberry Sauce (page 55) or Peach Butter (page 69).

Currants are sometimes available in supermarkets, and usually easy to find in health food stores. You may substitute raisins for the currants, but the pudding will not taste the same.

6 ounces French or Italian-style whole wheat bread, cut into 1-inch cubes
2 tablespoons currants
3 cups skim milk
1/3 cup sugar
3 eggs
2 teaspoons vanilla extract
1/4 teaspoon cinnamon

Preheat the oven to 350 degrees F.

Place the bread in a buttered 6-cup soufflé dish and scatter the currants over, around, and between the cubes. In a separate bowl, whisk the remaining ingredients together until well blended but not frothy. Pour over the bread, pressing the bread into the egg mixture so that all the bread is wet.

Bake until pudding is puffy and lightly browned on top, about 1 hour and 15 minutes.

Allow to cool for 10 minutes before serving.

Preserves and Fruit Butters

The counterculture's move from cities and campuses to communes, as well as its belief in an older, simpler way of cooking, led to a resurgence in canning and preserving, especially during the summer months when there were often huge, unexpected excesses of fruits and berries.

Making preserves and fruit butters is simple. Preserves need only about 15 minutes of preparation and about an hour of cooking; fruit butters need about half an hour of preparation, and about 8 hours in the oven. Fortunately, fruit butters need no stirring, so you can place the fruit mixture in the oven, set "time bake" so the oven turns itself off in 8 hours, and go about your day's business or night's sleep.

The sugar in the recipes below has been reduced by 75 percent to 90 percent from traditional preserves and butters. These lighter preserves and butters allow the ripe, fresh aromas and flavors of the berries or fruit, rather than sugar, to dominate their taste.

For the best results, use fresh, ripe, peak-season berries or fruit, which are often available in farmers' markets or roadside stands at reasonable prices.

Because preserves and fruit butters freeze well, freezing is recommended rather than the process of traditional canning. If you wish to put them in glass containers to give as presents, see chapter 11.

BLUEBERRY PRESERVES

Master Recipe

Makes about 4 cups

These lightly sweetened preserves have a fresh, intensely fruity flavor with an assertive lemon taste.

The best blueberries for preserving are the smaller, sweeter varieties, rather than the large commercial blueberries found in most supermarkets.

3 quarts (about 3¾ pounds) fresh blueberries
1½ cups sugar
1 cup water
Grated zest and juice of 1 lemon

In a large pot, combine the berries, sugar, and water. Place over medium heat and stir frequently until the sugar is dissolved and the mixture comes to a boil. Reduce the heat and simmer, stirring occasionally to prevent scorching, until the preserves have thickened and reached the proper jelling consistency, about 45 to 60 minutes.

Testing for proper consistency: After about 40 minutes, the berries will have partially dissolved into a thick, sometimes seething mixture. Stir the mixture, then scoop a little of the preserves into a clean teaspoon and set the spoon in the freezer for 5 minutes to chill. The liquid on the spoon around the berries should be thick and jelled, but not hard. If not, simmer for another 5 to 10 minutes, then test again.

When the berries have reached the proper consistency, remove from the heat, stir in the lemon zest and juice, cover loosely, and set aside to cool.

When cool, transfer a cup or so of the preserves to a jar, cover and refrigerate for current use. Divide the remaining amount into plastic freezer bags, seal airtight, and freeze until needed.

Preserves can be stored for up to 2 months in the refrigerator; up to 6 months in the freezer.

Huckleberry-Blueberry Preserves

Using all huckleberries for a preserve makes a very fibrous jam, so I suggest using 2 quarts huckleberries and 1 quart blueberries.

Fresh Raspberry Preserves

Substitute raspberries for the blueberries, increase the sugar to 2 cups, and begin testing for doneness after 30 minutes. Substitute the grated zest and juice of ½ orange for the lemon zest and juice. Or substitute ¼ cup Grand Marnier for the orange juice.

Fresh Blackberry Preserves

Substitute fresh blackberries for the blueberries, eliminate the zest, and add the juice of only ½ lemon.

Sour Cherry Preserves

Substitute 2 quarts pitted sour cherries for the blueberries, eliminate the lemon zest, and add the juice of only ½ lemon.

PEACH BUTTER

Makes about 6 cups

Ripe peaches from local farms that are so tender they have to be eaten the day they are purchased and so moist they drip all over your hands when you eat them are my favorite fruit of summer, and I always buy too many of them. The second day in my kitchen, they are soft and bruised and oozing, so I turn them into this butter before they destroy themselves with their own sweetness.

This sauce is not worth making with commercial, picked-green, supermarket peaches.

Use as a topping on ice cream, to accompany custards, with pancakes or waffles, as a spread for breads, or mixed into breakfast cereals. It can also be served alongside roast chicken or pork.

5 pounds tree-ripened peaches, washed, stems and leaves removed

1 cup sugar

1 teaspoon cinnamon

1 teaspoon ground ginger

1 teaspoon ground coriander or nutmeg

Juice of 1 to 2 lemons (optional, see note in procedure)

Cut the peaches into chunks by making 6 or 7 deep vertical cuts into the peach until the knife blade touches the pit. Next, make 2 horizontal cuts all the way around the peach, again cutting to the pit. With a little squeezing and pressing, the flesh will fall off the pit in chunks just the right size for puréeing.

Working over a very large bowl, pit all the peaches in this way, allowing juices to drip into the bowl.

Depending on the size of your food processor, transfer a cup or two of the peaches into the bowl and pulse until the peaches become a little liquidy but are still chunky. Do not purée until smooth. Unevenly chopped pieces are best, but there should be no pieces larger than a small marble. Repeat until all the peaches are processed.

Transfer the peaches to a nonaluminum roasting pan or ovenproof pot that is large enough to hold all the chopped peaches, 6 quarts or more. The larger the mouth of the pot, the faster the peach sauce will cook, so a deep, tall pot will take longest, and a large shallow roasting pan will take the least time.

When all of the peaches have been placed in the pan or pot, stir into them the sugar and spices, and lemon juice. (Sometimes I use the lemon juice, sometimes I don't. The sweeter the peaches, the more likely I am to use the lemon juice to balance the flavor.)

Place the pan uncovered in the lower third of a cold oven. Set the oven temperature to 250 degrees F and cook the peaches until a caramel-colored, thick but still runny sauce forms, about 8 hours. I generally stir and taste the sauce every 2 or 3 hours, though it isn't necessary.

When done, if the skin on the surface of the butter is very thick, remove it, and stir the peach butter well. Cool, loosely covered. Transfer some to a jar, cover, and refrigerate for current use; transfer the rest to plastic bags and freeze.

Peach butter can be stored in the refrigerator for up to 2 months, in the freezer for up to 6 months.

PEAR BUTTER

Makes about 6 cups

Pears, with their complex flavor, aroma, and texture, make a thick, rich butter that is best on simply flavored breads.

Juice of 5 lemons
2 cups fine quality Scotch, bourbon, dark rum, or apple cider or juice
2 cups granulated sugar
5 pounds tender, sweet, ripe but not mushy pears

In a large nonaluminum pot or kettle, stir together the lemon juice, liquid, and sugar. Bring to a boil over medium heat, stirring occasionally until sugar is dissolved. Reduce the heat and simmer very gently while you prepare the pears.

Remove the stems and cut the pears in half lengthwise. With a melon baller, remove and discard the cores. With a sharp knife, cut a wedge into the pear halves to remove the fibers that attach the core to the stem and blossom ends. Peel the pears and cut into 1½- to 2-inch chunks. Toss into the simmering cooking liquid.

When all the pears are in the pot, increase the heat to high and bring the mixture to a boil, then reduce the heat so that the pears boil very slowly. Cook, stirring and checking the heat occasionally, until the pears become the texture of a chunky applesauce, about 1 hour.

Purée the pear mixture in small batches in a food processor until very smooth. Transfer the pears to a large, shallow nonaluminum pan or pot and place in a cold oven, uncovered. The larger the mouth of the pot, the faster the sauce will cook.

Set the oven to 250 degrees F. Bake, stirring (and tasting) every 2 hours until a dark brown pear butter forms that is about as thick as sour cream, almost thick enough for a spoon to stand in it, about 8 hours.

When done, if the skin on the surface is thick, remove it, stir well, and set aside to cool, loosely covered. Transfer some to a jar, cover, and refrigerate for current use; transfer the rest to plastic bags and freeze.

Pear butter can be stored in the refrigerator for up to 2 months, in the freezer for up to 6 months.

APPLE BUTTER

Makes about 6 cups

The best apple butter is made with big, tart cooking apples, such as Jonathans or Pippins, and is just barely flavored and scented with spices. This is a thick butter, unlike the thin, oversweetened apple butters found in farmers' markets, health food stores, and sometimes in supermarket fresh produce sections.

Serve with whole grain breads such as Mixed-Grain Bread (page 257), or Everyday Whole Wheat Bread (page 251).

Juice of 2 lemons
2 cups apple cider or juice
4 cups sugar
5 pounds tart apples, peeled and cored
2 teaspoons ground cinnamon
$^{1}/_{2}$ teaspoon nutmeg
$^{3}/_{4}$ teaspoon ground ginger

Prepare as directed in the recipe for Pear Butter (page 71), stirring the spices into the apple mixture just before placing it in the oven.

Smoothies

Smoothies are cold, "frozen" drinks made from fresh or frozen fruit, fruit juices, milk, and yogurt. They are refreshing, full of body and texture, and laden with the intense flavors of the orchard. For breakfast, they are mostly warm-weather drinks. But they can also be used for after-school and after-the-gym snacks.

Smoothies were in vogue with the counterculture in the West in the late 1960s and 1970s. Later they became popular with athletes and weight lifters, who often added powdered protein supplements and raw eggs to make them healthier. Neither of those, however, is necessary or recommended. Indeed, protein supplements are placebos (though there is no evidence to indicate that they are dangerous) for those believing they will build muscles; and today eating raw eggs, many of which are contaminated with salmonella, could be dangerous.

There is some evidence to indicate that children who participate in preparing their own foods eat better and enjoy the food more. Smoothies are an excellent way to involve children in preparing their own after-school snacks. If they can pour juice, peel a banana, and perhaps cut up a fresh fruit, they can make their own smoothies.

Smoothies are a good source of calories, fiber, vitamins, and minerals, with the important virtue of having no fat.

My inspiration for this section of the book came from a friend and dietitian, Kristine Mehring, whose understanding of the rich nutritional value of smoothies, and whose love for food, led her to develop a great variety of these cold drinks for her patients.

Making Smoothies: All smoothies are made in the same way: Ingredients are combined in a blender and blended until smooth. Bananas, sherbets, sorbets, nonfat ice creams, and ice give the smoothies body; fruits, fruit juices, yogurt, and skim milk give the smoothies flavor. To create your own smoothies, combine a banana or $1/2$ cup of ice, sherbet, or sorbet with any large fruit and about $1 1/2$ cups of juice, nonfat milk, or yogurt, and blend until smooth.

STRAWBERRY-BANANA-ORANGE SMOOTHY

Makes 2 servings

8 large strawberries, washed and hulled
1 medium-sized ripe banana
1 cup calcium-enriched or freshly squeezed orange juice
1 cup ice cubes

Blend until smooth.

Raspberry-Banana-Orange Smoothy

Substitute 1/2 cup raspberries for the strawberries.

Blackberry Smoothy

Substitute 1/3 cup blackberries for the strawberries.

KIWI SMOOTHY

Makes 2 servings

4 ripe kiwis, peeled
1/2 cup pineapple juice
3/4 cup ice cubes

Blend until smooth.

Mango Smoothy

Substitute the flesh of 1 large mango for the kiwis, and use $1/4$ cup pineapple juice and $1/4$ cup apricot nectar.

Peach Smoothy

Substitute 1 large ripe peach for the kiwis and add a small ripe banana.

ORANGE CREAMSICLE SMOOTHY

Makes 2 servings

1 cup calcium-fortified or freshly squeezed orange juice
$3/4$ cup nonfat vanilla ice cream or nonfat vanilla yogurt
$1/2$ cup ice cubes

Blend until smooth.

Raspberry Creamsicle

Substitute 1 cup fresh or frozen raspberries for the orange juice and add $1/2$ cup skim milk to the other ingredients.

Lime Creamsicle

Substitute lime sherbet or sorbet for the orange juice and add $1/4$ cup skim milk to the other ingredients.

4

Soups

VEGETABLE SOUPS

Gently Curried Pumpkin Soup
Fresh Corn and Egg Drop Soup with Chives
Sweet Potato Soup
Carrot and Yam Bisque
Parsnip Bisque with Coconut
Wild Mushroom Soup with Barley
Winter Tomato Soup

BEAN AND LENTIL SOUPS

White Bean and Leek Bisque
Mixed Bean Soup
Tomato, Chicken, and Red Bean Soup
Lentil Soup

LIGHT SEAFOOD SOUPS

Thai-style Fish Soup with Lemongrass
Lobster Stew

MEAL-SIZE SOUPS

Aztec Chicken Soup
Provençal-style Fish Soup with Potatoes, Halibut, and Fennel
Mediterranean-style Fish Soup with Potatoes and Orzo
A Big Boiled Dinner for a Formal Party

STOCKS, BROTHS, AND CONSOMMÉS

Chicken Stock, or Broth, or Soup
Chicken Consommé
Brown Beef Stock, or Broth, or Soup
Vegetable Stock, or Broth, or Soup
Fish Stock, or Broth, or Soup

Introduction

Soups, because of their association with simple home cooking, were an essential part of counterculture cooking in the 1970s. For the students of the 1960s, as much as for all of us today, soups are comfort food. We were and sometimes still are nourished with soups our mothers made—thick, rich vegetable soups in winter; light bisques and cold soups in summer; chicken soups when we are sick.

There is almost never a time when it would be inappropriate to serve a soup. Fruit soups have been served at breakfasts, all manner of soups have been served to start a lunch, some soups are big enough to *be* a lunch. At dinner, formal cups of consommé begin elegant dinners; light fish soups introduce a company meal; hearty soups begin family dinners.

Soups have traditionally occupied a prized place in American eating. Now, with our awareness of a need for lower-fat foods, and for foods that are light on the environment, we are seeing a renewed interest in soup making.

In this chapter there are a variety of different kinds of soups: soups that can be made quickly, light bisques, meal-size soups from Mexico and the south of France, and bean and lentil soups. There are versions of classics, like Chinese egg drop soup and Thai fish soup. And finally, there are stocks, broths, and consommés.

Using Stocks and Broths in This Book

Many of the recipes in this book use a stock or broth. Ideally, these should be homemade, either from the recipes in this chapter or from your own favorite stock recipe.

When there isn't time to prepare your own stocks, real homemade chicken and beef stocks can be purchased in the frozen foods sections of many premium food specialty stores. Fish stock is sold by some premium fish markets.

Canned stock, broth, bouillon, and bouillon cubes really are not an acceptable substitute for homemade, or store-bought "homemade" stocks.

Vegetable Soups

GENTLY CURRIED PUMPKIN SOUP

Makes 4 to 6 servings

The pumpkin-eating "season" in my home begins just after Halloween and lasts until Thanksgiving. Very rarely do I use fresh pumpkin; its watery texture and flavor is so mild, it is difficult for most people to identify. Instead I use canned pumpkin, which is not made from jack-o'-lantern type pumpkins, but huge (usually over 20 pounds) gray-blue winter "pumpkin squashes," which have a very hard dark orange flesh.

This quick soup has a big, sweet pumpkin flavor balanced gently with a little curry powder. Serve it from a mug with a vegetarian sandwich for lunch, or as the starter for a family dinner.

Olive oil spray
1 medium-sized onion, peeled and chopped
1/2 teaspoon curry powder
2 cups (16 ounces) canned pumpkin
4 cups chicken stock

Lightly spray the bottom of a nonstick sauté pan with oil spray and set over medium heat. Add the onion, mist so that all the onion pieces are lightly coated, and sauté, stirring frequently, until onion becomes translucent, about 6 minutes. Sprinkle the curry over the onions and cook 2 minutes longer to remove the powdery flavor of the curry.

Scrape into the bowl of a food processor, add the remaining ingredients, and purée; or combine everything in a large bowl and purée, in batches, in a blender.

Heat, either in a saucepan or in the microwave, and serve.

Chilied Pumpkin Soup with Corn

Replace the curry with 1 tablespoon chili powder, $^1/_2$ teaspoon ground cumin, and $^1/_2$ teaspoon crushed dried oregano. After puréeing, stir in about $1^1/_2$ cups canned or frozen (and defrosted) corn.

Pumpkin Bisque

In either the recipe or variation above, to make a bisque, simply replace 2 cups of the stock with 2 cups of 2 percent or whole milk.

FRESH CORN AND EGG DROP SOUP
WITH CHIVES

Makes 6 servings

This fresh corn soup can be made in less than 15 minutes. It is a corn-filled version of egg drop soup—but not as thick, and with a richer broth flavor. If there are children in the house, let them watch as the egg whites are poured into the spinning soup to form the white threads.

In very cold weather, I sometimes stir a little hot Chinese mustard or mushroom soy sauce into the soup just before serving.

4 cups chicken stock
2 ears of corn, preferably white, shucked
1½ tablespoons (1 tablespoon plus 1½ teaspoons) cornstarch
2 tablespoons cold water
1 extra large egg white
2 tablespoons skim milk
2 tablespoons freshly chopped chives (scallions may be substituted if necessary)

In a large pot, bring the stock to a boil. While the stock is heating, stand the corn on one end, and with a sharp paring knife, cut off the kernels, slicing downward. Toss the kernels into the stock.

In a small bowl mix the cornstarch and water until smooth. In another bowl, beat the egg white and milk together until blended.

When the stock comes to a boil, stir in the cornstarch and bring back to a boil so the soup will thicken.

When it has reached a rolling boil, remove the soup from the heat and stir with a large spoon so that the soup is spinning around in a circle. While stirring with one hand to keep the soup moving, slowly pour the egg white mixture, in a very thin stream, into the center of the spinning soup. This will form the traditional threads called "egg drops."

Ladle into soup plates or bowls, sprinkle the top of each with a scant teaspoon of chives, and serve.

SWEET POTATO SOUP

Makes 2 to 3 servings

Many of us who free-lance and work alone at home have found ways to amuse ourselves by sending each other faxes—jokes, cartoons, or whatever. Occasionally, friends fax me recipes, like this utterly simple soup that takes almost no time to make and is an example of simple home cooking at its best.

This recipe was created to use up a leftover sweet potato. An 8-ounce sweet potato can be cooked in a microwave oven on high (100%) in 7 minutes, if like me, you virtually never find yourself with a leftover cooked sweet potato.

1 large cooked sweet potato, peeled
1½ cups strong chicken stock
¾ cup milk (1 percent or skim)
Salt and white pepper to taste

In a food processor, combine the sweet potato, stock, and milk. Process until smooth, pulsing frequently. Season with a little salt and pepper.

Either pour into a heavy-bottomed saucepan and cook over medium heat, stirring occasionally, until very hot, or pour into a microwave-safe bowl, cover tightly with plastic wrap, and microwave on high (100%) until very hot, about 4 minutes.

Ladle into soup bowls or mugs and serve.

CARROT AND YAM BISQUE

Makes 6 servings

This medium-thick, pale orange-colored soup has a sweet flavor accented with cinnamon and ginger. It is rich in beta carotene, an important nutrient. For the best flavor and aroma, allow the soup to mellow for about half an hour after it is puréed, then reheat.

Serve a small bowl of this soup before a large bowl of Vegetarian Chili (page 190), accompanied by thick slices of a Everyday Whole Wheat Bread or Mixed-Grain Bread (pages 251 and 257).

^{1}/2 pound carrots, trimmed, scrubbed, and cut into 2- to 3-inch pieces
1 small (about 8 ounces) yam, peeled and cut into chunks
1 small onion, trimmed, peeled, and quartered
A 2-inch cinnamon stick
1 quart skim milk
2 cups chicken broth
Grated zest of ^{1}/2 orange
^{1}/2 teaspoon ground ginger
A little ground white pepper

In a large soup pot, combine the carrots, yam, onion, cinnamon stick, milk, and broth. Bring to a boil over high heat, then reduce the heat and simmer for 50 to 60 minutes, until all the vegetables are very tender.

In small batches, purée in a blender until very smooth, holding the top of the blender very securely in place to prevent the soup from spewing out all over the kitchen.

Stir in the orange zest and ginger, taste, and season with pepper.

Return to the soup pot, reheat, and serve.

PARSNIP BISQUE WITH
COCONUT

Makes 6 to 8 servings

Unfortunately, parsnips have been relegated to a lowly status in culinary circles. Simply because they grow underground and aren't especially pretty is no reason to ignore this flavorful, nutritious winter wonder.

This soup has a velvety texture and a sweet flavor, with a coconut aroma and a subtle nip of cardamom and ginger.

Serve at a family or company dinner, with Clover Leaf Rolls (page 249), followed by Haricots Verts with Chanterelles (page 166), Seared Halibut with Chermoula Sauce (page 275), and some brown rice (see chapter 7).

1 large onion, trimmed, peeled, and quartered
1 large leek, white part only, thoroughly washed to remove all grit,
  but left whole
1 celery rib, washed and cut in half
1½ pounds medium-sized parsnips, washed, trimmed, peeled and cut
  into 1-inch pieces
3 cups chicken stock
3 cups skim milk
⅛ teaspoon ground cardamom
⅛ teaspoon ground ginger
¼ cup shredded, dried, sweetened coconut

In a large soup pot, combine everything and bring to a boil over high heat. Reduce the heat and simmer for 1 hour.

With a ladle and long tongs, carefully remove and discard the onion, leek, and celery. In small batches, purée the soup in a blender until very smooth, holding the top of the blender securely in place to prevent the soup from erupting all over the kitchen. Strain to remove the bits of coconut, then return to the pot and reheat.

Leftover soup can be refrigerated for up to 3 days or frozen for up to 3 months.

WILD MUSHROOM SOUP
WITH BARLEY

Makes 4 servings

Laden with strips of wild mushrooms and accented by barley, this soup has an unexpected gentleness. Serve at a small, special winter dinner, accompanied by warm sourdough bread, followed by small servings of a roasted chicken with 2 or 3 vegetables and a grain, such as the Sweet Red Pepper Ragout (page 177), a green beans preparation, and Whole Wheat Couscous with Wild Mushrooms (page 212).

1 celery rib, washed and cut into small dice
$1/2$ medium size onion, trimmed, peeled, and diced
1 large garlic clove, peeled and very finely chopped
2 tablespoons medium pearl barley
1 pound shiitake mushrooms, or a mixture of shiitake and chanterelle mushrooms, stems removed, washed and cut into $1/4$-inch wide strips
$3^1/2$ cups beef broth
$1/4$ teaspoon crushed dried thyme
$1/8$ teaspoon crushed dried marjoram
$1/8$ teaspoon crushed dried savory
A little salt
Freshly ground black pepper

Combine everything except the salt and pepper in a large soup pot. Bring to a boil over high heat, then reduce the heat and simmer for 45 minutes. Season with salt and pepper to taste.

WINTER TOMATO SOUP

Makes 8 servings

By January or February, when it has been five or six months since I have eaten a great, vine-ripened tomato, I make this soup, as a remembrance of summer. This is a simple, moderately thin soup with a rich tomato flavor. The sweet red peppers, rather than competing with the tomatoes, bring out their flavor.

Serve this as a light starter to a heavy winter meal.

Two 28-ounce cans peeled Italian-style plum tomatoes, undrained
1 tablespoon tomato paste
2 medium-sized sweet red bell peppers, cored and cut into 1-inch
  pieces
3 cups beef broth
1 teaspoon hot Hungarian paprika
A little salt
Freshly ground black pepper

In a large soup pot, combine everything except the salt and pepper and bring to a boil over high heat. Reduce the heat and simmer for 30 minutes, stirring occasionally to break up the tomatoes.

In a blender, in small batches, holding the cover securely in place to prevent the soup from spewing all over the kitchen, purée the soup until very smooth.

Return to the soup pot, season with salt and pepper to taste, and reheat before serving.

Leftover soup can be refrigerated for up to 3 days, and frozen for up to 4 months.

Bean and Lentil Soups

WHITE BEAN AND LEEK BISQUE

Makes 4 or 5 servings

This light bisque with a rich leek flavor is friendly enough to be served for a family meal or afternoon snack, and with the garnish of chopped chives, elegant enough for a wintertime company dinner.

2 tablespoons olive oil

3 large leeks, white parts only, split, thoroughly washed, and thinly sliced

1 small onion, peeled and thinly sliced

2 garlic cloves, peeled and finely chopped

1 cup cooked white beans (canned and drained, or prepared according to the recipe on page 216)

2 cups chicken stock

1/2 cup whole milk or half-and-half

2 teaspoons finely chopped chives (optional)

In a large saucepan, stir together the oil, leeks, onion and garlic. Place over medium low heat and cook, covered, stirring occasionally, until vegetables become tender and translucent, about 10 minutes.

Add the beans and 2 cups chicken stock, then purée in small batches in a blender, holding the top securely in place to prevent the soup from erupting all over the kitchen. Return to the saucepan, stir in the milk or half-and-half, and bring back to a boil.

To serve, ladle into bowls and sprinkle with chives.

White Bean Vichyssoise

After puréeing the soup, strain to make a fine, smooth purée, discarding any bean pulp that remains in the strainer. Stir in the milk or half-and-half and refrigerate, covered, until cold. Serve chilled, garnished with chopped chives.

MIXED BEAN SOUP

Makes 12 servings

The variety of beans, each with its own special flavor and texture, is accented with a handful of different vegetables and herbs to make this a hearty, very cold-weather soup. The final addition of vinegar and pepper pulls all the flavors together and eliminates the need for salt.

Beans are nutritional powerhouses, dense in fibers and nutrients with virtually no fat. Packages of mixed beans without seasonings are available in premium supermarkets and specialty food stores.

Serve a small bowl of this soup before a winter dinner, or with slices of toasted, crusty bread for a light winter lunch.

2 cups (about 12 ounces) dried mixed beans or other many-bean combination
2 quarts chicken stock
One 28-ounce can crushed tomatoes in purée
2 quarts water or vegetable stock
2 medium-sized carrots, trimmed, scrubbed, and, as much as possible, cut into 1/2-inch dice
2 celery ribs, washed and cut into 1/2-inch dice
1 medium-sized onion, peeled and chopped
1 small sweet green bell pepper, cored and cut into 1/2-inch dice
1 small sweet red bell pepper, cored and cut into 1/2-inch dice
8 small garlic cloves, peeled only
1 teaspoon crushed dried oregano
1 teaspoon crushed dried thyme
1 teaspoon crushed dried rosemary
2 teaspoons crushed dried basil
3 tablespoons balsamic vinegar
Freshly ground black pepper

In a large soup pot, combine everything except the vinegar and black pepper and bring to a boil over high heat. Reduce the heat to low and simmer, partially covered, until all the beans are tender, though some will be soft and others still firm, about 2 to 2½ hours, stirring the soup occasionally.

Stir in the vinegar, and season with pepper.

Leftover soup can be stored in the refrigerator for up to 4 days, or frozen for up to 6 months.

TOMATO, CHICKEN, AND
RED BEAN SOUP

Makes 4 to 6 servings

This is a meal in itself, mostly made from leftovers—a rich tomato, chicken, and bean soup flavored with paprika and herbs. It only takes about 15 minutes to prepare, assuming all the ingredients are on hand.

Homemade tomato sauce will give this soup its best flavor, but commercial tomato sauce can be used. Three cups of home-cooked beans can be substituted for the canned beans if ¹/₂ cup additional broth is added to the recipe. You can, of course, omit the chicken if you have none on hand.

Serve in a large bowl with a couple of thick slices of homemade bread for a family dinner.

Two 15-ounce cans red kidney beans, not drained
¹/₂ teaspoon dried thyme
¹/₂ teaspoon dried rosemary
1 tablespoon sweet or hot Hungarian paprika
1¹/₂ cups chicken broth
1 cup Tomato Sauce (page 228)
1 cup diced cooked chicken
Freshly ground black pepper

Combine 1 can of the kidney beans with the thyme, rosemary, and paprika in a blender and blend until smooth.

Transfer to a medium-sized saucepan and stir in the remaining can of beans, the broth, tomato sauce, and chicken. Bring to a boil over medium heat, season with pepper, and serve.

LENTIL SOUP

Makes 12 servings

Lentil soup, with its homey texture and simple, earthy aroma is traditional cold-weather fare. When cooked without the ham hock and puréed until smooth, then strained to make it even smoother, and chilled, this lentil soup can be served cold in warm weather, topped with a dollop of plain yogurt or light sour cream and some finely chopped fresh herbs.

2 cups dried lentils
2 carrots, scraped and cut into 1-inch lengths
1 large onion, peeled and quartered
2 celery ribs, washed and cut into 1-inch lengths
One 28-ounce can peeled Italian-style plum tomatoes, not drained
3 quarts hot tap water
2 garlic cloves, peeled
A 2-inch chunk fresh gingerroot, peeled and coarsely chopped
2 teaspoons crushed dried rosemary
1 teaspoon crushed dried thyme
1 teaspoon crushed dried oregano
1 small smoked ham hock
A little salt
Freshly ground black pepper

Combine everything except the salt and pepper in a large soup pot and bring to a boil over medium high heat, stirring once or twice. Reduce the heat and cook, partially covered, until lentils are very tender, about 1½ hours. Carefully remove the ham hock, and trim off any small pieces of meat still adhering to the bone. These can be added back to the soup, or saved for another use.

For a smooth soup, purée everything in batches in a blender or food processor.

For a chunky soup, carefully ladle about ⅓ of the lentils out of the pot and pour into a clean bowl. A little of the soup will come with the lentils. Next, purée the remaining soup, then put the reserved lentils back into the soup. Taste, and season with salt and pepper.

Reheat and serve.

Leftover soup can be stored in the refrigerator for up to 4 days, or frozen for up to 6 months.

Light Seafood Soups

THAI-STYLE FISH SOUP WITH LEMONGRASS

Makes 6 servings

This Thai-style soup is made by flavoring a light fish broth with lemongrass and ginger, then straining the broth and adding shrimp, scallops, tomato, and slivers of hot pepper. The seafood adds textural interest to the highly scented soup. The jalapeño pepper can be eliminated if you prefer a milder version.

Lemongrass is a fibrous grass with a straw color that is sold in sticks about two feet long. When cooked, it imparts a sweet, roundly flavored lemon taste, without any of the acidity of lemon juice. It is available in Thai markets and some premium supermarkets.

For a light dinner on a warm spring night, serve this soup followed by Thai Chicken Salad (page 284).

6 small fresh shrimp, peeled, shells reserved

8 cups Fish Stock (page 118)

3 sticks lemongrass, bottoms trimmed, tough, dry outer leaves removed, then cut crosswise (like scallions) with a very sharp chef's knife into ¼-inch pieces

3 quarter-sized disks fresh gingerroot

6 large fresh bay scallops, each carefully cut crosswise into 3 disks

1 small jalapeño pepper, ends trimmed, cut in half lengthwise, seeds removed, and cut into eighteen 1-inch slivers (the rest of the pepper can be saved for another use)

1 small tomato, cored and cut in half around its middle, then squeezed to remove the seeds, and finally cut into ½-inch dice with a serrated knife

Combine the shrimp shells, stock, lemongrass, and ginger in a large nonaluminum saucepan and bring to a boil over high heat. Lower the heat so the stock is boiling very gently and reduce to 6 cups.

Strain through a sieve lined with a dampened towel or cheesecloth and return to the saucepan. Bring back to a boil, add the shrimp, scallops, the jalapeño slivers, and the diced tomato. Adjust the heat so the stock simmers until the shrimp and scallops have just become opaque, about 90 seconds.

Ladle into heated soup bowls or plates. Each should have 3 pieces of scallop, 1 shrimp, and 3 slivers of the pepper.

Serve immediately.

LOBSTER STEW

This is like an oyster stew, but with lobster instead of oysters. It is simple, expensive, and very impressive, especially considering that it takes less than 10 minutes to make. As there are only 5 ingredients, and virtually no cooking, each ingredient for this elegant soup must be perfect. Use only homemade stocks, very fresh basil leaves, and the freshest lobster meat.

Many fish shops and fish markets in premium groceries sell raw lobster meat. To be certain it is fresh, ask if it has been frozen. Frozen meat will be tough, dry, and grainy.

1 cup Fish Stock (page 118)
1 cup Chicken Stock (page 110)
1 cup whole milk
12 ounces fresh lobster meat, cut into ½- to ¾-inch pieces
6 fresh basil leaves, stems removed, then rolled like a cigarette and cut
   crosswise into very thin threads with a very sharp chef's knife

In a nonaluminum saucepan, bring the fish stock, chicken stock, and milk to a boil. Add the lobster and basil, reduce the heat, and simmer until the lobster just becomes opaque, about 90 seconds.

Ladle into soup plates and serve immediately.

Meal-Size Soups

AZTEC CHICKEN SOUP

Makes 10 servings

A hot and cold combination of flavors and textures makes this Aztec-inspired chicken soup refreshing and vibrant. The spicy soup, which includes a variety of vegetables, rice, and chick-peas, is boldly flavored with garlic, spices, and herbs, and is topped, just before serving, with chunks of cold avocado mixed with tomatoes, scallions, and a hot pepper.

This is a meal in itself. There are 4 vegetables, chick-peas, and rice, as well as chicken, in each serving. Accompanied by thick slices of sourdough or whole wheat bread, lightly toasted or fresh from the oven, this is an extraordinary winter meal for family or friends.

This recipe, submitted by The Square D Company, was one of the winning guest chef recipes in the 1991 Chicago March of Dimes Gala. The original recipe called for 10 cups of chicken stock, more than most of us have on hand, so in this version, the first step is to make some simple stock. Use chicken bones, necks, and backs that have been frozen from previous chicken meals for future stock-making, or buy some inexpensive chicken backs or legs, or use turkey bones and necks.

12 cups cold water

4 pounds chicken or turkey bones, necks, or backs

One 2½-pound chicken, quartered

4 large garlic cloves, peeled and finely chopped

1 tablespoon crushed dried oregano

¼ teaspoon ground cloves

1 tablespoon ground cumin

1 sprig fresh basil

3 bay leaves, crumbled into 3 or 4 pieces each

1 pound zucchini, washed and sliced ¼ inch thick

2 large green peppers, cored, seeded, and cut into ¼-inch dice

4 celery ribs, washed and sliced ¼ inch thick

1 medium-sized onion, peeled, halved lengthwise, and thinly sliced

1½ cups home-cooked chick-peas (garbanzo beans), or a 15-, 16-, or 17-ounce can, drained

2½ cups cooked rice, preferably brown rice (see note on page 102)

For garnish:

1 small avocado, peeled, seeded, and cut into ½-inch dice

2 firm, ripe tomatoes, cored and cut into ¼-inch dice

4 thin scallions, washed and thinly sliced

1 small fresh jalapeño pepper, cored, seeded, and finely chopped

Half a small bunch of cilantro leaves, washed and finely chopped

In a large stock pot, bring the water and 4 pounds of chicken bones or parts to a boil over medium high heat. Reduce the heat and simmer for 1 hour, partially covered. Skim to remove as much of the fat and scum that has risen to the surface as possible, then strain and return the broth to the pot. Add the quartered chicken and simmer for 10 minutes.

In the meantime, combine the garlic, oregano, cloves, cumin, and basil in a food processor and process to form a paste.

Skim the top of the stock again, then stir in the garlic paste and bay leaves and simmer for 45 minutes, partly covered.

Carefully remove the chicken and set aside to cool. Skim the soup again. Skim off fat and bay leaves. There should be 10 cups of stock at this point. If not, add water to get that amount.

Add the zucchini, green peppers, celery, onion, and chick-peas to the soup and simmer until tender, about 15 minutes.

Remove the meat from the chicken, discarding the skin and bones. Using 2 forks, or your fingers, pull the chicken into shreds or pieces small enough to fit onto the spoon when the soup is eaten.

Add the chicken and rice to the soup and bring to a boil to reheat the soup.

In a small bowl, mix together the ingredients for the garnish.

To serve, ladle into bowls and top generously with the avocado-tomato garnish.

Leftover soup can be stored in the refrigerator for up to 3 days, or frozen for up to 4 months.

NOTE: To prepare the cooked rice, bring 2 cups of water or vegetable or chicken stock to a boil, add 1 cup of rice and simmer, partially covered, until liquid has been absorbed and rice is tender, about 35 minutes.

PROVENÇAL-STYLE FISH SOUP WITH POTATOES, HALIBUT, AND FENNEL

Makes 8 servings

This golden soup is textured with diced potatoes, tomatoes, and sliced onion, and flavored with chunks of halibut, orange zest, garlic, and parsley. Scented with orange and fennel, it reflects, in an unorthodox way, the kinds of everyday fish soups found in the south of France.

Alternative fish: Any firm white fish can be substituted for the halibut, such as snapper, mahimahi, grouper, haddock, or bass.

Serve this as a light, cool-weather lunch or dinner, accompanied by thick slices of a warm whole grain bread.

Olive oil spray
3 garlic cloves, peeled and very finely chopped
1 large onion, trimmed, peeled, cut in half lengthwise, then thinly sliced
1 pound small red or yellow potatoes (see headnote, page 178)
2 strips orange zest, peeled from an orange with a swivel-bladed vegetable peeler, each about 1 inch wide and 3 inches long
1 teaspoon fennel seeds, tied in cheesecloth
2 small tomatoes, cored and cut in half around the middle, then squeezed to remove the seeds, and cut into ¹/₂-inch dice
1 quart Fish Stock (page 118)
¹/₄ teaspoon crushed saffron threads
1 pound fresh halibut fillets, cut into ¹/₂-inch cubes
A little salt
Freshly ground black pepper
3 tablespoons finely chopped fresh parsley

Place a large nonstick sauté pan over medium heat. When hot, mist with olive oil spray and add the garlic and onion. Spray again so that all the onion and garlic are lightly coated in oil. Cook for 6 minutes, reducing the heat to prevent browning, and stirring frequently, until the onion is tender and translucent. Scrape into a nonaluminum soup pot.

Add the potatoes, orange zest, fennel seed, tomatoes, fish stock, and saffron. Bring to a boil over high heat, then reduce the heat and simmer for 20 minutes, stirring occasionally.

Add the halibut and simmer until fish is just tender, about 6 minutes. Taste and add a little salt, if necessary, and some pepper.

Ladle into soup bowls and sprinkle each with about a teaspoon of the chopped parsley. Serve immediately.

MEDITERRANEAN-STYLE FISH SOUP
WITH POTATOES AND ORZO

Makes 6 servings

This is a chunky, Mediterranean-style fish soup with the typical flavors and textures of that sun-drenched sea. This is an extravagant meal in itself.

Soups like this are often spiced up with a rouille, a fiery hot red pepper sauce from the south of France. The rouille is passed separately, and guests spoon a tablespoon or two (depending on tolerance) into their bowl of soup.

Orzo is a rice-shaped pasta available in most supermarkets. Any firm-fleshed white fish, such as grouper or mahimahi, can be substituted for the halibut.

Olive oil spray
1 large onion, peeled and chopped
2 medium-sized leeks, white parts only, split, thoroughly washed, and sliced
2 large garlic cloves, peeled and chopped
Two 28-ounce cans peeled Italian-style plum tomatoes, drained and squeezed to remove the seeds
1 teaspoon fennel seeds, slightly crushed
1 quart Fish Stock (page 118)
2 cups water
$^1/_8$ teaspoon crushed saffron threads
$^1/_2$ cup orzo
8 ounces halibut fillet, cut into $1^1/_2$-inch cubes
4 ounces medium-sized fresh shrimp, peeled and deveined
$^1/_2$ large bunch curly parsley, finely chopped (1 cup)
$^1/_4$ cup finely chopped feathery green threads from the top of a fennel bulb, or $^1/_4$ cup finely chopped fresh dill
Rouille (recipe follows)

Spray the inside of a large nonstick sauté pan with oil and set over medium heat. Add the onion, leeks, and garlic and spray so everything in the pan is lightly coated in oil. Cook until onion becomes translucent, about 6 to 8 minutes.

Scrape the onion mixture into a large nonaluminum pot. Add the tomatoes, fennel seeds, stock, and water and mix well. Bring to a boil over medium high heat, then add the saffron and orzo and cook until the orzo is almost tender, about 8 minutes. Add the halibut and cook for 3 minutes. Add the shrimp and cook another minute or so, until all the seafood is opaque.

Toss in the herbs, stir, and serve, passing the *rouille* separately.

Rouille

Makes about ²/₃ cup

6 large garlic cloves, peeled and roughly chopped
2 very small, fresh, hot red peppers (such as jalapeño or serrano), split
   and seeded
¹/₂ slice soft white bread, crusts removed
2 tablespoons tomato paste
1 tablespoon olive oil
Juice of ¹/₂ lemon
2 teaspoons hot Hungarian paprika
¹/₄ teaspoon freshly ground black pepper
¹/₂ cup fish or chicken stock

Purée everything in a food processor until very smooth. Taste carefully and adjust the seasonings.

A BIG BOILED DINNER FOR
A FORMAL PARTY

Makes 8 or more servings

Most cuisines have a soup like this that simply outgrew its pot. In Italy, it's a bollito misto, in France, a pot-au-feu, in this country, a New England boiled dinner. This recipe leans toward the Italian version, although there are no tortellini added to the soup. It is a formal, deep-winter meal that generates a broth as the first course, and slices of beef and chicken and an assortment of vegetables as the entrée.

Serve with a selection of mustards (a coarsely textured mustard, a smooth Dijon-style or Düsseldorf mustard, a Creole mustard, or a flavored mustard), thick slices of a warm, mixed-grain bread, and cornichons (tiny, tart pickles). This meal is worthy of your best china and silver.

This soup can be made a day or two ahead.

For the broth:

8 cups (2 quarts) chicken or vegetable stock
3 carrots, scrubbed, trimmed, and cut into 3 or 4 pieces each
2 celery ribs, washed and cut into 3 or 4 pieces each
2 large onions, ends trimmed, peeled, and quartered
3 garlic cloves, unpeeled
A 2-inch chunk of fresh gingerroot, unpeeled
2 bay leaves, crumbled
2 teaspoons dried thyme
1 teaspoon dried rosemary
1/2 teaspoon dried oregano

The meats:

A 2-pound rump roast or bottom round, trimmed of all excess fat
A 2½- to 3-pound chicken, excess fat pulled from the vent end, and
   trussed

The vegetables:

4 cups (1 quart) chicken or vegetable broth
24 very small red potatoes, washed and scrubbed
16 pearl onions, trimmed and peeled
3 medium-sized turnips, thickly peeled and cut into 6 wedges each
8 medium-sized leeks, white parts only, thoroughly washed (the ends
   can be split, if necessary, to rinse out the grit, but the leeks should
   be kept whole for serving)
4 fresh fennel bulbs, tops and cores removed, cut into quarters, sixths,
   or eighths, depending on the size (enough to make 2 or 3 wedges
   for each person)
2 medium-sized carrots, trimmed, scrubbed, and cut into 1½-inch
   lengths

In a very large soup kettle or stockpot, combine all the ingredients for the broth. Bring to a boil, then add the beef. Adjust the heat so the liquid simmers, and cook for 3 hours. The beef should feel almost tender when pierced with a carving fork.

While the beef is simmering, fill a large saucepan with the additional quart of broth. Bring to a boil, then add the potatoes. Cook until tender, about 15 to 20 minutes, then remove, cool under running cold water, and set aside. Bring the broth back to a boil and repeat with the remaining vegetables, cooking each separately. If preparing this meal several hours or even a day ahead, moisten the vegetables after they have been cooked and cooled with a little broth from the pot, cover tightly, and refrigerate.

After 3 hours, carefully slip the chicken into the simmering liquid in the stockpot, arranging it atop or next to the beef. There should be enough liquid to cover the chicken; if not, add more chicken stock or water. Simmer for 45 to 60 minutes longer to cook the chicken and finish cooking the beef.

Remove the beef and chicken to a platter and set aside. If preparing this meal several hours or even a day ahead, place the meats in a shallow dish, cover with plastic wrap, and refrigerate.

Strain the meat broth, discarding the vegetables that have been cooked for the last 4 hours. Remove all the fat from the top of the broth. Cool, then cover and refrigerate the broth if this meal is being made ahead.

About half an hour before serving (an hour if everything has been refrigerated), pour the broth back into the pot, bring to a boil over high heat, add the beef and chicken and all the vegetables, and adjust the heat so the broth simmers. Simmer for 20 to 30 minutes, until everything is very hot, then turn off the heat.

To begin the meal, carefully ladle a cup of the broth into hot soup plates and serve. Next, arrange the meats on a carving board, and the vegetables in a variety of large, attractive serving bowls. Carve the meats at the table, arranging a slice or two of the beef and a slice or two of the chicken on each plate, then surround with 2 or 3 pieces of each of the vegetables. Pass mustards and cornichons separately.

Stocks, Broths, and Consommés

CHICKEN STOCK, OR BROTH, OR SOUP

Makes 4 quarts

Although there are technical differences between a stock, a broth, and a soup—the stock is the weakest, the broth moderately flavored, and the soup well flavored—for home cooking those distinctions have essentially disappeared. Today, the words are used interchangeably to indicate a full-flavored liquid.

The best-flavored broth is made by using a generous amount of chicken, especially the bony parts, like necks, backs, and wings, with some vegetables added to balance the flavor. The secret to making a great stock is to simmer it for many hours. Three to 4 hours will make a good stock; 5 hours a fine broth; and 6 hours a great broth.

Chicken stock can be frozen for up to 3 months.

About 8 pounds of chicken and bones (ideally a 4- to 5-pound stewing
    fowl or roasting chicken, and 3 or 4 pounds of necks, backs, and
    wings, though 2 large roasters, cut into serving-size pieces, or all
    bones will do)
6 quarts cold tap water
4 celery ribs, washed and cut into 2- to 3-inch lengths
4 medium-sized carrots, trimmed, scrubbed, and cut into 2- to 3-inch
    lengths
3 medium-sized onions, trimmed, peeled, and quartered
1 large turnip, thickly peeled and quartered
3 large leeks, white parts only, slit, washed thoroughly to remove the
    grit, and cut into 2-inch chunks
2 large tomatoes, cored and cut in half
3 garlic cloves, peeled
2 teaspoons dried thyme
1 teaspoon dried rosemary
4 or 5 parsley sprigs
1 teaspoon black peppercorns
4 whole cloves
3 crumbled bay leaves

In a very large soup kettle or stockpot, combine all the ingredients. There should be
enough water to cover everything by at least an inch. If not, add more water.

    Bring to a boil over medium heat, then reduce the heat and simmer, partially
covered, for 4 to 6 hours. Occasionally, skim the stock to remove the fat, foam, and
sediment that have risen to the surface.

    When the stock has simmered for 1 or 2 hours and the meat is tender, remove
the meaty pieces (such as the breast and thighs), cut the meat off the bones, and
reserve for a recipe calling for cooked chicken, such as a chicken salad. Return the
bones and skin to the pot and continue cooking.

    Carefully ladle the stock through a strainer lined with cheesecloth or a damp-
ened, clean kitchen towel. Discard the vegetables and bones.

    Refrigerate the stock, then remove the fat that has congealed on the surface.

CHICKEN CONSOMMÉ

Makes 6 servings

A *consommé* is a crystal-clear soup made by simmering a broth until it reduces by half, and then clarifying it. The resulting shimmering, gelatin-rich smoothness and intense flavor have classically categorized consommés as the most elegant of all soups, usually reserved for formal dinners. To make beef or vegetable consommé, substitute beef or vegetable broth for the chicken broth.

Serve consommé in bouillon cups as a first course, or in soup plates for a more casual meal, or occasionally as an after-school snack, with a piece of toast.

3 quarts Chicken Stock (preceding recipe)
8 egg whites plus their shells

Pour the stock into a large pot and bring to a boil over medium high heat. Reduce the heat and simmer until reduced by about half, about 1½ hours. After about an hour of reducing, occasionally measure the soup by ladling it into a large liquid measuring cup until there is about 7 cups. Skim the stock periodically to remove any froth or sediment that has risen to the surface.

Place the egg whites and their shells in a large bowl. Beat with a whisk until the whites are very frothy and have about tripled in volume and the shells are crushed. Pour the whites and shells into the reduced broth and place over medium high heat. Beat and stir until the broth reaches a rolling boil. The egg whites and shells will have risen to the surface and will have formed a "raft," and all the particles in the broth will have attached themselves to the raft, leaving a crystal-clear consommé. Immediately turn off the heat and allow the consommé to rest, undisturbed, for 15 minutes, so all the solids can settle to the bottom or float up to the raft.

Ladle the stock gently into a large strainer lined with cheesecloth or a clean kitchen towel and set over a large container. Allow the soup to strain undisturbed. It will strain quite slowly.

Return to a saucepan and bring to a gentle boil over medium heat. Serve immediately.

Leftover consommé can be frozen for up to 3 months.

BROWN BEEF STOCK, OR BROTH, OR SOUP

Makes 4 quarts

Most home cooks rarely make beef stock, which requires browning the beef, bones, and vegetables in the oven, deglazing the roasting pan, and cooking for 24 hours. Unfortunately, there really is no substitute for homemade beef stock. Canned beef stock is a poor substitute, and rehydrated bouillon cubes are worse.

Begin the stock early in the morning. Just before bed, divide it into several bowls, cover, and refrigerate. In the morning, combine everything again, bring to a boil over high heat, reduce the heat, and continue simmering until done.

The beef bones and knuckles for this recipe need to be cut into pieces with a saw. Some supermarket butchers are cooperative enough to do this, as it cannot be done at home; a prime butcher will almost always be willing to cut up bones for you.

Like chicken stock, beef stock can be frozen for up to 3 months.

4 pounds beef chuck, trimmed of fat and cut into 4 or 5 pieces
3 pounds beef bones, sawed into 1-inch pieces
2 to 3 pounds veal knuckle bones, sawed into 1-inch pieces
2 medium-sized onions, trimmed, peeled, and halved
3 celery stalks, washed and cut into 3 or 4 pieces each
3 carrots, trimmed, scrubbed, and cut into 3 or 4 pieces each
3 large leeks, white parts only, ends split and washed thoroughly to
    remove all grit, but left whole
6 garlic cloves, unpeeled
1 quart hottest possible tap water
5 quarts cold tap water
1 teaspoon dried thyme
2 teaspoons dried rosemary
4 whole cloves
4 bay leaves, crumbled

Preheat the oven to 375 degrees F.

Evenly scatter the chuck, beef bones, veal knuckle, onions, celery, carrots, leeks, and garlic in a single layer in a large roasting pan.

Roast until the meat, bones, and vegetables are well browned but not burned, about 1½ hours, turning them 2 or 3 times during the roasting so they color evenly. It is essential that the bones do not burn.

With a large spoon and tongs, carefully transfer the meat, bones, and vegetables to a very large stockpot.

Pour the fat out of the roasting pan and place the pan across 2 burners set on high heat. Add the quart of hot water to the pan, and scrape the bottom of the pan so that all the brown, encrusted bits mix into the water as it comes to a boil. Carefully pour into the stockpot with the beef, bones, and vegetables.

Add the cold water, thyme, rosemary, cloves, and bay leaves to the stockpot and bring to a boil over medium high heat. Reduce the heat and simmer, partially covered, for 24 hours. Occasionally, skim the stock to remove the fat, foam, and sediment that have risen to the surface.

Carefully ladle the stock into a large bowl through a strainer lined with cheesecloth or a dampened, clean kitchen towel.

Refrigerate the stock, then remove the fat that has congealed on the surface.

VEGETABLE STOCK, OR
BROTH, OR SOUP

Makes about 2 quarts

Vegetable stock is the easiest stock to make, and it can be used in place of chicken or beef stock in any of the recipes in this book. The flavor will be lighter and more subtle.
   This is a rich stock with a golden coral color.

3 medium-sized carrots, trimmed, scrubbed, and cut into 5 or 6 pieces
   each
4 large leeks, white parts only, split lengthwise, thoroughly washed to
   remove all grit, and cut into 3 or 4 pieces each
3 large shallots, peeled
2 medium-sized onions, trimmed, peeled, and quartered
3 celery ribs, washed and cut into 4 or 5 pieces
1 pound zucchini, trimmed, washed, and cut into 1-inch lengths
2 large tomatoes, washed, cored, and quartered
1 large sweet red bell pepper, washed, cored, and cut into 6 or 8 pieces
1 medium-sized turnip, trimmed, peeled, and cut into 6 or 8 pieces
1 medium-sized parsnip, trimmed, peeled thickly, and cut into 6 or 8
   pieces
2 garlic cloves, peeled
A 1/2-inch chunk fresh gingerroot, peeled and cut in half lengthwise
3 sprigs fresh parsley
2 bay leaves
2 quarts cold tap water
1 teaspoon black peppercorns
A little salt

In a food processor, in batches that no more than half fill the bowl, finely chop the carrots, leeks, shallots, onions, celery, zucchini, tomatoes, red pepper, turnip, parsnip, garlic, ginger, parsley, and bay leaves. It is not necessary to chop each vegetable separately. As each batch is chopped, transfer it to a large stockpot.

Add the water and peppercorns and bring to a boil over medium high heat. Reduce the heat and simmer, partially covered, for 2 hours.

Carefully ladle the stock into a bowl through a strainer lined with cheesecloth or a dampened, clean kitchen towel, pressing firmly on the vegetables so they release all their liquid. Discard the vegetables and add salt to taste.

Vegetable stock can be refrigerated for 2 or 3 days, or frozen for up to 6 months.

FISH STOCK, OR
BROTH, OR SOUP

Makes 2 quarts

This is a full-flavored fish stock with flavor subtleties from the vegetables, herbs, lemon, and wine. It can be used as a broth or light soup, or as a liquid for poaching fish.

Use the heads, bones, and tails of white fish such as halibut, grouper, whitefish, or mahimahi. Remove the dark, burgundy brown gills from the heads and rinse the heads and bones well under running cold water to remove all the blood; gills and blood could make the stock bitter. Do not use heads or bones from oily fish such as tuna, swordfish, bluefish, or salmon, as they would give the stock an unpleasant, fishy flavor.

With a heavy kitchen knife, hack the heads of large fish in half, cut the tails off the bones, and cut the bones into pieces about 3 inches long, so all the flavor is extracted easily when the stock is simmered. This is a messy procedure, and I sometimes ask the salesclerk at the fish store to do it. It does not matter whether the heads and bones are washed before or after they are cut up.

4 pounds fish bones, cut up and thoroughly washed
1 medium-sized onion, trimmed, peeled, and chopped
1 large leek, white part only, split and thoroughly washed to remove the grit, and coarsely chopped
2 celery ribs, washed and thinly sliced or coarsely chopped
2 garlic cloves, peeled and coarsely chopped
3 parsley sprigs, washed
Three 1/4-inch-thick slices from the center of a lemon
1 sprig fresh thyme, or 1/4 teaspoon dried thyme
1 bay leaf, crumbled
1/2 teaspoon white peppercorns
1 1/2 cups fine-quality dry white wine
2 quarts cold tap water

Toss all the ingredients into a large nonaluminum pot and bring to a boil over medium heat. Reduce the heat and simmer, partially covered, for 45 minutes.

Carefully ladle the stock into a bowl through a strainer lined with cheesecloth or a dampened, clean kitchen towel, pressing firmly on the bones and vegetables so they release all their liquid. Discard the vegetables and bones.

Fish stock can be refrigerated for 2 or 3 days, or frozen for up to 2 or 3 months.

5

First Courses

APPETIZERS

Lightly Marinated Roasted Red Peppers
Croustades with Cheddar Cheese and Barbecued Beans
Polenta Croustades with Broccoli and Tomato Sauce
Summer Lentil Salad with Diced Country-cured Ham
Golden Beet Salad with Peaches and Pecans
Poached Finnan Haddie with Red Potato Salad
Clams Puttanesca

APPETIZER PIZZAS

Pizza alla Puttanesca
Shrimp Pizza with Chèvre
Vegetarian Chili Pizza

DIPS AND SPREADS

Honey-Mustard-Tarragon Dip
Mixed Herb, Caper, and Anchovy Dip
Vidalia Onion and Ginger Dip

Sun-dried Tomato and Dill Dip
Garlic Lover's Dip
Black Bean Dip
A Light Hummus
Eggplant Guacamole

Introduction

In a healthy, high-carbohydrate diet, an appetizer is simply a small portion of any dish that has enough character and dimension to be served on its own. Usually these will be dishes made from vegetables, legumes, cereals, and grains, though a small portion of some animal proteins, such as a few slices of decoratively arranged medium-rare grilled duck breast, or a small portion of chicken or shrimp salad, can be served as an appetizer if followed by a vegetarian entrée.

How people choose to order and sequence the foods they serve in a meal varies from country to country, from cuisine to cuisine. Traditionally, the Japanese nibble many different foods at one time, while Italians separate their foods into a long series of courses, and the French eat certain foods in a prescribed order. In the United States today, time restraints and health considerations have led us to rethink which foods we serve when, and many foods and dishes that were once served only as part of the entrée are now being served as appetizers.

Eating a healthy, high-carbohydrate diet rather than a high-fat, meat-centered diet means that meals are vegetable-, bean-, and cereal- and grain-centered. Thus these foods are made into dishes that are complete within themselves, able to stand independently, even though they are frequently served together. As a result, small portions of many of the recipes in chapters 6, 7, and 9 can be served as first courses. Here is a list of those recipes:

First Courses from Chapter 6, Vegetables:

Steamed Asparagus with Sun-dried Tomato Sauce (page 156)
Green Beans with Chermoula Sauce (page 163)
Haricots Verts with Chanterelles (page 166)
Mushroom and Snow Pea Stir-fry (page 172)
Russian Summer Vegetable Salad (page 186)

Cold Summer Vegetables with Miso Dressing (page 188)
Vegetarian Chili (page 190)

First Courses from Chapter 7, Rice, Beans, Grains, and Pasta:

Golden Asparagus Risotto (page 198)
Brown Rice Risotto with Azuki Beans (page 201)
Whole Wheat Couscous with Wild Mushrooms (page 212)
Bulgur Salad with Poblanos (page 215)
Summer Lentil Salad (page 220)
Saffron Pasta with Asian "Pesto" (page 223)
Whole Wheat Fettuccine with Wild Mushrooms and Dill (page 224)
Rigatoni with Puttanesca Sauce (page 226)

First Courses from Chapter 9, Animal Protein:

Spicy Salmon Fillets (page 271)
Maryland Crabcakes (page 272)
Fresh Tuna and White Bean Ceviche, Italian-style (page 274)
Thai Chicken Salad (page 284)

LIGHTLY MARINATED ROASTED
RED PEPPERS

Makes 4 to 6 servings

Light, fresh, and brightly colored, this simple but elegant appetizer reflects the sparkling sensitivity of Mediterranean cooking. The utter simplicity of this recipe demands that all the ingredients be carefully chosen. The peppers should be thick and meaty, with smooth skins and no bruises. The vinegar should be flavored with raspberries, not coloring and chemical flavoring, so check the ingredients on the label before buying the vinegar.

Use an imported, small, unpitted olive from France, Spain, or Greece, available in Mediterranean markets and many supermarkets and gourmet food shops.

Begin a formal vegetarian dinner with these roasted peppers, followed by a risotto (see Chapter 7), Whole Wheat Couscous with Wild Mushrooms (page 212), and Lemon Soufflé (page 292) for dessert.

For a change of pace, substitute ¼ cup Miso Dressing (page 189) for the raspberry vinegar, and replace the red peppers with sweet yellow or orange bell peppers.

4 to 6 large, firm, sweet red bell peppers
2 or 3 tablespoons raspberry vinegar
1 tablespoon finely chopped chives
1 tablespoon finely chopped parsley
Freshly ground black pepper
6 to 12 imported green olives

Heat the broiler.

Arrange the peppers, evenly spaced, in a foil-lined roasting pan. Slide onto a rack so that the peppers are close to the broiling unit. Broil until the skins of the peppers are almost completely black, turning as needed so that the skins char evenly. This can take 15 to 30 minutes.

Carefully transfer the peppers to a thick plastic bag and seal. The peppers will steam as they cool, making them easy to peel. When they are cool, carefully peel off the charred skin, trying not to tear the peppers. Remove the stems and seeds. If necessary, rinse quickly under running cold water.

Arrange the peppers outer sides down in a dish and sprinkle with the vinegar. Marinate for about an hour.

To serve, place each pepper, outer side up, in the center of a small plate, trimming the peppers, if necessary, to fit neatly onto the plates. Mix together the chives and parsley and sprinkle a teaspoonful over each pepper, then season with a little black pepper and garnish with an olive or two.

CROUSTADES WITH CHEDDAR CHEESE
AND BARBECUED BEANS

Makes about 12 to 15 croustades, 4 to 6 servings

Croustades are simply toasted slices of bread with a topping. They can be used as hors d'oeuvres, or 2 or 3 can be served on a plate as an appetizer. They can also be used to accompany an entrée or a bowl of soup.

The flavors and textures of these Cheddar and bean croustades are bold and enticing.

1 large loaf crusty Italian bread, cut on the bias into 3/4-inch-thick slices
3 ounces sharp Vermont Cheddar cheese, shredded
1 1/2 cups canned or home-cooked black beans
About 1/2 cup Barbecue Sauce (recipe follows)

Heat the broiler.

Arrange the bread on a baking sheet and toast lightly under the broiler on both sides.

While bread is toasting, stir together the beans and just enough barbecue sauce to thickly coat the beans.

Sprinkle each slice of toast with a tablespoon or so of cheese, and broil until melted. Watch carefully to ensure that neither the bread nor the cheese burns.

Spoon a generous mound of barbecued beans over each croustade and serve.

Barbecue Sauce

Makes 4 cups

This is a hot, spicy western-style barbecue sauce. It will keep for up to a month in the refrigerator, or it can be frozen for 2 or 3 months.

2 cups ketchup
2 cups chili sauce
2 cups dark beer
1/2 cup Worcestershire sauce
1/4 cup prepared mustard
1/4 cup brown sugar
2 tablespoons chili powder
2 teaspoons dried oregano
2 teaspoons hot pepper sauce

In a medium-sized saucepan, whisk together all the ingredients and simmer for 15 minutes. Set aside to cool.

POLENTA CROUSTADES WITH BROCCOLI
AND TOMATO SAUCE

Makes 8 servings

While croustades are traditionally made with slices of toasted bread, gently sautéed slices of polenta can be used in place of the toast.

During much of the winter, I keep a tightly covered pan of polenta in the refrigerator, ready to be sliced and turned into croustades, or just sautéed and served as a side dish.

Almost any kind of leftover, a few pieces of diced chicken, some mushrooms, chopped cooked vegetables, or canned beans can be mixed lightly with a sauce and spread onto sliced polenta for a quick first course. Puttanesca Sauce (page 226) makes a spicy topping for polenta.

8 cups water
2 cups polenta (not instant) or yellow cornmeal
1 tablespoon unsalted butter
A little salt
Freshly ground black pepper
Vegetable oil spray
1 small bunch of broccoli, cut into tiny florets, and steamed or cooked
    in boiling water until tender just before serving
1 cup Tomato Sauce (page 228), heated until very hot just before
    serving

Traditional procedure: Bring half the water to a boil. Meanwhile, in a separate bowl, stir together the remaining water and polenta. Pour the polenta mixture into the boiling water, stirring constantly until it comes to a boil. Pour into the top of a large double boiler set over slowly boiling water. Cook, stirring almost constantly, for 45 to 60 minutes, until the polenta is very thick. Beat in the butter, and salt and pepper to taste.

129

Microwave procedure: Combine the water and polenta in a very large microwave-safe bowl and microwave on high (100%) for 15 minutes, carefully uncovering and whisking hard every 5 minutes to prevent lumping. When cooked, whisk in the butter and salt and pepper to taste, beating until smooth.

Lightly mist the inside of a large loaf pan with vegetable oil spray. Scoop the hot polenta into the pan, smooth the top, and cover tightly. Refrigerate until solid, at least 4 hours.

To serve, mist the inside of a large nonstick skillet with vegetable oil spray and place over medium heat. Cut the polenta into slices about ⅓ to ½ inch thick. When the skillet is hot, slide in the polenta and cook until golden brown on one side, then turn carefully and cook until golden brown on the other side and heated through. Reduce the heat, if necessary, to prevent burning. Alternatively, the sliced polenta can be arranged on a foil-lined baking sheet and broiled until nicely browned on both sides.

Mix the broccoli with just enough tomato sauce to coat the florets thickly. Spoon on top of the polenta and serve immediately.

Polenta with Golden Caviar

Cool the sautéed or broiled polenta until just slightly warm, then arrange on plates topped with a little light (not imitation) sour cream, some very finely chopped fresh chives, and a dollop of golden caviar (whitefish roe, which is moderately priced and only slightly salty). Garnish with a wedge of lemon, if you wish.

SUMMER LENTIL SALAD WITH
DICED COUNTRY-CURED HAM

Makes 6 servings

Although lentils are most often thought of as winter fare, this salad makes an unexpected summer treat with a big squirt of lemon and the addition of fresh summer herbs and vine-ripened tomatoes.

Country-cured hams are available in some specialty food stores, premium department store food sections, premium markets, and mail order catalogs. A pound of ham, trimmed of all its fat, will generously yield the 2/3 cup needed for this recipe.

Alternatives to the ham could include diced Marinated Flank Steak (page 277), grilled chicken breast, or cooked white navy beans.

Serve this as a starter before a light summer meal, or as a side dish to accompany a vegetarian sandwich.

Olive oil spray
2 medium-sized carrots, trimmed, scrubbed, and cut into 1/4- to 1/3-inch dice
2 celery ribs, trimmed, scrubbed, and cut into 1/4- to 1/3-inch dice
1 small onion, peeled and diced
2 garlic cloves, peeled and chopped
1 cup green or brown lentils
3 cups chicken or vegetable stock
1 tablespoon virgin or extra virgin olive oil
Juice of 1 small lemon
2 large tomatoes, cored, seeded, and neatly diced
2/3 cup diced (1/4- to 1/3-inch) Virginia, Missouri, or Kentucky country-cured ham
2 tablespoons finely chopped fresh basil
2 tablespoons finely chopped fresh parsley

Mist a large nonstick sauté pan with olive oil spray and set over medium heat. Add the carrots, celery, onion, and garlic, and spray so all the vegetables are lightly coated with oil. Cook, stirring frequently, for 8 to 10 minutes, reducing the heat as needed to prevent browning.

Transfer the vegetables to a large saucepan, add the lentils and stock, bring to a boil, then reduce the heat and simmer until lentils are tender, about 40 minutes. Drain, then gently toss with the oil and lemon juice.

Refrigerate until cool, then stir in the tomatoes, ham, basil, and parsley. Serve slightly chilled, or at room temperature.

GOLDEN BEET SALAD WITH
PEACHES AND PECANS

Makes 4 servings

Golden or yellow beets, once quite exotic and difficult to find, are now periodically available in specialty food stores and some premium supermarkets. They have a fine, firm texture and a honeylike sweetness.

This salad, with its variety of colors and sweet and nutty flavors, has enough strength of character to be served as an appetizer, but it could also be used as a side dish.

There's a formal quality to this recipe, with an autumnal feeling. Serve it warm or cold before a bowl of homemade pasta followed by Fresh Pear Compote (page 43).

2/3 cup moist dried peaches or apricots, cut into 1/4-inch julienne
1/2 cup dark rum, Grand Marnier, or apple juice
1 pound golden beets, rinsed under running cold water, then
    trimmed, thinly peeled, and halved
1/4 cup pecan pieces, very coarsely chopped
1 tablespoon virgin olive oil
2 teaspoons freshly squeezed lemon juice
Freshly ground black pepper to taste

In a nonaluminum saucepan, heat the dried peaches or apricots and the rum, Grand Marnier, or apple juice until just hot to the touch, then pour into a small measuring cup and set aside so the fruit can absorb the liquid and soften.

Bring about a quart of hot tap water to a boil in a large saucepan, add the beets, and when the water returns to a boil, reduce the heat and simmer until beets are tender, about 10 minutes. Drain, and return to the saucepan if serving hot, or transfer to a mixing bowl if serving cold.

Drain the peaches or apricots. Add to the beets along with the remaining ingredients, mix well, and season with pepper.

To serve warm, heat gently over a low flame; to serve cold, cover and refrigerate until needed.

POACHED FINNAN HADDIE
WITH RED POTATO SALAD

Makes 4 servings

Finnan haddie, that is, Scottish smoked haddock, has a pale yellow color, a sweet flavor, and a nutty peat fragrance. Here a colorful red-and-green potato salad is added to the smoked haddock, which has been very gently cooked in milk to remove some of its saltiness, giving the plate a variety of textures and complementary flavors.

You can find finnan haddie in premium fish markets and the fish sections of some specialty food markets.

½ pound small red potatoes, scrubbed, cut into ¼-inch dice, and
    tossed into a bowl of cold water to prevent discoloration
2 tablespoons light (not imitation) sour cream
1 teaspoon finely chopped fresh tarragon
1 teaspoon finely chopped fresh parsley
1 teaspoon finely chopped fresh chives
A little salt
Freshly ground black pepper
¾ pound skinless and boneless smoked haddock, cut into ¼-inch
    slices
1½ cups skim milk
4 small lemon wedges

Bring a large saucepan of water to a boil over high heat. Add the potatoes, and when the water returns to a boil, reduce the heat and simmer until the potatoes are just tender, about 8 minutes. Drain and rinse under running cold tap water until potatoes are cool. Pat dry, then gently mix with the sour cream, herbs, and salt and pepper to taste. Cover and set aside.

Arrange the haddock slices in a large skillet, in a single layer if possible, and add enough skim milk to just barely cover the fish. Place over medium heat and cook until the milk just begins to boil. Immediately remove from the heat. With a spatula, carefully transfer the slices to a plate lined with paper toweling to drain and cool.

Arrange finnan haddie and a small mound of the potato salad on each plate. Add a lemon wedge and serve.

CLAMS PUTTANESCA

Makes 4 servings

Small clams, gently simmered in a thick, rich, and spicy tomato sauce, and served in a deep soup bowl with lots of toasted whole wheat or sourdough bread for mopping up the sauce, make a robust cold-weather starter to a meal full of vegetables and cereal or rice dishes. You can also cook the clams in Tomato Sauce (page 228).

2 cups Puttanesca Sauce (page 226)
$1/2$ cup dry red or white wine, or water
26 littleneck clams, washed and scrubbed well with a brush to remove
    all sand and grit
2 tablespoons coarsely chopped fresh basil

In a very large saucepan, stir together the Puttanesca Sauce and wine or water, and set over medium heat. Cook, stirring steadily, until sauce reaches the boiling point. Add the clams, stir, cover, and cook until the clams open, about 5 or 6 minutes, stirring once after 2 or 3 minutes to ensure that the clams cook evenly. Discard any clams that do not open after 6 or 7 minutes at the most.

With a slotted spoon, divide the clams into serving bowls. Stir the basil into the sauce, mixing well, and ladle over the clams.

Serve immediately.

Appetizer Pizzas

PIZZA ALLA PUTTANESCA

*Makes 1 large (14-inch) round pizza, 6 small appetizer-size (6-inch) pizzas,
or a 10-inch × 16-inch rectangular pizza*

*Even though this pizza abounds with the everyday flavors of central to southern Italy, it is
utterly American, utterly satisfying, and utterly delicious.*

1 recipe Whole Wheat Pizza Dough (page 264)
²⁄₃ cup Puttanesca Sauce (page 226)
¹⁄₄ cup grated fontina cheese
¹⁄₄ cup grated, reduced fat (part skim) mozzarella cheese
2 tablespoons freshly grated Romano cheese
12 small fresh basil leaves

Preheat the oven to 500 degrees F.

On a clean work surface, roll the dough into a circle about 14 inches in diameter, or divide into 6 pieces and roll each into a circle about 6 inches in diameter, or roll to fit a rectangular baking pan 10 × 16 inches. Place the dough on a baking sheet, or fit into a baking pan, gently pressing it to the edges.

Spread the sauce evenly over the pizza, leaving a ¹⁄₂-inch border. Mix the 3 cheeses together, then sprinkle over the sauce. Arrange the basil leaves decoratively on top of the cheese.

Bake until the cheese is bubbly and beginning to become golden brown, about 10 minutes.

Remove from the oven, cut into slices, and serve immediately.

Traditional Pizza

Use the Traditional Pizza Dough variation (page 265), substitute Tomato Sauce
(page 228) for the Puttanesca Sauce, and use 1 cup of grated mozzarella instead of
the mixture of fontina, mozzarella, and Romano.

SHRIMP PIZZA WITH CHÈVRE

Makes one large (14-inch) round pizza, 6 small appetizer-size (6-inch) pizzas,
or a 10-inch × 16-inch rectangular pizza

This is a white pizza (meaning it has no tomato sauce), lightly topped with goat cheese and
shrimp, and gently seasoned with fresh rosemary.

1 recipe Traditional Pizza Dough (variation of Whole Wheat Pizza
    Dough, page 265)
2 tablespoons virgin or extra virgin olive oil
12 large fresh shrimp, peeled and deveined
¾ cup crumbled French goat cheese
2 tablespoons finely chopped fresh rosemary

Preheat the oven to 500 degrees F.

On a clean work surface, roll the dough into a circle about 14 inches in diameter, or divide into 6 pieces and roll each into a circle about 6 inches in diameter, or roll to fit a rectangular baking pan 10 × 16 inches. Place the dough on a baking sheet, or fit into a baking pan, gently pressing it to the edges.

Brush the olive oil evenly over the pizza, leaving a ½-inch border.

Butterfly the shrimp: Cut each shrimp almost in half lengthwise, leaving the 2 pieces just attached at the tail end. Decoratively arrange the shrimp, cut sides down, on the dough. Scatter the cheese over the pizza, again leaving a ½-inch border. Sprinkle with the rosemary.

Bake until the cheese is bubbly and beginning to become golden brown, about 8 minutes.

Remove from the oven, cut into slices, and serve immediately.

VEGETARIAN CHILI PIZZA

Makes one large (14-inch) round pizza, 6 small appetizer-size (6-inch) pizzas,
or a 10-inch × 16-inch rectangular pizza

This is a hearty, spicy pizza. It is an excellent way to use up leftover vegetarian chili. It makes for somewhat messy, playful eating; children love it.

1 recipe Whole Wheat Pizza Dough (page 264)
2 cups Vegetarian Chili (page 190)
$^{1}/_{3}$ cup grated Vermont (or other sharp) Cheddar cheese

Preheat the oven to 500 degrees F.

On a clean work surface, roll the dough into a circle, about 14 inches in diameter, or divide into 6 pieces and roll each into a circle about 6 inches in diameter, or roll to fit a rectangular baking pan 10 × 16 inches. Place the dough on a baking sheet, or fit into a baking pan, gently pressing it to the edges.

Place the chili in a large strainer and press gently but firmly to remove the excess liquid, then spread evenly over the pizza, leaving a $^{1}/_{2}$-inch border. Sprinkle the cheese decoratively over the top of the chili. Bake until the cheese is bubbly and beginning to become golden brown, about 10 minutes.

Remove from the oven, cut into slices, and serve immediately.

Dips and Spreads

Intensely flavored dips, rather than just being an accent on the edge of an overly salted, greasy chip or cracker, can be a culinary center of attention when spread, like Italian croustades, on toast rounds made from homemade breads, toasted pita points, or broken pieces of whole-grain Scandinavian flat and crisp breads.

We should not let the American tradition of serving dips in bowls in the living room during cocktail parties stop us from experimenting with croustades (see page 127). They provide almost unlimited possibilities for great-tasting hors d'oeuvres and appetizers, often using little more than leftover beans and vegetables atop a dip spread on a bread.

Several of the following recipes use a thick, strained yogurt as a base, rather than mayonnaise or sour cream. Some yogurts are more acidic than others, some quite sweet. Experiment with a few different brands until you find the yogurt flavor you prefer.

All of the dips in this section can be prepared 2 or 3 days ahead. Store them in a covered dish or jar in the refrigerator, and stir just before serving.

HONEY-MUSTARD-TARRAGON DIP

Makes about 2 cups

Every type of honey, kind of mustard, and brand of yogurt is different, so it may be necessary for you to taste and adjust after mixing the ingredients together in order to achieve an even balance of flavor.

2 cups plain, unflavored yogurt
¼ cup honey
¼ cup Dijon mustard
3 tablespoons finely chopped fresh tarragon, or 1 tablespoon crushed
    dried tarragon

Line a strainer with a clean kitchen towel and set it over a bowl. Scoop the yogurt into the towel, cover loosely with a piece of plastic wrap, and set aside until about ¾ cup of liquid has drained off the yogurt, about 4 hours.

Whisk the honey, mustard, and tarragon into the yogurt. Taste and adjust the flavors.

Refrigerate in a covered container until needed.

MIXED HERB, CAPER, AND ANCHOVY DIP

Makes about 2 cups

This dip abounds with the flavors often found in Italian green sauces, and like those sauces, it can be served as a garnish for poached fish or chicken.

2 cups plain, unflavored yogurt
3 tablespoons Dijon mustard
¼ cup capers, rinsed well under running cold water
2 garlic cloves, peeled
6 anchovy fillets, rinsed well under running cold water
¼ cup coarsely chopped fresh basil
¼ cup coarsely chopped fresh parsley
¼ cup coarsely chopped fresh dill
2 thin scallions, cut into 2-inch pieces
Juice of 1 small lemon
Freshly ground black pepper

Line a strainer with a clean kitchen towel and set it over a bowl. Scoop the yogurt into the towel, cover loosely with a piece of plastic wrap, and set aside until about ¾ cup of liquid has drained off the yogurt, about 4 hours.

In a food processor, combine the drained yogurt with the mustard, capers, garlic, anchovies, basil, parsley, dill, scallions, and lemon juice. Process, pulsing frequently, until everything is very finely chopped. Season with pepper.

Refrigerate in a covered container until needed.

VIDALIA ONION AND GINGER DIP

Makes about 1½ cups

This is a sweet dip with a gentle onion flavor and a mild ginger aftertaste. Vidalia onion jellies and relishes (made from the very sweet onion grown in Vidalia, Georgia) are available in premium supermarkets and specialty food stores.

With its sweet, warm flavor, this dip is excellent spread on vegetarian sandwiches, or served with cold vegetables in the summer.

2 cups plain, unflavored yogurt
½ cup Vidalia onion jelly or relish
3 quarter-size pieces of fresh gingerroot, peeled
¼ cup coarsely chopped fresh chives
Freshly ground black pepper (optional)

Line a strainer with a clean kitchen towel and set it over a bowl. Scoop the yogurt into the towel, cover loosely with a piece of plastic wrap, and set aside until about ¾ cup of liquid has drained off the yogurt, about 4 hours.

In a food processor, combine the yogurt with the jelly or relish, ginger, and chives. Process, pulsing frequently, until chives are finely chopped. Taste and season with pepper if you wish.

Refrigerate in a covered container until needed.

SUN-DRIED TOMATO AND DILL DIP

Makes 1¹/₂ cups

This is a thick dip, richly flavored with sun-dried tomatoes and accented with fresh dill.

To make a spicier dip, add 1 teaspoon chili powder, 1 teaspoon hot or sweet Hungarian paprika, and ¹/₂ teaspoon crushed dried oregano to the food processor with the other ingredients.

2 cups plain, unflavored yogurt
¹/₂ cup sun-dried tomatoes
2 tablespoons coarsely chopped fresh dill
1 garlic clove, peeled
Freshly ground black pepper

Line a strainer with a clean kitchen towel and set it over a bowl. Scoop the yogurt into the towel, cover loosely with a piece of plastic wrap, and set aside until about ³/₄ cup of liquid has drained off the yogurt, about 4 hours.

Soak the dried tomatoes in a cup or so of the hottest possible tap water for 3 minutes to soften, then drain and pat dry.

In a food processor, combine the yogurt with the tomatoes, dill, and garlic. Process, pulsing frequently, until the tomatoes have been puréed and the dip is smooth, though speckled with finely chopped dill. Taste and season with pepper.

GARLIC LOVER'S DIP

Makes about 1 cup

This golden-colored dip is intensely flavored with garlic and saffron, two of the major flavors of the Mediterranean. For garlic bread, eliminate the saffron and spread the dip on toasted bread slices.

2 cups plain, unflavored yogurt
6 garlic cloves, peeled
Generous ¼ teaspoon saffron threads
2 teaspoons lemon juice
2 tablespoons coarsely chopped fresh parsley
A little salt
Freshly ground black pepper

Line a strainer with a clean kitchen towel and set it over a bowl. Scoop the yogurt into the towel, cover loosely with a piece of plastic wrap, and set aside until about ¾ cup of liquid has drained off the yogurt, about 4 hours.

In a food processor, combine the yogurt with the garlic, saffron, lemon juice, and parsley. Process, pulsing frequently, until garlic has been completely puréed. Season with salt and pepper to taste.

BLACK BEAN DIP

Makes 4 cups

Tender black beans are moistened with yogurt and flavored with 4 herbs to make this soft dip.

4 cups very tender cooked black beans (about 60 ounces canned,
    drained, and rinsed well under cold tap water)
1/3 cup nonfat plain yogurt
1/4 cup coarsely chopped fresh chives
1/8 teaspoon dried oregano
1/8 teaspoon dried thyme
1/4 teaspoon dried tarragon
Salt
Freshly ground black pepper

Combine the beans, yogurt, chives, oregano, thyme, and tarragon in a food processor and process until a thick, smooth paste forms. Taste, adding more dried herbs if necessary for the mixture to have a mild herbed flavor, and season with salt and pepper.

Serve at room temperature.

A LIGHT HUMMUS

Makes 8 servings

Considerably lower in fat than the usual hummus, this chick-pea spread is full of fresh flavors, like lemon and lime, garlic, and 3 fresh herbs.

Although hummus is traditionally served as a dip with bread or crackers, this light version is lively enough to make into a summer appetizer, mounded on a plate with thickly sliced vine-ripened tomatoes, tender young scallions, and other peak-season summer vegetables.

Tahini is a paste or butter made from ground and puréed sesame seeds. It is available in most supermarkets and Middle Eastern markets. If the oil has separated from the paste, simply stir together before using.

1/2 pound (1 1/4 cups) dried chick-peas (garbanzo beans), or 4 cups
    canned chick-peas (see procedure below)
3 quarts water
1/3 cup tahini
Juice of 1 lime
Juice of 1/2 lemon
3 large garlic cloves, peeled
1/4 teaspoon cayenne
1/4 cup tightly pressed parsley leaves
1/4 cup tightly pressed cilantro leaves
1/4 cup tightly pressed mint leaves
Freshly ground black pepper

If using dried chick-peas, place a large pot of hot tap water over high heat and add the chick-peas. Bring to a boil, then reduce the heat and simmer until the chick-peas are tender, about 2 hours. Drain and reserve 1 cup of the cooking liquid.

If using canned chick-peas, drain and reserve 1 cup of the liquid from the cans.

149

In a food processor, purée the chick-peas, tahini, lime and lemon juices, garlic, and cayenne, pouring through the feed tube enough of the reserved liquid (about ³/₄ cup) to make the hummus smooth and to give it the texture of a light sour cream. Add the parsley, cilantro, and mint leaves, and pulse on and off rapidly so herbs are very well chopped and evenly distributed. Season to taste with black pepper.

EGGPLANT GUACAMOLE

Makes about 3 cups

This light guacamole made with eggplant rather than avocado can be used as a spread or dip, either cold or at room temperature. In winter, when I originally developed this recipe, I substituted sweet red bell peppers for the tomatoes. Sometimes I eliminate the hot pepper.

One 2-pound eggplant, stem trimmed, cut in half lengthwise
2 large tomatoes, washed, cored, seeded, and cut into 1/4-inch dice
1/4 small serrano or other hot red pepper, trimmed, seeded, and finely
    chopped
3 scallions, finely chopped
1 tablespoon olive oil
1 small bunch cilantro, washed and finely chopped
Juice of 1/2 lime
Freshly ground black pepper

Cook the eggplant: Place half the eggplant, cut side down, in a microwave-safe baking dish, cover, and microwave on high (100%) until tender, about 15 minutes; or place the eggplant, cut side down, on a baking sheet (which has been very lightly rubbed or sprayed with oil) and bake in a 350-degree oven until tender when pierced deeply with a toothpick, about 45 minutes.

In the meantime, mix together in a large bowl the tomato, hot pepper, scallions, oil, cilantro, and lime juice.

When eggplant is cooked, with a large spoon, scrape out the flesh onto a cutting board and chop into fine pieces. Discard the skin. Stir into the tomato and scallion mixture, taste, adjust the flavors, adding more cilantro or lime juice if needed to make the taste bouncy and alive, and season generously with pepper.

6

Vegetables

Steamed Asparagus with Sun-dried Tomato Sauce
Broccoli with Onions
Brussels Sprouts with Nutmeg
Steamed Baby Carrots with Jean-Louis Palladin's Versatile Onion Sauce
Green Beans with Chermoula Sauce
Green Beans and Fennel
Haricots Verts with Chanterelles
Red Cabbage Braised with Cranberries
Curried Cauliflower
Corn on the Cob
Spring Dandelion Greens with Mushrooms
Mushroom and Snow Pea Stir-fry
Stewed Okra and Tomatoes with Cilantro
Parsnip Purée
Sweet Red Pepper Ragout
Fluffy Whipped Potatoes
Emerald Spinach with Hidden Herbs

Spicy Butternut Squash
Julienned Summer Squash Skins
Three Summer Squash Sautés
Russian Summer Vegetable Salad
Cold Summer Vegetables with Miso Dressing
Vegetarian Chili
Mixed Winter Root Vegetables

Introduction

Nothing in the culinary world enlivens our meals as much as vegetables, which provide us with a great variety of fibers and nutrients as well as an enticing array of colors. It is particularly important to remember to try to include a red or orange vegetable in each day's meals, as vegetables with these colors are rich in certain important nutrients such as vitamin A and beta carotene.

Ideally, we should be eating 3 or 4 vegetables a day, choosing organically grown vegetables as much as possible, and, overall, we should be leaning away from meat-centered meals and toward meals that are vegetable-centered.

We go from asparagus to zucchini in this chapter, but the recipes here only hint at the infinite possibilities of today's bounty of fresh vegetables available in farmers' markets, supermarkets, and food specialty shops.

STEAMED ASPARAGUS
WITH SUN-DRIED TOMATO SAUCE

Makes 4 servings

This is a sprightly and dramatic-looking appetizer for a cool spring day, a simple, light, sensual combination of tastes and textures. Sun-dried California tomatoes, with their slightly acidic flavor and rich, natural sweetness, are softened in some broth and quickly made into a thick chutneylike sauce that is spooned over fresh asparagus. You can substitute broccoli florets for the asparagus spears.

1 pound asparagus, washed and lower halves peeled if stalks are thick and woody
Sun-dried Tomato Sauce (recipe follows)

Place 2 inches of hot tap water in the bottom of a steamer, insert the steaming basket, cover, and bring to a boil. When the steamer is filled with steam, add the asparagus, cover, reduce the heat to medium, and steam until just tender, about 6 to 8 minutes.

Stack the asparagus neatly on serving plates and spoon the warm sauce over them.

Serve immediately.

Sun-dried Tomato Sauce

Makes about 1 cup

Because this sauce is virtually fat-free yet lusciously bold in flavor, a small amount of it can be used to top baked potatoes (in place of sour cream), or it can be thinned with a little stock and used as a pasta sauce. I like it over hot, fresh fettuccine (there's enough for 2 large or 4 small servings), though it can also be used in cold pasta salads.

12 sun-dried tomatoes
1¼ cups beef, chicken, or vegetable broth
1 tablespoon balsamic or sherry vinegar
1 tablespoon finely chopped fresh basil or cilantro
Freshly ground black pepper

In a small saucepan set over high heat, bring the broth to a boil. Add the tomatoes and set aside for 10 minutes, until tomatoes rehydrate and become very soft.

Pour the tomatoes and broth into a blender and add the vinegar. Holding the cover securely in place to prevent the sauce from erupting all over the kitchen, purée to form a thick, slightly chunky sauce. Transfer the sauce to a bowl, stir in the basil or cilantro, and season generously with pepper.

BROCCOLI WITH ONIONS

Makes 4 servings

Broccoli florets enmeshed in tender strands of sweet onion and flavored with fresh herbs make a simple, pure dish, more impressive and good tasting than its humble ingredients would indicate.

Vegetable oil spray
2 medium onions, peeled, cut in half lengthwise, then very thinly sliced
1 garlic clove, peeled and finely chopped
1 bunch broccoli, cut into florets
3 tablespoons finely chopped fresh parsley, basil, or cilantro
Freshly ground black pepper

Lightly mist the inside of a large nonstick skillet with vegetable oil spray. Add the onions and garlic and spray so that they are lightly coated in oil. Cook over medium low heat, stirring frequently, until very limp and almost tender but not browned, about 15 to 20 minutes.

Meanwhile, cook the broccoli in boiling water until tender, about 8 to 10 minutes. Drain and cool under running cold tap water to set the color and stop the cooking. Drain thoroughly and pat dry.

Mix the broccoli into the onions, increase the heat to moderate, and toss until very hot. Add the herbs and black pepper and mix well.

Serve immediately.

BRUSSELS SPROUTS WITH NUTMEG

Makes 4 servings

Small, young brussels sprouts have a sweet, fragrant, slightly nutlike character. Older sprouts develop a strong cabbage flavor and "off" odor. Choose the youngest, smallest sprouts available at a local farmers' market or health food store.

Whole nutmegs, shaped like an inch-long football, are available in the spice section of many premium supermarkets, and in health food stores. You can usually find an inexpensive aluminum grater. Freshly grated nutmeg has a sweet, nutty fragrance, unlike the powdery, lackluster ground nutmeg in spice rack jars.

Serve with Spicy Butternut Squash (page 181) and a brown rice preparation.

4 cups chicken stock
1 pound fresh young brussels sprouts, any damaged outer leaves re-
　　moved, bottoms trimmed
Olive oil spray
A little salt
Freshly grated nutmeg

In a medium-sized saucepan, bring the stock to a boil over high heat. There should be enough stock to cover the sprouts when they are added. Add the sprouts, and when the stock returns to a boil, reduce the heat and simmer until the sprouts are just tender, about 6 minutes.

Immediately drain, mist with just enough oil for the sprouts to glisten, then season lightly with salt and grate a little nutmeg ($1/8$ to $1/4$ teaspoon) over the sprouts, just enough to give them a fragrance of nutmeg. Do not overflavor them, or the nutmeg will hide the sweetness of the vegetable.

STEAMED BABY CARROTS WITH
JEAN-LOUIS PALLADIN'S VERSATILE
ONION SAUCE

Makes 4 servings

Baby carrots, with their delicate, sweet flavor and pale pumpkin orange color are gently blanketed with a sweet onion sauce, which adds sensuality and warmth to this otherwise humble vegetable.

Serve with Julienned Summer Squash Skins (page 182) and basmati rice.

1 pound baby carrots, washed and peeled
1 recipe Jean-Louis Palladin's Versatile Onion Sauce (recipe follows)

Place 2 inches of hot tap water in the bottom of a steamer, insert the steaming basket, cover, and bring to a boil. When the steamer is filled with steam, add the carrots, cover, reduce the heat to medium, and steam carrots until just tender, about 6 minutes.

Using tongs, carefully arrange the carrots in neat bundles and decoratively spoon the sauce over them.

Serve immediately.

Jean-Louis Palladin's
Versatile Onion Sauce

A Microwave Recipe

Makes 1 1/2 cups, 4 to 6 servings

Jean-Louis Palladin, the chef and owner of Jean-Louis at the Watergate in Washington, D.C., and arguably the greatest chef in America, developed this recipe one afternoon when he was experimenting with cooking in the microwave. The delicate, sweet flavor, smooth texture, and golden color of the sauce reminded me of a hollandaise, so I developed variations for a light hollandaise and béarnaise.

As an onion sauce, it can be used almost any time you would use a traditional white sauce. Serve this sauce on pasta or fish, on vegetables such as asparagus, broccoli, or brussels sprouts, or prepare as a light béarnaise (see variation) and serve with meat.

Fish, vegetable, or beef broth can be substituted for the chicken broth, depending on the food being sauced.

This recipe works only in a microwave.

1 pound (2 large) yellow onions, peeled and quartered
1/4 teaspoon turmeric
1/2 cup chicken broth
1 tablespoon unsalted butter or olive oil
A little salt
Freshly ground black pepper

Place the onions in a large microwave-safe bowl, cover, and microwave on high (100%) for 8 minutes.

In a blender, combine the cooked onions with the turmeric, broth, and butter or oil and blend until very smooth. With the back of a spoon, press through a fine strainer.

Taste the sauce and season with salt and pepper.

Curried Onion Sauce

Substitute ¼ to ½ teaspoon curry powder for the turmeric.

Herbed Onion Sauce

Stir 1 to 2 tablespoons of finely chopped fresh herbs into the sauce after straining.

Light Hollandaise

Increase the butter to 2 tablespoons (do not use oil).

Light Béarnaise

Increase the butter (do not use oil) to 2 tablespoons and reduce the broth to ⅓ cup.

In a small saucepan set over medium heat, cook 1 small shallot, peeled and finely chopped, with 3 tablespoons tarragon vinegar and ¾ teaspoon crushed dried tarragon until vinegar is reduced by half—to about 1½ tablespoons. Strain immediately, pressing on the shallots with the back of a spoon to extract all the liquid. Pour this reduced vinegar into the sauce before puréeing. Discard shallots.

GREEN BEANS
WITH CHERMOULA SAUCE

Makes 6 servings

Tender, small pieces of fresh green beans are gently coated here with chermoula, the lemony, mildly spicy sauce from North Africa. The balance of flavors is sprightly and will add a sparkle to almost any meal.

**1 1/2 pounds green beans, ends trimmed and strung if necessary, then
     cut into 1-inch pieces
1 recipe Chermoula Sauce (recipe follows)**

Fill a large saucepan with hot tap water and bring to a boil over high heat. Add the green beans, reduce the heat to medium, and boil until beans are quite tender, about 10 to 12 minutes.

Drain thoroughly, then toss with enough chermoula (about 5 tablespoons) so all the beans are lightly coated. Serve immediately.

Chermoula Sauce

Makes about 1 cup

This is the North African version of Mexico's salsa—hot, sometimes fiery; balanced, acidic, and bold.

Drizzle on vegetables, hot or cold; serve over potatoes; or use to accompany poached fish.

1/2 bunch cilantro, washed and thick stems removed, to make 1/2 cup
1/2 bunch fresh parsley, washed and thick stems removed, to make 1/2 cup
6 garlic cloves, peeled
Juice of 1 large lemon
Juice of 2 small limes
1 tablespoon tomato paste
1/2 teaspoon salt (optional)
2 tablespoons hot Hungarian paprika
1 1/2 teaspoons ground cumin
1/4 teaspoon cayenne, or more to taste

Combine all the ingredients in a food processor and process until the herbs are very finely chopped and a thick, well-blended sauce forms. Taste, adding more cayenne if necessary to give the sauce a nice kick.

Chermoula can be stored in a tightly covered jar for up to 4 days in the refrigerator.

Recipe Archives

Improve your diet with healthy fish!
click here

Recipe Archives->Fish->**Pan Fried Fish**

<-Oven Fried Fish 03-   **Pan Fried Fish**   -Pan Fried Fish 02->

Newsgroups: rec.food.recipes
Subject: Pan Fried Lake Fish
Message-ID: <HHATC37@taronga.com>
Date: Wed, 4 Aug 93 22:27:29 CDT

Pan-Fried Lake Fish

4 8-to-10 oz fresh or frozen pan-dressed trout, lake perch, or other whitefish
3/4 cup finely crushed saltine crackers (21 crackers)
1/4 cup grated Parmesan cheese
1 tablespoon snipped parsley
1/3 cup all-purpose flour

1/8 teaspoon pepper
3 tablespoons lemon juice
1 beaten egg
3 to 4 tablespoons shortening or cooking oil
Lemon slices, halved (optional)

Thaw fish, if frozen. In a shallow bowl, combine the crushed
crackers, grated Parmesan cheese, and snipped parsley. In another
shallow bowl, combine the flour and pepper. Place lemon juice and
egg in separate bowls. Dip fish in lemon juice, then in flour
mixture, then in egg, and finally in the cracker mixture.

In a 12-inch skillet heat shortening or cooking oil. Add fish in
a single layer. Fry over medium heat for 5 to 7 minutes or till
brown. Turn fish; fry for 5 to 7 minutes more or till fish flakes
easily when tested with a fork. Drain on paper towels. Serve fish
with lemon. Garnish with parsley, rosemary, and dill if desired.
Serves 4.

Printable version: pan-fried-fish.txt.

<-Oven Fried Fish 03-   **Search**   -Pan Fried Fish 02->

GREEN BEANS AND FENNEL

Makes 4 servings

Green beans and fennel, both cut the same size and cooked until tender, are a natural pair, enhancing each other's sweetness. The light cream and dill dressing binds them, enhancing the mild anise flavor of the fennel and relating it to the beans. Fresh peas also go nicely with fennel and dill.

Serve with Parsnip Purée (page 176) and steamed baby carrots.

12 ounces green beans, washed, snapped and cut into 1-inch lengths
2 large fennel bulbs, stalks trimmed, discolored outer layers and cones of the bulbs discarded, and inner layers cut into $1/3$-inch-wide julienne, then cut into 1-inch lengths (the fennel pieces should be about the same size as the cut beans)
2 tablespoons finely chopped fresh dill
2 tablespoons light (not imitation) sour cream
1 teaspoon honey

Bring a large saucepan of hot tap water to a boil over high heat. Add the beans and cook until tender and not at all crisp, about 9 minutes. Immediately drain and cool under running cold water. Drain and set aside.

Cook the fennel in the same manner until tender, about 7 to 9 minutes.

Meanwhile, mix together the dill, sour cream, and honey.

When fennel is tender, add the cooked beans to the pot with the fennel and cook just long enough for the beans to heat. Drain well, toss with the dill and sour cream mixture, and serve.

HARICOTS VERTS WITH CHANTERELLES

Makes 4 servings

Haricots verts *are a thin, deep green, young French bean. They are available in many supermarkets and specialty stores. Chanterelles are an amber to umber orange-colored wild mushroom prized by the French, now available in many premium supermarkets, at farmers' markets, and in specialty stores. The woodsy flavor of chanterelle mushrooms balances perfectly with the crunch of the beans to make a strikingly fresh-looking autumn dish.*

For a more modest version of this recipe, substitute young green beans for the haricots verts, *and cultivated white or brown mushrooms, quartered, for the chanterelles.*

Serve as an appetizer, or as part of dinner accompanied by Parsnip Purée (page 176) and Steamed Baby Carrots with Jean-Louis Palladin's Versatile Onion Sauce (page 160).

10 ounces *haricots verts*, washed and ends neatly trimmed with a knife
10 ounces fresh chanterelles, quickly rinsed under running cold water, patted dry, and cut into bite-sized (about 1-inch) pieces
²/₃ cup beef broth
1 tablespoon finely chopped fresh tarragon
1 tablespoon finely chopped fresh parsley
Freshly ground black pepper

Carefully drop the beans into a large saucepan of rapidly boiling water and cook until just tender, about 6 minutes.

Meanwhile, combine the chanterelles and broth in a sauté pan, cover, and set over high heat. Allow the chanterelles to steam-cook this way for 2 minutes, until just tender when pierced with the tip of a knife. Uncover, increase the heat to high, and reduce until there is just a thin film of broth on the bottom of the saucepan, just enough to moisten the beans when they are added.

Drain the beans, add to the chanterelles, and cook until heated through. Mix in the herbs and season with a little pepper.

Serve immediately.

RED CABBAGE BRAISED
WITH CRANBERRIES

Makes 10 to 12 servings

Here are two of my winter favorites in a fruity version of sweet-and-sour red cabbage. During the cooking, the cabbage becomes tender without losing its integrity and the cranberries disintegrate, binding the purple-red shreds gently together.

Other than shredding the cabbage, there is virtually no work involved in making this recipe. Just toss everything into a large pot and cook until done.

I usually make this cabbage for a big Thanksgiving or Christmas dinner, when all 12 servings disappear, even if there are only 8 guests. For a smaller dinner, prepare the whole recipe anyway, and freeze the extra. It freezes well for up to 4 months.

Serve this as part of a winter holiday meal, with Green Beans and Fennel (page 165), and Parsnip Purée (page 176), and a roasted bird.

One 2½-pound head red cabbage, outer leaves removed, cut in half,
    cored, and thinly sliced or shredded
2 large onions, peeled and thinly sliced
3 cups fresh or frozen cranberries (about 12 ounces by weight)
1½ cups chicken, beef, or vegetable broth
¼ cup raspberry vinegar
½ cup brown sugar

Combine all the ingredients in a large pot, cover, and bring to a boil. Reduce the heat and simmer, stirring about every 10 or 15 minutes, until cabbage is tender and cranberries have disintegrated, about 1¼ hours.

CURRIED CAULIFLOWER

Makes 6 servings

Curried cauliflower, with its bright yellow color and mild-tasting spiciness, is a full-flavored yet sweet and flowery, tender-tasting, vegetable.

Serve with Spring Dandelion Greens with Mushrooms (page 171) and Broccoli with Onions (page 158).

Vegetable oil spray
1 large onion, peeled and finely chopped
A 1-inch piece fresh gingerroot, peeled and finely chopped
1 large garlic clove, peeled and finely chopped
Juice of 1/2 large lemon
1/4 cup chicken stock
1 tablespoon curry powder
1/2 teaspoon ground cumin
1/2 teaspoon ground coriander
1/4 teaspoon ground cardamom
1 medium-sized head cauliflower, cored and cut into small florets

Place a large nonstick sauté pan over medium heat. When hot, mist with vegetable oil spray. Add the onion, ginger, and garlic and mist again, tossing the onions, garlic, and ginger well, and misting again if necessary, so that they are all very lightly coated with oil.

Reduce the heat to medium low and cook, stirring frequently, for 10 minutes without browning the onion.

In a small bowl, stir together the lemon juice, stock, curry powder, cumin, coriander, and cardamom. Pour into the sauté pan and swirl around to mix well. Add the cauliflower and toss until evenly colored. Reduce the heat to low, cover, and cook until cauliflower is tender, about 6 to 8 minutes, shaking the pan or stirring once or twice.

CORN ON THE COB

There are frivolous debates among some of my friends about the proper way to eat corn on the cob. Some insist that it must be chewed along its length in straight rows, typewriter-style, while others argue it should be eaten downward, four or five kernels at a time, the cob being turned until it has been eaten clean in one-inch bands. For me, though, the problem with corn on the cob isn't procedural (I eat typewriter-style); it is nutritional and aesthetic.

Traditionally, corn on the cob is used as a vehicle for moving melted butter and salt from plate to mouth. Since we need to reduce both of those in our diets, I began to explore alternatives.

Instead of butter, spread the corn with a hot red or green pepper jelly, or with sweet pineapple jelly. The fibrous texture and sweetness of the corn can support a gentle lathering in something hot and sweet, as in the pepper jellies, or something acidic and sweet, as in the pineapple jelly. Although sauces won't generally adhere to corn on the cob, harissa, the spicy red pepper and tomato sauce of North Africa, is pasty enough to be brushed onto corn.

If corn on the cob and jelly seems just too bizarre, try running a wedge of lemon or lime over the kernels. The acidity of those two juices will give a flavor balance to the sweetness of the corn.

Also, the corn can be brushed ever so lightly with a highly flavored oil, like an extra virgin olive oil or a dark sesame oil. Because those oils are so strongly flavored, a quarter to a half teaspoon on a pastry brush will flavor a whole ear of corn. A hot Chinese oil, if you dare, could also be used, as could Chinese hoisin sauce.

Alternatives to salt are abundant: Sprinkle with curry powder, chili powder, or Chinese five-spice powder; with a sweet or hot Hungarian paprika, or a little turmeric, or ground ginger, or coriander, or cardamom, or any other spice you are fond of.

Combinations then become possible: lemon wedge and curry powder; lemon wedge and cumin; sesame oil and black pepper; olive oil and turmeric, and so on.

SPRING DANDELION GREENS
WITH MUSHROOMS

Makes 4 servings

Tender young dandelion greens, sometimes called spring dandelion greens, need considerably less cooking time than older greens, and are intense but not bitter in flavor. Here they are gently stewed with mushrooms and flavored with a little garlic and ginger.

1 very large onion, peeled and chopped
2 large garlic cloves, peeled and chopped
A 1-inch chunk fresh gingerroot, peeled and very finely chopped
Vegetable oil spray
8 ounces small mushrooms, washed and quartered
16 ounces spring dandelion greens, thoroughly washed and thick
    stems cut off, then gathered together tightly and cut into ½-inch
    shreds
A little salt
Freshly ground black pepper

Place a very large pot over medium low heat. Add the onions, garlic, and ginger; mist them with oil spray and cook, stirring occasionally, until the onions are translucent, about 6 minutes. Add the mushrooms and greens, mix well, cover loosely, and cook until greens are just tender, about 15 minutes. Season with salt and pepper to taste.

MUSHROOM AND SNOW PEA STIR-FRY

Makes 6 servings

The sweetness and crisp texture of the snow peas contrasts with the earthy flavor and soft texture of the mushrooms to produce a wonderful dish. The final seasonings of Chinese oyster and soy sauces add unity to the assorted tastes and accents.

Any combination of fresh mushrooms can be used in this recipe. In winter, use the more strongly flavored mushrooms such as cremini and shiitake, to make the stir-fry bigger, warmer, earthier. In summer, to lighten it, use primarily domestic white mushrooms and, if you wish, add a big handful of finely chopped fresh herbs, such as cilantro or basil, just before serving.

For a one-dish family lunch or supper, serve this stir-fry on a bed of rice.

10 sun-dried tomatoes
1 to 1½ tablespoons peanut oil
1 large onion, peeled and chopped
2 large garlic cloves, peeled and finely chopped
2 quarter-sized disks fresh gingerroot, finely chopped
3 celery ribs, sliced on the bias about ¼ to ⅓ inch thick
1 pound fresh mushrooms, thickly sliced
1 pound snow peas, washed, the stem end of each pod broken and pulled off with the string that runs the length of each pod, and sliced on the bias in ½-inch pieces
3 scallions, washed, trimmed, and cut on bias into 1-inch pieces
½ pound spinach, washed, thick stems removed, and roughly chopped
3 tablespoons Chinese oyster sauce
2 tablespoons soy sauce
Freshly ground black pepper

Place the dried tomatoes in a small bowl or measuring cup and add just enough of the hottest possible tap water to cover. Set aside for 3 minutes to rehydrate. Drain and pat dry. Cut the tomatoes into $1/2$-inch pieces. Set aside.

Oil a large wok and place over high heat. Add the onion, garlic, and ginger, and mix well. Cook, stirring frequently, until onion develops a slightly yellow color without browning, about 4 minutes. Lift the onions up the side of the wok and allow any oil and liquid to drain down. Transfer onions to a large bowl.

Add the celery to the wok. Add a tiny amount of oil, if necessary. Cook, stirring frequently, until celery develops a bright kelly green color and is mostly tender, though a little crisp, about 3 or 4 minutes. Lift up the side of the wok and allow any oil and liquid to drain down. Add the celery to the bowl with the onions.

Toss the mushrooms into the wok. Add a little oil, if necessary. Cook, stirring frequently, until the mushrooms darken in color and have just become tender, about 3 minutes. Stop cooking the mushrooms immediately if they begin to give off their liquid. Lift up the side of the wok and allow any oil and liquid to drain down. Add the mushrooms to the bowl with the celery and onions.

Cook the snow peas with the scallions in the same way. When they glisten, become bright green, and are crisply tender, in about 3 minutes, add them to the other cooked vegetables.

Add the spinach to the wok and cook, stirring frequently, until just wilted, about 1 or 2 minutes. Add to the other cooked vegetables.

Add the sun-dried tomatoes, oyster sauce, and soy sauce to the vegetables and mix well. Season generously with pepper.

Reheat the stir-fry in the wok just before serving.

STEWED OKRA AND TOMATOES
WITH CILANTRO

Makes 6 servings

Properly cooked, okra, with its fresh, suave, sensual texture, is one of the great joys of the summer garden. Here, it is stewed with lots of onions and tomatoes and flavored with cilantro, ginger, lime juice, and a few shreds of jalapeño. The combination bursts with energy.

Buy fresh, young, unblemished okra no more than about 2 inches in length, and when trimming, cut off the stem without exposing the soft inside to ensure the okra is tender. Longer, older, often brown-gray blotched okra can be both tough and slimy.

Serve with rice.

Olive oil spray
3 garlic cloves, peeled and chopped
$^{1}/_{2}$ small jalapeño pepper, trimmed, seeded, and cut into the thinnest
    possible threads (optional)
A $^{3}/_{4}$-inch piece fresh gingerroot, peeled and very finely chopped
1 medium-sized onion, peeled and finely chopped
$1^{1}/_{2}$ pounds fresh okra, stem ends trimmed
One 28-ounce can crushed tomatoes in purée
Juice of 1 lime
1 small bunch cilantro, coarsely chopped
A little freshly ground black pepper

Place a large saucepan or small pot over medium heat. Mist with oil spray, then add the garlic, jalapeño, ginger, and onion and mist again, tossing so that everything is evenly coated with oil. Reduce the heat to medium low and cook for 6 minutes, stirring frequently and reducing the heat again if necessary to prevent browning.

Add the okra, tomatoes, and lime juice, mix well, and bring to a boil over medium high heat, stirring occasionally to prevent scorching. Reduce the heat and simmer, partially covered, until okra is tender, about 25 minutes, stirring occasionally.

Stir in the cilantro and season very lightly with pepper.

PARSNIP PURÉE

Makes 4 servings

Parsnips are deliciously mild and when onion, leek, and garlic are added, they make an excellent alternative to mashed potatoes.

Olive oil spray
1 small onion, peeled and finely chopped
1 small leek, white part only, split and washed to remove all grit, then
    thinly sliced
1 garlic clove, peeled and finely chopped
1 pound parsnips, peeled, trimmed, and cut into quarters
²/₃ cup skim milk

Place a large nonstick sauté pan over medium heat. When hot, mist lightly with oil spray, then add the onion, leek, and garlic. Mist again so that all the chopped vegetables are lightly coated with oil, stirring once or twice. Reduce the heat to medium low and cook for 10 minutes, stirring frequently to prevent sticking, and reducing the heat again if necessary to prevent browning.

While the onions are cooking, drop the parsnips into a large pot of boiling water and cook until very tender, about 12 minutes. Drain well.

In a food processor, combine the parsnips with the cooked onion mixture. Pulse rapidly 2 or 3 times to combine, then add the milk and process until smooth, about 1¹/₂ to 2 minutes.

Reheat before serving.

SWEET RED PEPPER RAGOUT

Makes 6 servings

Hungarian paprika adds a shadow of warmth to this richly textured, sweet pepper stew, with lemon juice balancing the flavors. The peppers become very soft as they stew, but retain their fire-engine red color. This is one of my favorite recipes.

You can change this ragout into a spread that can be used for moistening and flavoring sandwiches simply by cutting the peppers in ¹/₂-inch dice instead of strips. The spread also can be spooned onto thick slices of lightly toasted homemade bread and be served as an appetizer or to accompany a bowl of soup or a light supper. For an interesting variation, use yellow or orange peppers with curry powder instead of paprika.

Serve with Emerald Spinach with Hidden Herbs (page 180) and Fluffy Whipped Potatoes (page 178), garnished with Spicy Salmon Fillets (page 271).

2 garlic cloves, peeled and finely chopped
1 large red onion, peeled and thinly sliced
Vegetable oil spray
1 tablespoon sweet Hungarian paprika
3 pounds large sweet red bell peppers, washed, cored, and cut into ¹/₄-inch strips
Juice of 1 lemon
Freshly ground black pepper

Combine the garlic and onion in a large, heavy pot set over medium heat. Spray lightly with oil, mix well, cover, and cook until wilted, about 5 minutes, stirring once or twice.

Add the paprika and mix well (the onions will become tangled). Cover and cook for 1 minute. Add the peppers and lemon juice, stir to break up the clumps of onion, cover, and cook until tender and wilted down to about half the original volume, 15 to 20 minutes, stirring occasionally.

Season with black pepper and cook, uncovered, stirring occasionally, until most of the liquid has evaporated, about 15 minutes.

FLUFFY WHIPPED POTATOES

Makes 6 servings

These softly textured whipped potatoes are lightly flavored with chicken stock and milk. This is winter comfort food, excellent for parties and holiday meals, or for casual family dinners. The potatoes can be made several hours or even days ahead, and refrigerated or frozen until needed.

Russets (often labeled "Idaho") have been suggested in the recipe because they make the lightest and fluffiest whipped potatoes. But any of the yellow potatoes, such as Yukon Golds and Kennebecs, which are available from late summer until early spring, could be used instead, producing a creamy texture and light buttery flavor without needing the fat and cholesterol of whole milk or sour cream.

1½ pounds large russet (Idaho) potatoes, scrubbed in cold water and
   patted dry
⅓ cup Chicken Stock (page 110)
¼ cup skim milk
A little salt, if you wish, and freshly ground black pepper

Bake the potatoes, either in a microwave or conventional oven. Using the microwave will save about half an hour of cooking time.

Microwave method: Prick each potato in 2 or 3 places to prevent the very remote possibility of the potato exploding in the microwave. Arrange the potatoes in a circle (no pan or dish is necessary) on the oven floor. Microwave on high for 16 minutes. Midway through the cooking, carefully flip the potatoes (so the bottoms resting on the oven floor become the tops) to ensure even cooking. Set aside to cool.

Conventional method: Place the potatoes on the rack of a conventional oven heated to 350 to 400 degrees F and bake until tender when pierced with the tip of a sharp knife, 45 to 60 minutes.

178

When they are cool enough to handle, peel the potatoes. With an electric mixer, whip the potatoes with the stock and milk until light and lump-free. Taste and season with salt and pepper.

Transfer to a double boiler and cook over medium heat until very hot, then beat well with a whisk to refluff, and serve.

EMERALD SPINACH WITH
HIDDEN HERBS

Makes 4 servings

This exceptionally delicious spinach recipe sparkles with flavor, the hidden herbs adding an unexpected depth to the brilliant green leaves.

Serve with Sweet Red Pepper Ragout (page 177) and Crookneck Squash Sauté (page 183).

1 pound fresh spinach, thick stems removed, thoroughly washed, drained, and coarsely chopped
A bunch fresh coriander, rinsed under running cold water
A bunch fresh chives, rinsed under running cold water
Freshly ground black pepper

Toss the spinach in a large pot set over medium high heat, cover, and cook until just wilted, about 5 minutes, stirring once or twice. Meanwhile, coarsely chop enough of the coriander and chives to make about $1/2$ cup. Stir the herbs into the spinach and season with pepper.

Serve immediately.

SPICY BUTTERNUT SQUASH

A Microwave Recipe

Makes 6 servings

The spicy coating on these cubes of rich butternut squash can be either sweet or hot, depending on the kind of chili powder used. When the chili powder is barely hot, the sweet taste of the squash will dominate; if it is fiery hot, it will add contrast to this autumn vegetable.

This versatile recipe can be served as part of a cold meal in August, when the first winter squashes appear in the market, or hot from the oven during the winter months.

3 tablespoons chili powder (pages 191 and 192)
Juice of 1 large lemon
One 3-pound butternut squash, split lengthwise with a sharp, heavy
    chef's knife, the seeds and fibrous center scooped out of the cavity
    with a spoon, peeled, and cut into 3/4-inch dice

In a small bowl, mix together the chili powder and lemon juice. Place the squash in a very large microwave-safe bowl and pour the mixture over it. Toss until all the cubes are evenly coated, and push them toward the sides of the bowl (rather than leaving them heaped in the center) so they will cook evenly.

Cover and microwave on high (100%) for 14 minutes. Test for doneness by carefully uncovering and inserting the tip of a small sharp knife or toothpick into a few of the cubes. It should slide through easily. If not, cover and microwave for another 2 minutes, then retest.

If serving hot, scoop onto plate with a large serving spoon and serve immediately. If serving cold, refrigerate until cool.

181

JULIENNED SUMMER SQUASH SKINS

Makes 6 servings

I was never fond of the summer squashes; they always seemed more wet than savory. Then, at a lunch in Washington, D.C., prepared by Chef David Fye, I discovered that their skins, where all the flavor is, could be julienned and served as a vegetable (the mushy insides can be saved for soup), so I am now a summer squash fan.

Serve on a cool spring or summer evening, as part of a formal dinner.

3 pounds yellow crookneck summer squash (preferably about 1¼ to 1½ inches in diameter), washed, ends trimmed, and cut into 3-inch lengths
2 pounds zucchini (preferably about 1¼ to 1½ inches in diameter), washed, ends trimmed, and cut into 3-inch lengths
1 tablespoon very finely chopped fresh chives
1 tablespoon unsalted butter, or virgin or extra virgin olive oil
A little salt
Freshly ground black pepper

Using a mandoline or plastic vegetable cutter, julienne just the squash skins, reserving the flesh of the squashes for soup or a vegetable stew.

Bring a large pot of hot tap water to a rapid boil. Drop all the julienned skins into the water at once, stir, and cook until just about tender, about 1½ minutes. Drain immediately, toss gently with the chives and butter, and season with a little salt and very little pepper.

Serve immediately.

THREE SUMMER SQUASH SAUTÉS

Makes 6 servings

This is a miniformula for cooking summer squash. Depending on availability of small, young summer squashes, I use either all crookneck squashes, all zucchini, or a combination of both; and I adjust the flavoring accordingly: garlic and red onions with crookneck; lime and parsley, in addition, with zucchini; and red onion and parsley or lemon thyme (see headnote, page 272) with a combination of the two.

The procedure is always the same, cutting the squash into triangular shaped pieces and quickly sautéing them. After you've prepared squash this way once or twice, you may want to experiment with different herbs and flavorings, using the basic proportions from the ingredient lists below as a guide in your experiments.

Leftovers can be tossed with fettuccine the next day, perhaps with a seeded and diced tomato, to make a quick pasta primavera.

Crookneck Squash Sauté:

Olive oil spray
1 large garlic clove, peeled and finely chopped
1 small red onion, trimmed, peeled, quartered lengthwise, then thinly sliced
2 pounds yellow crookneck squash, as evenly shaped as possible, about 1½ to 2 inches in diameter, ends trimmed, cut in quarters lengthwise, then sliced about ⅓ inch thick
A little salt
Freshly ground black pepper

Zucchini Sauté:

Olive oil spray
1 large garlic clove, peeled and finely chopped
1 small red onion, trimmed, peeled, quartered lengthwise, then thinly
    sliced
2 pounds zucchini, evenly shaped, about 1½ to 2 inches in diameter,
    ends trimmed, cut in quarters lengthwise, then sliced about ⅓ inch
    thick
Juice of 1 small lime
2 tablespoons finely chopped parsley
A little salt
Freshly ground black pepper

Mixed Squash Sauté:

Olive oil spray
1 small red onion, trimmed, peeled, quartered lengthwise, then thinly
    sliced
1 pound yellow crookneck squash, as evenly shaped as possible, about
    1½ to 2 inches in diameter, ends trimmed, cut in quarters length-
    wise, then sliced about ⅓ inch thick
1 pound zucchini, as evenly shaped as possible, about 1½ to 2 inches
    in diameter, ends trimmed, cut in quarters lengthwise, then sliced
    about ⅓ inch thick
2 tablespoons finely chopped parsley
1 tablespoon finely chopped lemon thyme (if available)
A little salt
Freshly ground black pepper

Place a large nonstick sauté pan over medium heat. When hot, mist lightly with olive oil spray and add the garlic, if using, and the onion. Spray again so that the onion and garlic are lightly coated in oil. Cook, stirring frequently, for 5 minutes, reducing the heat as needed to prevent browning.

Add the squash, mix well, loosely cover, and cook, stirring occasionally, until squash is tender, about 6 to 8 minutes. Stir in the herbs and citrus juice, if using, and season with salt and quite generously with pepper.

Serve immediately.

Leftovers can be stored, tightly covered, in the refrigerator for up to 3 days.

RUSSIAN SUMMER VEGETABLE SALAD

Makes 6 to 8 servings

With vegetables fresh from the garden, or the farm, or the farmers' market, this is one of the most refreshing ways to celebrate summer. Although I usually find I have nibbled my way through a third of this salad before it gets into the refrigerator, it should be served cold.

Texturally, the salad is best when all the vegetables are cut to the same size, about 1/2-inch dice. For a more subtle flavor, cut the vegetables into 1/4-inch dice. For a rustic feel, chop them coarsely and unevenly.

Use this as a garnish for sandwiches, or whenever you would traditionally serve coleslaw or potato salad; or serve it with thick slices of toasted whole wheat or sourdough bread as an entrée for lunch. It makes a refreshing, colorful addition to buffets and brunch menus. As an appetizer, serve very cold with thin slices of dark pumpernickel bread.

4 large vine-ripened tomatoes, washed, cored, seeded, and diced
4 medium-sized pickling (Kirby) cucumbers, scrubbed and diced, or 1
    large cucumber, peeled, seeded, and diced
1 small bunch scallions, root ends trimmed, washed and very thinly
    sliced
1 sweet bell pepper (green, red, yellow, or orange, washed, cored,
    seeded, and diced)
1 large bunch fresh dill, washed, shaken dry, and finely chopped
    (about 1 cup)
About 1/3 cup light (not imitation) sour cream
A little salt
Freshly ground black pepper

In a large bowl, mix together the tomatoes, cucumbers, scallions, bell pepper, and dill. Add half the sour cream and toss gently. All the vegetables should be just barely coated. If not, add a little more sour cream. Taste and season with salt and pepper.

Refrigerate the salad for an hour or two before serving, to allow the flavors to mellow.

COLD SUMMER VEGETABLES
WITH MISO DRESSING

The counterculture first encountered miso, a Japanese fermented bean paste with a distinctive vegetable flavor, when it discovered macrobiotic cooking in the late 1960s. At that time miso was assigned almost mystical healing and spiritual powers, and was used almost exclusively for making soup. Here the miso is used to make a nonfat dressing, which is wonderfully alive and fruity, with unexpected balance and zing. Sometimes I pass large platters of vegetables with the dressing served on the side. Sometimes I arrange the vegetables "artfully," as a friend describes it, on plates.

What is miso? Imagine brewing a cup of coffee with ground soybeans instead of coffee beans, and with salted water instead of tap water. To give extra flavor, imagine letting the soybeans ferment before draining off the water. When you filtered or strained the brew, the liquid would become soy sauce, the grounds would become miso.

Miso ranges from cream to dark chocolate in color—the lighter the color, the milder the flavor—and in texture from smooth to quite grainy. Yellow miso, which is readily available in Japanese (and some other Asian) markets and health food stores, is on the mild side of the miso spectrum, and has a smooth texture.

Use the miso dressing on salads of all kinds, from simple green salads to potato salads, from fish salads to beef salads. Use it as a spread on sandwiches, as a sauce for hot vegetables in winter, or as a dip. For an herbal version of this dressing, add ¼ cup finely chopped chives, parsley, and cilantro.

Vegetables

A selection of summer vegetables, such as crisp-cooked asparagus, crisp-cooked broccoli, vine-ripened yellow or red tomatoes, seeded cucumbers, roasted peppers, tiny florets of cauliflower, cooked or uncooked baby or miniature vegetables, beautiful tender heads of lettuces, and anything else fresh from the garden or farmers' market

Miso Dressing

Makes 1 cup (about 8 servings) dressing

3 tablespoons Dijon mustard
3 tablespoons yellow miso
Juice of 1½ lemons
⅓ cup chicken stock
Freshly ground black pepper

Arrange the vegetables decoratively on a platter or plates.

In a small bowl, whisk together the mustard, miso, lemon juice, and stock. Taste and season with pepper. Spoon over vegetables.

Extra dressing can be stored in a tightly covered jar in the refrigerator for several weeks.

VEGETARIAN CHILI

Makes 8 servings

Mildly spicy, with a robust winter flavor and a variety of textures, this chili can be used as a side dish or as a meal in itself; it can be mixed into rice or risottos, or made into a pizza topping.

2 tablespoons safflower oil
1 very large red onion, peeled and diced
4 large garlic cloves, peeled and finely chopped
A 1-inch piece fresh gingerroot, peeled and finely chopped
4 medium carrots, peeled and cut into $1/4$-inch dice
2 cups vegetable stock or water
2 to 4 tablespoons chili powder (recipes follow)
5 celery ribs, cut into $1/3$-inch dice
2 cups corn kernels, either cut from 3 large ears of yellow corn or
   canned and drained
2 poblano peppers, stems removed, cored and seeded, cut into $1/3$-inch
   dice
1 cup home-cooked white beans or canned white beans, drained
1 cup home-cooked black beans or canned black beans, drained
One 28-ounce can crushed tomatoes

Pour the oil into a large pot set over medium low heat. Stir in the onion, garlic, and ginger and cook without browning for 6 minutes. Add the carrots and stock and cook until carrots are almost tender, about 8 minutes. Add the remaining ingredients all at once, stir well, bring to a boil over medium heat, then reduce the heat and simmer for 45 minutes. Stir occasionally to prevent scorching, and add another $1/2$ cup of stock or water if chili seems to be getting too thick.

Hot Chili Powder

Makes about ¹/₂ cup

This hot but not scorching chili powder has a freshness and a depth of flavor not found in commercial chili powders. Once made, the mixture will stay fresh for about 3 months in a tightly covered jar stored at room temperature. To make the chili powder very hot, add ¹/₂ teaspoon cayenne and an additional ¹/₂ teaspoon of black pepper to the mixture.

An attractively labeled jar of homemade chili powder makes an excellent house gift or winter holiday gift.

Ancho chili powder is available in Mexican markets.

¹/₄ cup ancho chili powder
2 tablespoons hot Hungarian paprika
1 tablespoon ground cumin
1 tablespoon onion powder
1 tablespoon garlic powder
1 teaspoon ground white pepper
1 teaspoon ground black pepper
2 teaspoons crushed dried thyme
1 teaspoon crushed dried oregano
1 teaspoon crushed dried rosemary
2 teaspoons crushed dried marjoram

In a small jar or container, mix all the ingredients until thoroughly blended. Cover tightly and store at room temperature.

Sweet Chili Powder

Makes about ⅓ cup

This is a "sweet" version of the preceding recipe, with a completely different balance. Here, the hot ancho chili powder has been significantly reduced and partly replaced by sweet Hungarian paprika, which gives the mixture a lighter overall flavor. In addition there is more herb taste in this mixture.

2 tablespoons ancho chili powder
3 tablespoons sweet Hungarian paprika
2 teaspoons ground cumin
1 tablespoon onion powder
1 tablespoon garlic powder
¼ teaspoon ground white pepper
¼ teaspoon ground black pepper
1 teaspoon crushed dried thyme
1 teaspoon crushed dried rosemary
1 teaspoon crushed dried oregano
1½ teaspoons crushed dried marjoram

In a small jar or container, mix all the ingredients until thoroughly blended. Cover tightly and store at room temperature.

MIXED WINTER ROOT VEGETABLES

Makes 6 servings

The humbler root vegetables, like parsnips and the round, often dirt-coated celery root, are all too frequently overlooked, or shunned, after the buoyant vegetable bounty of summer. With their natural succulence and aromas, they would be sought after were it not that they grow underground and are knobby and dirty.

Here 3 of these winter vegetables are steamed and then mashed to make an inexpensive, unexpectedly lively and fragrant vegetable dish.

Serve as you would mashed potatoes.

1¼ cups Chicken or Vegetable Stock (pages 110 and 116)
1¼ pounds parsnips, peeled and diced
¼ pound celery root, peeled and diced
¾ pounds waxy potatoes, preferably not Idaho russets (see headnote, page 178), peeled and diced
A little salt (optional)
Freshly ground black pepper

Pour the stock into the bottom of a large steamer and bring to a boil. Toss the vegetables into the steamer basket, set in place, cover and let the steamer fill with steam, then reduce the heat and simmer until vegetables are tender, about 15 minutes.

Carefully remove the steamed vegetables and beat well in an electric mixer or press through a potato ricer to make a texture like mashed potatoes. Stir in a little of the stock used for steaming if the mixture seems very thick. Season with salt and pepper, and reheat, either in the microwave or in a double boiler.

Serve immediately.

7

Rice, Beans, Grains, and Pasta

RICE

Golden Asparagus Risotto
Brown Rice Risotto with Azuki Beans
Cold Rice Salad for a Picnic
Gently Spiced Brown Basmati Rice
Baked Jasmine Rice with Coconut
Everyday Brown Rice Casserole
Persian Rice with Dill and Saffron
Creamy Rice with Fresh Peas
Rice with Black-eyed Peas and Tomatoes

OTHER GRAINS

Whole Wheat Couscous with Wild Mushrooms
Barley with Wild Rice
Bulgur Salad with Poblanos

BEANS AND LENTILS

Basic Preparation of Dried Beans
Quick Black Beans with Chili
Flageolets in Rosemary Cream
Summer Lentil Salad

PASTA

Basic Pasta Dough
Saffron Pasta with Asian "Pesto"
Whole Wheat Fettuccine with Wild Mushrooms and Dill
Rigatoni with Puttanesca Sauce
Penne with Tomato Sauce

Introduction

For "back to nature" cooks in the 1970s, rice, beans, cereals, and grains were a part of almost every meal. These were the most "natural" of foods, they were inexpensive, and as Lappé had pointed out in *Diet for a Small Planet*, they were the most acceptable form of protein for anyone who cared about feeding the world and preserving the planet.

Brown rice was believed to be "healthier" than white rice, for it signified an unprocessed, natural condition, while white represented the evils of processed food and a processed life. Using brown rather than white rice not only increases the nutritional value of the dishes by adding more fiber, but it produces rice dishes with a nuttier, earthier flavor and richer texture. The dense, heavy, brown rice and other grain and bean concoctions of early counterculture cooking have become today's lighter brown rice casseroles and risottos.

Today we know that we should serve rice, cereal, beans, or grain with almost every meal. Even at breakfast rice can become a delicious cereal.

In this chapter, there are a dozen rice recipes and variations, from an elegant risotto with asparagus to an everyday brown rice casserole as well as recipes for couscous, barley, bulgur, a variety of beans, and pastas.

Rice

GOLDEN ASPARAGUS RISOTTO

Makes 6 appetizer servings, 4 main course servings

Risotto, the elegant, creamy rice specialty of Northern Italy, has become increasingly popular in this country's restaurants, though it has remained outside the home cook's ken largely because the traditional cooking method requires constant stirring. But with the microwave, you can make an excellent risotto, better than you will be served in most restaurants, quickly and easily.

This risotto is flavored with fresh asparagus and saffron. A great many variations are possible—almost any fresh vegetable can be used, with the minor flavorings (the cheese, saffron, and herbs) being appropriately adjusted. A few possibilities are presented in the variations that follow.

Only medium-grain rice, which produces the creamy texture in a risotto, can be used for this recipe. Medium-grain rices are shorter and plumper than traditional long-grain rice, and should appear to be translucent with an opaque white center. They are generally imported, and although they are sometimes confusingly named and labeled, look for Arborio rice or other risotto rices.

Do not rinse risotto rice before cooking; the starch that coats the grains is in part responsible for the natural creamy texture of a risotto.

Serve this as a light summer appetizer before a formal meal, or as a spring and early summer entrée.

2 shallots, peeled and finely chopped

1 small garlic clove, peeled and finely chopped

A ½-inch chunk fresh gingerroot, peeled and grated

1 tablespoon olive oil

1 cup medium-grain rice, unwashed

¼ teaspoon crushed saffron threads

2¾ cups chicken stock if microwaving, 4 cups if preparing traditionally

6 ounces asparagus, trimmed of woody bottom ends and cut on the bias into ½-inch pieces

2 tablespoons grated Romano cheese

1 tablespoon finely chopped fresh tarragon

Traditional Procedure:

In a large saucepan set over medium heat, sauté the shallots, garlic, and ginger in the oil for 5 minutes. Stir in the rice and sauté until the rice becomes white and opaque, about 2 minutes.

While the shallots and rice are being sautéed, bring the stock and saffron to a boil in a medium-sized pot, then reduce the heat and keep at a simmer.

Slowly ladle about a cup of the stock into the pot containing the rice (which should be over medium low heat), stirring occasionally until the stock is absorbed.

Continue adding stock, about half a cup at a time, keeping the stock very hot and the risotto at a simmer the whole time. It should take about 30 to 35 minutes to incorporate all the stock. After 25 minutes, add the asparagus. Just before serving, stir in the Romano and tarragon.

If the stock is added too quickly, the rice will be mushy on the outside and chalky inside; if it is added too slowly, the risotto will become pasty. After about half the stock has been absorbed, the risotto will need almost constant stirring.

Microwave Procedure:

In a large, microwave-safe bowl, stir together the shallots, garlic, ginger, rice, and oil, stirring until the rice is evenly coated with the oil. Cover tightly and microwave on high for 4 minutes.

While rice is cooking, stir the saffron into the stock and set aside.

Uncover the rice and add the stock. Cover tightly and microwave on high (100%) for 17 minutes.

Carefully uncover, and using a fork, gently stir in the asparagus (the rice will be slightly undercooked and the risotto somewhat soupy at this point). Cover again and microwave on high (100%) for 6 minutes.

The risotto should be creamy and moist, but not soupy; if not, return to the microwave for another 1 or 2 minutes. When it is ready, stir in the cheese and tarragon with a fork and serve immediately.

Wild Mushroom Risotto with Sun-dried Tomatoes

Use beef broth instead of chicken broth and eliminate the saffron. Substitute shiitake mushrooms, stems removed and caps thinly sliced, for the asparagus. Add 5 or 6 thinly sliced sun-dried tomatoes to the risotto with the mushrooms. Substitute Parmesan for the Romano; and instead of the 2 tablespoons of tarragon, use 2 tablespoons of parsley and a generous teaspoon of very finely chopped fresh rosemary.

Seafood Risotto

Use fish stock instead of chicken broth. Substitute raw shelled small shrimp (or shrimp cut into ³/₄-inch pieces), or half shrimp and half bay scallops, for the asparagus. Eliminate the cheese, if you wish (Italians don't use cheese with seafood risottos), and use 1 tablespoon of finely chopped fresh parsley and 1 tablespoon of finely chopped fresh dill instead of all tarragon.

BROWN RICE RISOTTO WITH AZUKI BEANS

A Microwave Recipe

Makes 8 servings

Using brown rather than white rice for making risottos not only increases the nutritional value of the risotto, but it produces a nuttier, earthier-tasting risotto with a richer texture. In this recipe, azuki beans (the small, dark burgundy to brown beans that are everyday food in much of Asia) add warmth and sweetness to the risotto.

Brown risotto rice, or medium-grain brown rice, is available in health food stores and some premium supermarkets. It takes almost twice as long to cook as white risotto rice. Do not rinse the rice before cooking; the starch that coats the grains gives the risotto its creamy texture.

1 small onion, peeled and finely chopped
1 small garlic clove, peeled and finely chopped
1 tablespoon olive oil
1 cup medium-grain brown rice, unwashed
2³/₄ cups beef, chicken, or vegetable stock if microwaving, 7 cups if
    preparing traditionally
3 tablespoons grated Gruyère cheese
2 tablespoons finely chopped fresh parsley
¹/₂ cup cooked azuki beans (see page 216)
A little salt
Freshly ground black pepper

In a large, microwave-safe bowl, combine the onion, garlic, rice, and oil, stirring until the rice is evenly coated with the oil. Cover tightly and microwave on high for 4 minutes.

Carefully uncover the rice and add the stock. Cover tightly and microwave on high until most of the liquid is absorbed and the rice is just cooked through, about

201

35 minutes. The rice should be slightly chewy and there should be a little soupiness in the risotto; if not, return to the microwave for another 1 or 2 minutes to finish the cooking. When ready, stir in the cheese, parsley, and beans with a fork, taste, and season with a little salt and pepper.

Brown Rice Risotto with Duck

Use beef or chicken broth, or a combination of the two. Add only ½ cup cooked azuki beans and stir 1 cup of diced, cooked-medium-rare duck breast into the risotto with the parsley.

COLD RICE SALAD FOR A PICNIC

Makes 6 servings

This colorful rice salad, high in fiber and very low in fat, is a mix of lively textures and flavors. Use it for hot or cold buffets, or for potlucks or picnics.

3 cups chicken stock or water
1½ cups long-grain rice
Olive oil spray
½ small onion, peeled and finely chopped
2 small garlic cloves, peeled and finely chopped
A ½-inch piece fresh gingerroot, peeled and finely chopped
½ small sweet red bell pepper, cored and cut into ⅓-inch dice
½ small sweet yellow bell pepper, cored and cut into ⅓-inch dice
½ small sweet green bell pepper, cored and cut into ⅓-inch dice
¼ cup finely chopped fresh parsley
¼ cup finely chopped fresh cilantro
¼ cup finely chopped fresh dill
1 thin scallion, finely chopped
1 cup home-cooked white beans, or canned and drained white beans
2 tablespoons raspberry vinegar
1 tablespoon virgin or extra virgin olive oil
A little salt
Freshly ground black pepper

In a large pot, bring the stock or water to a boil over high heat. Stir in the rice, cover, reduce the heat, and simmer until rice is just tender and all the liquid has been absorbed, about 20 minutes.

Meanwhile, place a large nonstick sauté pan over medium heat. When hot, mist generously with cooking oil spray, then add the onion, garlic, ginger, and the red, yellow, and green peppers. Spray, stirring and tossing, until all these chopped vegetables are lightly coated with oil.

Cook for 10 minutes, reducing the heat to prevent browning, to soften (though not make completely tender) the onions and peppers. Scrape into a very large bowl and set aside.

When rice is cooked, stir with a fork and set aside to cool, then add to the bowl with the cooked onion and peppers. Add the parsley, cilantro, dill, and scallions to the bowl and toss very gently with a large fork, mixing everything but trying not to crush the rice. Sprinkle the white beans, vinegar, and oil over the rice and mix again with the fork, distributing the beans without crushing them.

Taste and season with salt and pepper, and a little more vinegar, if you wish. Serve at room temperature.

To serve hot, mix everything together without cooling the rice and serve immediately.

GENTLY SPICED BROWN BASMATI RICE

Makes 6 servings

This is a warming cool-weather rice dish, richly flavored with tomatoes. The texture is loose and creamy.

Serve with vegetarian chili and a couple of thick slices of toast for a winter lunch or dinner.

2½ cups chicken stock or water
1 cup long-grain brown basmati rice
Grated zest of ½ small orange
1 tablespoon sweet Hungarian paprika
½ cup tomato-vegetable juice
2 tablespoons tomato paste
Freshly ground black pepper

In a large saucepan, bring the stock or water to a boil over high heat. Stir in the rice, orange zest, and paprika, reduce the heat, cover, and simmer until rice is tender but still a little chewy, about 35 minutes.

With a fork, stir in the tomato-vegetable juice and tomato paste and simmer for 3 or 4 minutes to allow the flavors to merge and most of the liquid to be absorbed. Season with pepper.

Serve immediately.

BAKED JASMINE RICE WITH COCONUT

Makes 4 servings

This tender, fluffy rice has the texture of the elegant basmati rices of Persia, with a flowery aroma. In this simple casserole, coconut sweetens the rice and adds complexity to the bouquet.

Thai jasmine rice is a scented, prized rice from Southeast Asia available in Thai and some Asian groceries, and at some premium food shops. Unsweetened dried coconut is available in health food stores.

Serve with Haricots Verts with Chanterelles (page 166) and Steamed Asparagus with Sun-dried Tomato Sauce (page 156).

1½ cups hottest possible tap water
¾ cup Thai jasmine rice
3 tablespoons dried unsweetened coconut
A little salt

Preheat the oven to 400 degrees F.

Pour the water into a medium-sized stovetop and ovenproof covered casserole or serving dish. Bring to a boil over high heat. While water is heating, pick over the rice to remove any small pebbles, then rise off the powder that coats the rice.

When water reaches the boil, stir in the rice and coconut, cover, and place in the oven. Cook until rice is tender and all the water has been absorbed, about 18 minutes.

Uncover, fluff with a fork, season with salt, and serve.

EVERYDAY BROWN RICE CASSEROLE

Makes 6 servings

This is my brown rice equivalent to a rice pilaf, tender brown rice flavored with aromatic vegetables, garlic, and a little thyme.

Vegetable oil spray
1/2 medium-sized carrot, scrubbed, peeled, and finely chopped
1 small onion, peeled and finely chopped
1 celery rib, finely chopped
1 garlic clove, peeled and finely chopped
1 cup long-grain brown rice
1/4 teaspoon crushed dried thyme or rosemary
2 1/2 cups chicken stock
1 bay leaf

Preheat the oven to 375 degrees F.

Place a large nonstick sauté pan over medium heat. When it is hot, mist with vegetable oil spray and add the carrot. Lightly mist the carrot pieces, then reduce the heat and cook without browning for 4 minutes, stirring frequently. Add the onion, celery, and garlic, mist to coat lightly with oil, then cook, stirring frequently, for 6 minutes without browning. Stir in the rice and thyme or rosemary and cook for 1 minute.

Meanwhile, in a large stovetop and ovenproof covered casserole, bring the stock and bay leaf to a boil. Add the sautéed rice and vegetables, stir, cover, and slide into the oven. Cook until all the stock has been absorbed and the rice is tender, about 40 minutes.

Fluff with a fork and serve.

207

PERSIAN RICE WITH DILL AND SAFFRON

Makes 4 servings

My neighborhood Persian restaurant serves heaping plates of this pure, snow-white basmati rice with almost every entrée. Basmati rice, a fragrant rice prized in Persia and parts of Asia for its nutty aroma and fluffy texture, is available in specialty food markets at very high prices, in health food stores at moderate prices, and in Indian and Persian markets rather inexpensively.

2 cups water
1/8 teaspoon crushed saffron threads
3/4 cup basmati rice, rinsed
1/4 cup very finely chopped fresh dill

In a large saucepan, bring the water to a boil. Stir in the saffron and rice, partially cover, reduce the heat, and simmer until rice is very tender and all the water has been absorbed, about 25 minutes.

Fluff the rice with a fork, transfer to a large serving platter or dinner plates, and sprinkle with the dill, making a single line of dill across the rice.

Serve immediately.

CREAMY RICE WITH FRESH PEAS

Makes 4 servings

This is a wonderful, old-fashioned combination of flavors and textures. Using medium-grain (risotto) rice rather than long grain gives this recipe its creamy texture, and fresh peas give it color and balance. If you want a richer dish, stir 3 tablespoons grated Romano or Asiago cheese into the rice just before serving.

Domestic medium-grain rice can be found in many supermarkets, usually tucked away among the long-grain rices. It is considerably less expensive than the imported medium-grain risotto rices.

2 quarts water
Olive oil spray
1 small onion, peeled and finely chopped
1 garlic clove, peeled and finely chopped
¾ cup medium-grain rice
2 cups chicken stock or water
1 pound fresh peas, shelled to make about 1 cup peas

Bring 2 quarts of water to a boil in a large pot.

Meanwhile, place a large saucepan over medium heat. When hot, mist generously with olive oil spray, then add the onion and garlic. Spray again, stirring well, so that all the onion and garlic pieces are lightly coated in oil. Cook for 6 minutes, reducing the heat so the onions do not brown. Stir the rice into the onions, mist again to coat the rice, and cook until the rice changes from its vaguely translucent color to an opaque white.

Pour the stock over the rice and bring to a boil. Cover, reduce the heat, and simmer until rice is just barely tender, about 22 minutes. Some of the stock or water should not have been absorbed, leaving the rice soft, creamy, and slightly soupy in texture.

While the rice is cooking, drop the peas into 2 quarts boiling water and cook until tender, about 6 minutes. Immediately drain and cool under running cold water to stop the cooking and set the color.

Drain the peas and set aside. When rice is ready, with a fork, stir in the peas, cook for a minute or to heat the peas, and serve immediately.

RICE WITH BLACK-EYED PEAS AND TOMATOES

Makes 8 servings

This is one of my favorite rice recipes, and I occasionally keep a bowl of it in the refrigerator just for myself. I am particularly fond of the mildly spicy flavor and the interplay of textures between the rice and the peas.

Once it is cooked, I doctor it up by adding some canned corn, or leftover diced chicken or slivered ham, or some cooked green beans, nuke it until it is warm, and I have, with a couple of slices of toast, a quick meal.

Vegetable oil spray
1 large onion, peeled and finely chopped
1 garlic clove, peeled and finely chopped
1 1/2 cups long-grain white rice
One 16-ounce can black-eyed peas, undrained
One 28-ounce can peeled tomatoes, drained
1 1/2 tablespoons chili powder
1/2 teaspoon cumin
1 teaspoon crushed dried oregano
1/4 teaspoon cayenne (optional)
3 cups water

Mist the bottom of a large nonstick sauté pan with oil spray. Add the onion and garlic and mist again so that everything is lightly coated with oil. Set over medium heat and sauté until translucent, about 5 minutes, reducing the heat to prevent browning.

Scrape into a large pot, add the remaining ingredients, and bring to a boil over medium high heat, stirring occasionally. Reduce the heat and simmer, partially covered, until the rice is tender, about 30 minutes, stirring occasionally to ensure that everything is evenly distributed.

Other Grains

WHOLE WHEAT COUSCOUS
WITH WILD MUSHROOMS

Makes 12 appetizer servings, 6 main-course servings

The hearty, earthy flavors of whole wheat and woody wild mushrooms combine here with some sun-dried tomatoes and chopped dill to make a deeply satisfying autumn meal. To vary the dish, eliminate the mushrooms, stir $1/2$ cup cooked green lentils into the broth with the couscous, and substitute parsley for the dill.

Couscous, the cereal staple of much of North Africa, is a granulated form of semolina, a very hard (high protein), yellow-colored wheat. Most packaged couscous is precooked and then dehydrated, so it cooks almost on contact with a hot liquid. With today's increasing interest in Mediterranean cooking, sometimes for health reasons, sometimes for aesthetic reasons, couscous has become popular enough to appear on the shelves of most supermarkets; whole wheat couscous, however, requires a trip to a health food store.

For a formal dinner party, start with quickly marinated roasted yellow peppers, followed by a risotto, and then this whole wheat couscous.

$2^{1}/_{2}$ cups beef or chicken stock
3 tablespoons coarsely chopped sun-dried tomatoes
6 ounces small, woody wild mushrooms, such as morels, chanterelles, or shiitakes, washed, and stem ends trimmed but left in place (if mushrooms are large, cut into 1-inch pieces)
$1^{1}/_{2}$ cups whole wheat couscous
3 tablespoons chopped fresh dill
Salt
Freshly ground black pepper

In a large shallow pot, bring the stock and tomatoes to a boil. Add the mushrooms and simmer until just tender, about 3 minutes. Stir in the couscous, cover, remove from the heat, and set aside for 5 minutes. Stir in the dill, taste, and season with a little salt, if necessary, and pepper.

Serve immediately.

BARLEY WITH WILD RICE

Makes 4 servings

Barley, a grain used primarily in making beer and bread, has a soft, comforting texture, which is given a little nuttiness by the wild rice in this recipe.

Serve this with one of the summer squash sautés (pages 183–185) and Whole Wheat Fettuccine with Wild Mushrooms and Dill (page 224).

2³/₄ cups Brown Beef, Chicken, or Vegetable Stock (pages 114, 110, and 116)
¹/₂ cup medium pearl barley (not quick cooking)
¹/₃ cup wild rice
1 small onion, peeled and finely chopped
Olive oil spray
Freshly ground black pepper

In a large saucepan, bring the stock to a boil, stir in the barley and wild rice, cover, and reduce the heat. Simmer, stirring every 10 or 15 minutes, until grains are tender and the stock is absorbed, about 40 minutes.

Meanwhile, place the onion in a sauté pan and spray with just enough oil so that all the onion pieces are very lightly coated. Sauté over medium high heat until the onion just starts to brown, about 12 minutes. Set aside.

When the barley and wild rice are cooked, stir in the onion, taste, and season with pepper.

Serve immediately.

BULGUR SALAD WITH POBLANOS

Makes 6 servings

Bulgur has an interesting, nutty character, with a gentle chewiness. Made bolder, deeper, and richer in taste with the addition of a poblano pepper, then balanced with tomatoes, herbs, and lime juice, this is a lively summer salad, served cold or at room temperature.

Poblano peppers are available in many supermarkets and Mexican markets. They are shiny, dark green, and while not sweet like a bell pepper, they are not hot either.

Serve this to accompany sandwiches for lunch, or a cup of cold summer soup.

2 cups hottest possible tap water
1 cup bulgur (cracked wheat)
2 tablespoons virgin or extra virgin olive oil
1 medium-sized poblano pepper, cored, seeded, and finely chopped
1/4 cup coarsely chopped fresh basil
3 tablespoons coarsely chopped garlic chives or 1 scallion
1 large, ripe but firm tomato, cored, cut in half across the belly, and
    squeezed to remove the seeds, then cut into 1/2-inch dice
Juice of 1/2 large lime
A little salt
Freshly ground black pepper

In a saucepan, bring the water to a boil over high heat. Add the bulgur, stir once, and reduce the heat to a simmer. Simmer until most of the water has been absorbed and the wheat begins to seethe, about 6 minutes. Remove from the heat, cover, and set aside for 15 minutes. The bulgur will absorb the rest of the water and become tender. Put the bulgur in a large strainer or colander and cool under running cold water. Shake and gently press out all the excess water. Dump into a large bowl.

With a large fork, stir in the oil to help keep the grains separated, then add the poblano, basil, chives or scallion, tomato, and lime juice. Season with a little salt and pepper.

215

Beans and Lentils

BASIC PREPARATION OF DRIED BEANS

Makes 4 cups

Beans are among the few foods that everyone, from public health officials to leftover health food cultists, agrees should have a more prominent place in our eating. Not only are beans nutritional powerhouses, they are virtually fat-free, inexpensive, and "natural" enough to satisfy the philosophic remnants of the counterculture.

All dried beans with the exception of lentils cook in the same way. The traditional method is soaking in water overnight, then simmering. There is a shortcut method, starting in boiling water, resting for a couple of hours, then simmering, and there is a microwave method. Lentils do not need soaking before cooking.

Of the three, the traditional method shows the most respect for the beans, leaving them with the most texture. Cooking dried beans is just one of those things you shouldn't rush. When there isn't time to soak overnight and cook the next day (the beans can be soaked for a second day, if you don't get to them the first day), use canned beans, drained and rinsed under running cold water.

There are dozens of varieties of dried beans available in supermarkets, health food stores, natural foods stores, and ethnic markets, each with its own particular flavor and texture. Generally, larger beans cook more quickly than smaller beans.

Beans belong everywhere—in cereals for breakfast, in salads for lunch, in rice and pasta dishes, in dips and on toast as hors d'oeuvres, or seasoned and served alone as a vegetable.

2 cups (12 ounces by weight) dried beans

Soaking: Place the beans in a bowl or container and add cold tap water to cover. There should be enough water to come about 1 inch above the surface of the beans.

216

Cover the bowl or container loosely and set aside at room temperature to soak overnight (12 to 24 hours).

Drain and rinse under running tap water.

Cooking: In a large pot, bring 10 to 12 cups of hot tap water to a boil. Add the beans, stir, and reduce the heat so the beans simmer until just tender, 45 to 90 minutes. Drain.

QUICK BLACK BEANS WITH CHILI

Makes 6 servings

Having a half-dozen different kinds of canned beans in the kitchen cabinet allows me to serve beans on those days when I haven't soaked them the night before.

This recipe, and the curried white bean variation below, are two of my quick bean favorites. Either can be ready to serve in about 5 minutes.

Two 15-ounce cans black beans (or 1¼ cups home-cooked black beans), drained of most of the liquid in the cans
2 tablespoons chili powder
1½ tablespoons balsamic vinegar
Freshly ground black pepper

In a small saucepan, stir together the beans, chili powder, and vinegar. Add pepper to taste and cook over medium heat until very hot, stirring occasionally to prevent scorching.

Leftover beans can be refrigerated, in a tightly covered jar, for up to a week.

Quick Curried White Beans

Substitute any of the white beans (cannellini, Great Northern, or navy) for the black beans; use curry powder instead of chili powder; and use the juice of 1 lemon instead of vinegar.

FLAGEOLETS IN ROSEMARY CREAM

Makes 6 servings

Flageolets are small kidney-shaped beans with a delicate, almost sweet flavor. They are the most elegant and understated member of the bean community, occupying a place of reverence in French cooking. You can substitute any variety of cooked white beans if flageolets are not available.

Serve these as part of a formal dinner.

3 cups home-cooked flageolets (page 216)
3 tablespoons light cream
1 tablespoon very finely chopped fresh rosemary, or 1 teaspoon very
    well crushed dried rosemary
1 tablespoon finely chopped fresh parsley
Freshly ground white or black pepper

In a large saucepan, combine the cooked beans and cream and bring to a boil over medium heat, stirring gently with a fork to prevent crushing and scorching the beans. Boil for 1 minute, then off the heat, stir in the herbs and season with pepper.

Serve immediately.

SUMMER LENTIL SALAD

Makes 6 servings

This lively, sprightly lentil salad is perfect warm-weather eating. Lentils all too often are left for cold weather, where they are overcooked and denied their character in mushy soups. Here the lentils remain individuals. This makes great picnic fare.

1 cup green lentils

1 small red onion, peeled and halved lengthwise, then very thinly sliced

1 large European cucumber, peeled, halved lengthwise, then each half cut into thirds lengthwise to make 6 strips, the strips lined up and cut into ¼-inch pieces

1 poblano pepper, cored, seeded, quartered lengthwise, and cut cross-wise into thin slices

4 or 5 tablespoons balsamic or raspberry vinegar

2 tablespoons virgin olive oil

A little salt

Freshly ground black pepper

Bring a large saucepan of hot tap water to a boil over high heat. When it boils, add the lentils, stir, and reduce the heat so that the lentils simmer until they are just tender, about 20 minutes.

Meanwhile, in a large bowl, mix together the onion, cucumber, poblano, vinegar, and oil.

When cooked, drain the lentils and immediately cool under running cold tap water. Shake well to remove as much water as possible from the lentils, then mix well with the onion mixture. Season with a little salt and pepper.

Serve at room temperature, or refrigerator cold.

Pasta

BASIC PASTA DOUGH

Makes 4 servings

I suspect that the great interest in bread making in the late 1960s and early 1970s led to the interest in pasta making in the late 1970s and early 1980s. A good loaf of bread would take the better part of a day to make, but a batch of homemade pasta, which was in many ways just as satisfying aesthetically and philosophically, could be made in less than half an hour.

This basic dough is made with whole wheat flour and more egg whites than yolks, giving it added fiber and lower fat and cholesterol than traditional homemade egg pastas.

1²/₃ cups whole wheat flour
2 whole eggs
1 egg white
1 tablespoon cold water

Place the flour in the bowl of a food processor. In a small bowl, lightly beat together the eggs, egg white, and water. Pour into the food processor, turn on, and process until a dough forms and is about to gather itself together and jump onto the top of the blades. If, after 10 seconds, the dough is grainy or looks as if it is struggling to form itself into a ball, add another teaspoon of water.

Remove the dough from the processor. Knead it together, if necessary; otherwise, form it into a rectangle about ¹/₂ inch thick and wrap in plastic film. Refrigerate for at least 20 minutes, or as long as overnight.

To roll out the dough, set up a pasta machine following the manufacturer's directions.

Cut the dough into 3 approximately equal pieces. Set 2 pieces aside, draped loosely with a clean kitchen towel.

Very lightly flour the outside of the piece of dough about to be rolled, and squash down on the edge of the dough so it feeds into the rollers easily. With the machine set at its widest setting, feed in the dough and roll out. Fold in half lengthwise and roll out again. Repeat this twice more. The dough will begin to become smooth and resilient.

Adjust the rollers so they are 1 setting closer. Insert the dough (this time without folding it) and roll out. Fold and roll out. Repeat twice more.

Each time the rollers are adjusted, the dough is fed through them 4 times, the first time without being folded, the other 3 folded.

Continue until the dough is as thin as you want. On the narrowest setting, however, roll the dough only once. Generally, you should almost be able to see through the dough when it is the proper thinness. On my machine, which has settings between 1 and 7, it is either 6 or 7.

When the dough is sufficiently thin, hang it up to dry. I drape it across a large rolling pin suspended between two chairs, but any kind of home-rigged contraption like that will work just as well—a broomstick between two chairs, a laundry drying rack, or even one of the special pasta drying racks sold at some housewares shops.

Repeat with the remaining pieces of dough, then cut the dough (obviously in the same order that it was rolled out) by feeding each piece through the cutting rollers, or by hand.

Light Egg Pasta

Use 2 cups all-purpose flour and eliminate the whole wheat flour.

Saffron Pasta

Prepare either the basic pasta dough or the light egg pasta, stirring 1/4 teaspoon crushed saffron threads into the water before adding it to the egg mixture.

SAFFRON PASTA WITH ASIAN "PESTO"

Makes 4 servings

Golden pasta flavored with saffron is the perfect complement to the vibrancy of the Asian pesto sauce.

1 small bunch fresh basil, washed and thick stems removed, to make about 1 cup leaves

2 bunches cilantro, washed and thick stems removed, to make about 2 cups leaves

2 large garlic cloves, peeled

1/2 small jalapeño pepper, cored and seeded

A 1-inch piece fresh gingerroot, peeled

Juice of 1 lemon

2 teaspoons soy sauce

1/4 cup dark sesame oil

1/4 cup unsalted dry-roasted peanuts

Freshly ground black pepper to taste

1 recipe Saffron Pasta, cut into fettuccine (page 222)

Combine all the ingredients for the sauce in a food processor and process until nuts are finely chopped and a thick, bright green sauce forms.

Over high heat, bring a large pot of hot tap water to a boil. Add the pasta and cook until just barely tender, about 2 minutes.

Drain, divide into bowls for serving, and top with the pesto sauce.

Serve immediately; the pasta cools very quickly.

WHOLE WHEAT FETTUCCINE
WITH WILD MUSHROOMS AND DILL

Makes 4 servings

This is a mildly nutty, oak-flavored recipe that implies the cool times and turning leaves of autumn.

It is best when a combination of two or three fresh wild mushrooms is used, rather than just one type. Cremini mushrooms, sometimes called brown mushrooms, can be used here, though they are not "wild," even in the loosest sense in which we use that word today.

Cultivated wild mushrooms are available year round in premium supermarkets and specialty produce stores; occasionally forest-picked wild mushrooms are found in autumn farmers' markets.

Serve as the second course in a formal dinner, starting with a light bisque and followed by Spicy Salmon Fillets (page 271) and Emerald Spinach with Hidden Herbs (page 180).

Olive oil spray

½ small onion, peeled and finely chopped

2 large shallots, peeled and finely chopped

1 large garlic clove, peeled and finely chopped

A ½-inch chunk fresh gingerroot, peeled and finely chopped

1 pound fresh, firm-textured, deeply colored wild mushrooms, such as shiitakes, chanterelles, morels, or lobster mushrooms, quickly rinsed under running cold water, patted dry, and cut into ½-inch pieces

1¼ cup chicken or beef broth

1 tablespoon finely chopped fresh dill

1 recipe Basic Pasta Dough, cut into fettuccine (page 221)

Place a large nonstick sauté pan over medium heat. When hot, mist with olive oil spray, add the onion, shallots, garlic, and ginger and spray lightly, stirring so that all the vegetables are gently coated in oil. Reduce the heat to medium low and cook, stirring and reducing the heat as needed to prevent browning, for 5 minutes.

Add the mushrooms and broth to the sauté pan, cover, and set over high heat. Allow the mushrooms to steam-cook this way until just tender when pierced with the tip of a knife, about 2 minutes. Uncover, increase the heat to high, and reduce the broth until there is about ½ cup left on the bottom of the pan.

While broth is reducing, cook the fettuccine until tender in a large pot of boiling water, about 2 minutes. Immediately drain and add to the sauté pan with the mushrooms. Mix well, divide into bowls for serving, sprinkle with dill, and serve immediately, as the pasta cools quickly.

RIGATONI WITH PUTTANESCA SAUCE

Makes 6 servings

This is a vivacious dish, full of the poignant flavors of central Italy. It is one of my favorite pastas. According to myth, this was the dish tossed together by the prostitutes of Rome when the police came banging at the door. The former customer then became a dinner guest, and the suspicious police left without an arrest. It's a wild, brash sauce, aptly named.

Fresh rigatoni is available in many supermarkets, pasta stores, and premium groceries. Twelve ounces of dried rigatoni can be substituted if fresh is not available. Fresh rotini, penne, or fusilli can be substituted for the rigatoni in this recipe.

Serve this as a winter lunch, or as an appetizer for a company dinner.

Olive oil spray
1 small onion, peeled and coarsely chopped
2 large garlic cloves, peeled and coarsely chopped
One 35-ounce can peeled Italian plum tomatoes, drained and very
    coarsely chopped
$1/4$ cup tomato paste
2 tablespoons balsamic vinegar
6 to 8 anchovy fillets, very coarsely chopped
2 tablespoons capers
$1/2$ cup Kalamata olives, pitted and broken into 4 or 5 pieces each
$1/8$ to $1/4$ teaspoon hot red pepper flakes (optional)
Freshly ground black pepper

$1^1/2$ pounds fresh rigatoni

Place a very large saucepan over medium heat. When it is hot, mist lightly with olive oil spray, then add the onion and garlic. Spray again, stirring well, so that all the onion and garlic pieces are lightly coated in oil. Cook for 6 minutes, stirring almost constantly and reducing the heat so the onions do not brown.

Add the tomatoes, tomato paste, and vinegar and mix well. Increase the heat long enough to bring the tomato sauce to a boil, then reduce the heat and simmer for 5 minutes, uncovered, stirring often. Stir in the anchovies, capers, olives, and red pepper, if using. Simmer for another 8 to 10 minutes to form a thick, chunky sauce.

Taste and adjust the flavors. There should be a distinct flavor of capers and anchovies, supported by the olives. Ideally, the sauce should taste just a little hot (from the red pepper flakes). When all the flavors are lively, season with black pepper.

Bring a large pot of water to a boil over high heat. Add the rigatoni all at once, stir, and boil until tender, about 2 minutes. Drain well and mix into the puttanesca sauce.

Reheat and serve.

PENNE WITH TOMATO SAUCE

Makes 4 to 6 servings

It is easy to keep some tomato sauce on hand, either in the refrigerator or in the freezer. Combining the sauce with penne, the inch-long quill-shaped pasta, gives you a quick meal anytime, or an appetizer or a light lunch. (You can reheat the sauce in the microwave.)

This is a rich, slightly acidic basic tomato sauce.

2 tablespoons olive oil
3 large garlic cloves, peeled and finely chopped
2 medium onions, peeled and finely chopped
One 2-pound can Italian-style plum tomatoes, undrained
Two 14-ounce cans tomato purée
1 teaspoon dried thyme
1/2 teaspoon crushed dried rosemary
1 tablespoon crushed dried basil
A little salt
Freshly ground black pepper to taste

16 ounces dried penne

Pour the oil into a large saucepan and set over medium heat. When it is hot, add the garlic and onion and mix well. Cook for 8 minutes, stirring frequently and reducing the heat as needed to prevent browning.

Add the tomatoes, purée, thyme, and rosemary to the saucepan and bring to a boil over medium high heat, stirring occasionally and breaking up the tomatoes as you stir. Bring the sauce to a boil, then reduce the heat and simmer for 1 hour. Add the basil and simmer another 15 minutes.

In small batches, purée the sauce in a blender or food processor. Strain the sauce into a clean saucepan. Return to a boil, then simmer until a medium thick sauce forms, about another 15 minutes. Season with salt and pepper.

Transfer 2 cups of the sauce to a saucepan. The remaining sauce can be refrigerated in a tightly covered jar for 1 week, or can be frozen for up to 6 months. Reheat the sauce over medium low heat just after the penne are tossed into the water to cook.

Bring a large pot of the hottest possible tap water to a boil. Add the penne, stir, and cook until tender, stirring occasionally to prevent the pasta from sticking to the bottom of the pot, about 8 minutes.

Immediately pour through a strainer, shaking well to drain the water caught inside the penne.

Divide among serving plates, and top each with $^1/_3$ to $^1/_2$ cup tomato sauce.

8

Breads

QUICK BREADS

Mixed-Grain Buttermilk Quick Bread
Whole Wheat Soda Bread

YEAST BREADS

Your First Loaf of Bread
Sour Cream White Bread
Clover Leaf Rolls
Everyday Whole Wheat Bread
Mixed-Grain Farmhouse Loaf
Old-fashioned White Bread
Mixed-Grain Bread
Whole Wheat Fig Bread
Olive Bread
Whole Wheat Pizza Dough
White Pizza Bread
A Microwave-baked English Muffin Bread

Introduction

I learned to make bread from one of the great bread makers of the world, James Beard, who once looked at a half-filled glass of orange juice on the breakfast table and turned it into a loaf of bread in time for lunch. Not everyone can turn some leftover orange juice into a great loaf of bread, but you can make delicious breads, even if you have never tried before, because, fundamentally, bread making is a simple three-step procedure. All of the principles and techniques that you need to know to make your first loaf of bread are explained in detail on page 237.

But making bread is more than a technical skill. It is a wondrous and emotionally satisfying event. Nothing you do in the kitchen is quite like the magic of making bread. One of the reasons the counterculture of the 1970s became so enthralled with bread making was that it teaches you to be a sensually aware and responsive person. It teaches you to use your hands with a new sensitivity, to feel and to react, slowly and deliberately, to the ever-changing texture of the dough as you knead it into a bouncy, resilient ball. It teaches you to think about the weather, for the humidity in the air and the temperature in the room all affect the dough. It teaches you to enjoy working with your hands. And because bread making requires patience, it teaches self-discipline.

As you mix the ingredients together and watch the dough develop, the magic will begin, and you will feel it. You'll smell the heady aroma of the yeast as it activates, a fragrance that connotes the joys of good foods and family meals. And you'll soon begin to feel a quiet, personal satisfaction as the dough is kneaded and comes to life under your hands. Kneading, with its meditative, repetitious motion—push-turn-fold, push-turn-fold, push-turn-fold—perhaps because it demands so much attention, perhaps because it is a bit arduous, will ultimately relax you and relieve your stress. One student, on learning to knead her first loaf of bread, whispered to me: "This did more for me in fifteen minutes than an hour with my shrink."

Bread making is also fun. It is a time to let go and loosen up. And it is a time when you can welcome friends and children into the kitchen for some communal cooking. What better way to teach a 9-year-old, ready to study microorganisms, about yeast, one of the friendly microorganisms, than to work with it and transform it into a loaf of bread.

Two quick bread recipes start this chapter. If you have never made a bread before, begin with one of these. Quick breads use baking powder and baking soda rather than yeast for leavening, and as almost no kneading is necessary, they are the simplest breads to make. They are excellent breads to make with children.

There are 10 major yeast bread recipes, which, if prepared in sequence, form a mini-bread-baking course. Everything you need to know to make your first loaf of bread is explained in the first recipe. This is a sour cream white bread that is easy to make, develops quickly and responsively under your hands as you knead, and will give you a better "feel" for bread making than any other recipe I know. Although the counterculture categorically rejected white bread in the same breath that it rejected the White House, we now know that a variety of breads, including white breads, should be part of our daily eating.

The next two recipes, which are made in the same way as the first loaf, will show you how to use different flours and how to combine mixed grains to make light, high-rising loaves.

To make a loaf of bread with a thick, crumbly crust and a chewy crumb—breads that aficionados consider the best—the yeast must be started in a sponge (a kind of yeast batter) and allowed to age for a couple of days at room temperature so it turns into a sourdough starter. The next two recipes in the chapter explain how to prepare and work with a sponge.

When the counterculture added ingredients to their breads, they made them denser, heavier, "more nutritious." Soy pulp and wheat germ, for example, were favorite additives to 1970s breads. By the 1980s, however, lighter breads had become fashionable, and the dense additives changed into major flavorings. The fig and olive breads that appear in this chapter illustrate this new idea in bread making.

And finally, there is a pizza dough made with a sponge (though not aged into sourdough) and a very unusual microwave-baked English muffin bread that is one of my favorites in the chapter.

In 1900, 95 percent of all flour sold was for home use. In 1970, only 15 percent of the flour in this country was sold for home use. The return to homemade breads was the counterculture's attempt to reverse this trend, and it seems as important, if not more so, to continue to fight for that reversal today.

Quick Breads

MIXED-GRAIN BUTTERMILK QUICK BREAD

Makes 1 loaf

It takes less than 10 minutes to prepare the dough for this recipe, and just 35 minutes to bake, so you can have this bread on the table with very little effort in about an hour. Unfortunately, the bread goes stale quickly, and it doesn't toast well.

This is an excellent bread for making with children in the 8- to 12-year-old range. They have the understanding, coordination, and just about enough of an attention span to make it and see it come out of the oven before they become lost in some other activity of the moment.

For a breakfast version of this bread, add ⅓ cup golden raisins and 2 tablespoons brown sugar to the dry ingredients.

Vegetable oil spray
2 cups unbleached white flour, plus a little additional flour for kneading
1 cup whole wheat flour
1 cup rolled oats
1 teaspoon baking soda
2 teaspoons baking powder
1½ cups nonfat (or lowfat) buttermilk
1 egg

Preheat the oven to 350 degrees F. Mist the inside of a standard loaf pan with vegetable oil spray and set aside.

In a large bowl, mix together the white flour, whole wheat flour, oats, baking soda, and baking powder.

In a separate bowl, beat the buttermilk and egg until blended, then pour onto the dry ingredients. With a large spoon, stir, gently at first, then more firmly, to form a moist ball of dough. With your hands, press any dry bits into the dough. Dump the dough onto a work surface and knead the dough lightly, adding a little flour if needed, to form a damp-feeling but evenly textured dough that is just firm enough not to stick to the counter. Unlike yeast breads, in which the kneading is used to develop the springy texture of the loaf, the kneading here is used only to ensure that the ingredients are thoroughly blended and that the loaf isn't too moist.

Pull the dough under itself, pinching it on the bottom, to form a smooth, uncracked loaf. Fit into the pan and, with your fingertips, push to the sides so the dough fills the pan.

Bake for 35 minutes. The bread will be lightly and evenly browned, and will have shrunk in from the sides of the pan. Turn out of the pan and cool on a rack for at least 30 minutes so the bread can cool and the texture can set before slicing.

Serve within an hour of baking.

WHOLE WHEAT SODA BREAD

Makes 1 loaf

This easy-to-make Irish soda bread is a moderately dense, full-flavored whole wheat bread with a moist texture and a hard crust. Its essence is more that of a gigantic biscuit than a bread.

Vegetable oil spray
2 cups whole wheat flour
About 2½ cups all-purpose flour
1 teaspoon salt
1 teaspoon baking soda
1 teaspoon baking powder
2 cups lowfat buttermilk

Preheat the oven to 375 degrees F. Lightly spray the inside of an 8-inch cake pan with vegetable oil spray.

In a large bowl, mix together the whole wheat flour, 2 cups of the all-purpose flour, the salt, baking soda, and baking powder. Pour in the buttermilk and stir to form a ball of dough.

Dump the dough onto a floured work surface and knead for about 2 minutes, adding a little more flour if necessary to make a well-blended dough with the texture of a biscuit dough. It should be moist but firm enough to hold its shape.

Holding the dough in your hands, form it into a ball about 7 inches in diameter by pulling the dough under itself and pinching it on the bottom. Place in the center of the prepared cake pan, pressing down lightly so it spreads to just about fill the pan. With a very sharp knife or single-edged razor, cut an X across the top of the bread, slashing about ½ inch into the dough.

Bake for 40 minutes.

Remove from the pan and cool on a rack.

Yeast Breads

YOUR FIRST LOAF OF BREAD

Nothing you do in the kitchen is more wondrous or more satisfying than making your first loaf of bread.

No matter how many loaves of bread I make, there is always a feeling of magic and wonder as I feel the dough develop under my hands and later as the kitchen fills with the aroma of a freshly baked loaf. Yet bread making is neither mysterious nor difficult; the entire process can be reduced to 3 simple steps: proofing (activating the yeast), kneading (mixing the dough), and rising and punching down (inflating and deflating the dough). That's all there is to it.

Proofing

Yeast, which is a fungus—a living organism—is used both to leaven and to flavor bread. When purchased, yeast is dormant, or inactive. To activate, or "proof" yeast, simply dissolve it in warm water.

For the best results, the temperature of the water should be about 100 degrees F, which is a little more than lukewarm to the touch. Anywhere in the lukewarm range is fine, but if the water is hot, it will kill the yeast. You can test the water in the same way you would milk in a baby's bottle. If you are worried, or have been scared into undue concern by warnings in other bread recipes you have read, check the temperature of the water with an instant-read kitchen thermometer.

After nearly six thousand years of troublesome bread making, due mostly to variable yeast quality, we now have the luxury of absolutely dependable, self-stable yeast. No longer is it necessary to test the yeast, to add sugar or flour to it, or to watch for bubbles. Simple rehydration is sufficient.

Types of Yeast

Dried yeast is available in granules, called active dry yeast; or shaped like tiny splinters, called rapid- or quick-rise yeast. Although the latter was developed so that it could be mixed directly with the flour, eliminating the need for proofing, I have found that using it that way sometimes presents more problems with rehydration, and so I suggest, if you are using one of the quick-rise yeasts, that you proof it as directed in these recipes. The two types of dried yeast are interchangeable.

Fresh (compressed) yeast is sometimes available in small claylike cakes. Fresh yeast is more fragile than dried yeast, and must be stored under refrigeration. Although I know bread makers who prefer fresh yeast, I prefer dried yeast, which is more readily available and easier to store. Both produce breads of equal quality.

One package (about 1 tablespoon) of dried yeast is equal to about $\frac{1}{2}$ ounce of fresh yeast.

Kneading

Kneading is simply the way to mix a dough that has become too stiff to stir with a spoon. Once most of the flour has been stirred into the liquid in the recipe, the dough is dumped onto a work surface and is kneaded—rhythmically manipulated with your hands—to incorporate whatever additional flour is necessary to bring the dough to the right degree of firmness.

Kneading then continues until the proteins in flour (called gluten) form into long strands, making the dough elastic and resilient. This elasticity is important because it allows the dough to stretch evenly as it rises and bakes. A fully kneaded batch of dough will feel like a baby's rump, or like an earlobe.

It is virtually impossible to overknead a dough by hand, so if you feel the dough could be a little more satiny in feeling, a little more springy and bouncy under your palms, knead it a little longer. The final texture of the dough is what's important, not whether the recipe said to knead for 4 or 5 minutes and you kneaded it for 8 to 10 minutes. Kneading is a bit arduous until you become comfortable with the rhythmic movement, so stop and rest any time your hands feel tired. Don't be surprised or concerned if it takes you 20 minutes or more to knead your first loaf.

Kneading can be done by hand, in a heavy-duty electric mixer equipped with a dough hook, or in a food processor. All 3 techniques produce excellent results, and all 3 are explained in detail in the recipe that follows.

Hand kneading is the most satisfying, and will give you the greatest sense for the "feel" of a dough, so take the time to knead your first loaf by hand.

Types of Flour

No special flours are needed for your first loaf of bread. The all-purpose white flour you have in your kitchen is fine for your first loaf.

The best breads, however, are made with hard wheat flour, which is high in gluten (the protein in the flour that forms the elastic web that ultimately determines the texture of the loaf).

Unbleached or presifted all-purpose flour is higher in gluten than the bleached or nonpresifted varieties, and is therefore preferable, though by no stretch of the imagination is it necessary for a good loaf of bread.

The flours that are highest in gluten are called bread flour, high-gluten flour, patent flour, or hard wheat flour. Most supermarkets sell bread flour. Health food stores, however, usually sell a wide variety of high-gluten flours. In addition, there are small mills around the country that sell extraordinarily fine quality high-gluten flours by mail order.

After you have become comfortable with the process of bread making, you may want to experiment with different white flours. For your first loaf, however, use whatever is on hand or readily available.

Rising and Punching Down

When the yeast grows in the dough, it produces tiny bubbles of gas that inflate and stretch the dough, causing it to rise. Allowing a bread to rise serves 2 purposes. It gives the yeast time to develop its flavor, and it determines the final size and texture of the bread.

A bread dough should rise until it is "doubled in bulk," which actually means until it has increased to about 2½ to 3 times its original volume. At room temperature, this usually takes about 2½ hours for the first rising, and about 1¼ hours for the second rising.

You can slow down or speed up the risings to fit your schedule. In a cold closet with exposed outside walls in winter, the first rising will take 5 to 6 hours. In a warm spot, such as inside a gas oven with the pilot lighted or inside an electric oven with the light on, the first rising will take about $1\frac{1}{2}$ hours. Should you wish to stop the rising until the next day, simply place the dough in the refrigerator. The cold will retard the yeast growth and slow the rising almost to a standstill. In the morning, just let the dough come back to room temperature, which will take about 2 hours, and then proceed with the recipe. With experience, you will be able to control the rising times so you can comfortably fit bread making into your schedule.

When the dough is fully risen, it is "punched down." If you are feeling aggressive, you can literally punch the dough a few times to deflate it, or you can simply press or knead until no gas remains in the dough.

Some breads rise only once, most rise twice, and a few breads rise 3 times. The best-flavored and textured breads need 2 or 3 risings.

A Glance at the Chemical Mysteries of Bread Making

Before you start your first loaf, let's briefly unravel the chemical mysteries of bread making.

The simplest bread is a mixture of yeast, water, and flour flavored with a little salt. When yeast is activated in water and mixed with flour, it feeds on the carbohydrates in the flour and gives off carbon dioxide gas, causing the dough to rise. The gas becomes trapped in the elastic web that was formed by the gluten (protein) in the flour when the dough was mixed (kneaded). When the bread is placed in the oven, the heat causes the yeast to grow rapidly and the bread to spring up until the gluten strands in the flour dry and become hard, trapping the tiny bubbles of gas in fine pockets that give the bread its final texture. As the bread continues to bake, the yeast dries and a crust forms.

Bread Pans

You can bake bread in almost any kind of ovenproof pan. Just remember that the dough should not fill the pan more than $2/3$ full when you set it to rise. Traditional rectangular bread pans come in slightly varying sizes, but they usually measure about $9 \times 5 \times 3$ inches.

For the best crust and the most evenly textured crumb, use either the ugly, heavy black metal pans used by professional bakers, or terra cotta earthenware pans. But fine loaves can be baked in lightweight aluminum pans, or even a glass loaf pan. I have settled, after years of experimenting with different bread pans, on medium weight aluminum pans with a nonstick coating for most of my bread making.

SOUR CREAM WHITE BREAD

Master Recipe

Makes 1 loaf or 12 rolls

This is a rich bread with a hint of acidity in flavor, a soft crumb, and a thin crust. It is an excellent choice for the first-time bread maker because it is one of the easiest breads to make and it bakes well in any shape.

1 package (1 tablespoon) dry yeast or ½ ounce fresh yeast
½ cup warm water, about 100 degrees F
About 4 cups white flour
¾ teaspoon salt
8 ounces light or reduced fat (not imitation) sour cream
Vegetable oil spray

For the glaze:

1 egg white
1 teaspoon cold water

Add the yeast to the water and allow it to soften while you mix the flour and salt.

In a large mixing bowl, combine 3 cups of the flour with the salt and mix well.

Stir or mash the softened yeast until it is completely dissolved and a fragrant, smooth, chalky mixture forms. The yeast is ready to use.

Add the yeast and sour cream to the flour and stir with a big spoon to form a soft, shaggy, moist dough. With your hands, gather up the flakes and bits of dough on the bottom of the bowl and squeeze them into a ball.

Sprinkle a work surface with about ¼ cup of flour and dump the dough onto it.

Sprinkle the top of the dough heavily with flour if it feels very moist and sticky, or lightly if the dough is fairly firm. Dust your hands lightly with flour and begin kneading the dough.

How to Knead

By hand: Place the dough in the middle of the work surface and begin kneading.

With the heels of your palms close together, press down firmly on the edge of the dough closest to you. Flatten and extend the dough slightly by pushing down and forward. Give the dough a quarter turn, fold it in half so that the 2 edges are closest to you, then press as before, pushing down on the 2 edges so they adhere.

That's all there is to kneading: push, turn, fold; push, turn, fold. As you knead, the dough will absorb the flour from the work surface (any smooth work surface is fine). Continue to sprinkle the dough with flour until the dough is firm and manageable and no longer sticks to either your hands or the work surface.

Kneading may seem a little awkward at first, but once enough flour has been absorbed to eliminate the sticking, kneading becomes faster and easier, and you'll develop a natural rhythm of push-turn-fold, push-turn-fold, push-turn-fold.

This is a small batch of dough, so you may find it easier to knead with one hand. Experiment with the movement until you are comfortable with kneading.

Unfortunately, it isn't possible to predetermine the exact amount of flour needed for a batch of dough. The amount depends on such variables as the temperature of the kitchen, the humidity, how the flour is measured, the type and brand of the flour, the texture of the sour cream, and so on. A good estimate, though, is that you will use about $3^3/4$ to 4 cups of flour for this loaf.

Continue to knead the dough until it becomes very smooth and elastic, until it feels bouncy and playful under your hands, about another 8 to 10 minutes. Should the dough become sticky again as you knead, sprinkle it with a little more flour, about a tablespoon, and continue kneading. The stickiness should disappear.

You can stop and give your arms a rest at any time. It takes considerable effort to knead a dough for 10 minutes, but there is no reason to tire yourself out and become so frustrated that you never make bread again. Just stop, toss a clean kitchen towel over the dough, and do something else for a few minutes, then return to the kneading. What's important here is that the dough becomes supple and elastic, not how long it takes.

When the dough has been sufficiently kneaded, when you feel that it is as resilient and bouncy as it will get, the dough is ready to rise.

Although I believe it is important for you to knead your first loaf by hand, so you can gain a clear understanding of how a dough develops and feels, there are 2 other ways to knead, both of which are easier and faster, though to me not as satisfying.

Using a food processor: Proof the yeast as directed in the recipe above. Combine 3½ cups of the flour with the salt in a heavy-duty food processor fitted with its metal blade. Pulse once or twice to blend the flour and salt. Uncover and add the yeast and sour cream. Process until a ball of dough forms on top of the blades.

Feel the dough. If it is sticky, sprinkle with 2 tablespoons of additional flour and process for a few seconds, just long enough to incorporate the flour. Repeat until you have added enough flour to produce a firm dough that no longer feels sticky. Then process, with the dough banging around in the bowl, still in a ball on top of the blades, for 25 to 30 seconds. Stop processing immediately if the dough becomes too soft to hold together in a ball on top of the blades. Remove the dough from the processor and shape into a ball. The dough is now ready to rise.

Using an electric mixer with a dough hook: Proof the yeast as directed in the recipe above. Combine 3½ cups of the flour with the salt in the bowl of the mixer and secure the dough hook in place. Mix together the flour and salt on slow speed. Add the yeast and sour cream and allow the dough hook to whirl around slowly until a slightly sticky wad of dough forms and no lumps of dry flour remain in the bottom of the bowl.

Gradually add enough additional flour, 2 tablespoons at a time, until the dough is no longer sticky. Increase the speed to medium and allow the dough to knead by bouncing around the dough hook and by banging against the side of the bowl until it develops a smooth, elastic texture, about 3 or 4 minutes. The dough is now ready to rise.

Risings and Punching Down

Risings are an aging and maturing process that gives the yeast time to grow and the bread time to develop its full flavor.

First Rising: Choose a bowl that is large enough to hold the dough when it has risen to 3 times its present size. Spray the inside of the bowl lightly with vegetable oil spray. Press the dough down into the bowl. Tightly cover the bowl with plastic wrap. (This will trap the moisture given off during the rising and prevent the top of the dough from developing a dry, crusty skin.) Set aside to rise until double in bulk (generously twice its original volume), about 1½ to 2 hours.

The standard way to test the dough to determine if it has risen sufficiently is to poke your finger about an inch into the dough. If the dough has risen enough, the indentation will remain when your finger is withdrawn. If not, if the dough quickly expands, and looks as if it is filling the indentation, even if only partway, then the dough needs to rise longer.

For your first loaf, I suggest you use this simple test for the first and second risings. After that, you can just eyeball it.

When the dough has doubled in bulk, punch it down, deflating the dough completely.

Should the dough feel sticky, indicating that not enough flour was added during the kneading, knead in another tablespoon or so of flour to eliminate the stickiness.

Second rising: You could, if you wanted, if you are pressed for time, skip this second rising and proceed to the next step (shaping and third rising). I don't mean to suggest that this second rising is unimportant, because it gives the bread a finer flavor and texture than is possible without it, but many bread makers, and many bread recipes, do skip this middle rising, and the breads are still quite good.

Lightly mist the inside of the bowl with vegetable oil spray, press the dough into place, as you did for the first rising, cover, and set aside until doubled in bulk, which will take only about 1 hour this time. Test by poking it with your finger. When it has risen sufficiently, the dough is ready to be shaped and given its third rising.

Shaping and the third rising: This recipe makes a batch of dough that will fit perfectly into a traditional loaf pan.

Place the dough on the counter and form it with your hands into a rectangle, bulging high at the center, tapering toward the ends, and just a little larger than the loaf pan.

Lift the dough into the air and gently stretch it to form a smooth, unbroken top, pulling the sides under and tucking the dough into its underside. Pinch any cracks or seams securely into the bottom of the dough. Place the dough, seam side down, on the counter and spray the loaf pan lightly with vegetable oil.

Place the dough in the loaf pan, seam side down. Cup your hand and press the dough just hard enough to settle it firmly in the pan. With your fingertips, press around the perimeter of the dough so it touches the pan on all sides. It may spring back slightly, especially if you have accidentally overworked it in shaping it to this point. The dough should just about fill the pan (it may pull back slightly at the corners) and should have a nicely rounded, convex top. If it is uneven, or not bulging up at the center, remove the dough from the pan, place it on the counter, and toss a clean kitchen towel over it. Let it rest for about 5 to 8 minutes, then try shaping it again.

Spray the top of the dough very lightly with oil, then drape (do not seal it around the edges) a piece of plastic wrap over the pan and set it aside to rise until the center of the dough pushes just above the top of the pan, about 45 to 60 minutes.

If you want to make an old-fashioned loaf, one that rises up and mushrooms over the top of the pan, use a smaller pan (about $7 \times 4 \times 2^{1}/_{2}$ inches) and allow the dough to rise until the center of the loaf is about $1^{1}/_{2}$ to 2 inches higher than the edge of the pan.

Heat the oven: About 20 minutes before the bread finishes rising in the pan, heat the oven to 375 degrees F.

Glazing and Cracking

If you want a shiny, thin glaze on top of bread, when the dough has finished rising in the loaf pan, mix together 1 egg white and 1 teaspoon cold water, and brush this glaze lightly over the top of the dough. Try not to let any of the glaze drip down and touch the sides of the pan, where it will cause sticking.

The bread will rise once more when it is placed in the oven. This final rising is called the "oven spring," and is caused by the rapid growth of the yeast in its new warmer environment. During the oven spring, the top of the bread sometimes cracks. I usually just accept the crack as a promise of homemade goodness in the loaf. But you can easily prevent the cracking by decoratively slashing the top of the dough: Just before popping the bread into the oven (whether glazed or unglazed), with a very sharp knife or a single-edged razor blade, carefully make 2 or 3 diagonal slashes ½ inch deep in the top of the dough.

Baking

Bake the loaf in the center of the oven for 35 minutes. In about half an hour, the kitchen will fill with the aroma of freshly baked bread. When the bread has finished baking, remove it from the oven and turn it out of the pan.

Testing for Doneness

At this point, bread recipes traditionally instruct you test the bread for doneness by thumping the bottom of the loaf. If it sounds hollow, you're told, then it's done. Unfortunately, a bread will sometimes sound hollow even if it isn't done; and in order to test the bread, it must be removed from the pan, which is not always possible. There are other ways to test a bread for doneness, such as inserting a toothpick into the center of the loaf, testing the bread like a cake, but I have found that testing for doneness is unnecessary.

Even if you are baking 2 loaves at once, it takes a standard-size loaf 35 minutes to bake at 375 degrees F. Use that as your guide, and you'll always have perfectly done breads.

Cool the bread on a rack to prevent moisture from accumulating under the loaf and making the bottom of the bread gummy. (If you want a soft crust, spray the bread very lightly with vegetable oil and toss a towel over the loaf.)

Allow the bread to cool for at least ½ hour so the texture of the crumb can set. Be patient and wait at least that long before you slice into it.

A Few Other Things You Might Want to Know About Bread

Slicing breads: The best way to slice a bread is to lay the loaf on its side. Slicing from the side allows you to see where the knife is going, so you can cut evenly. It also allows you to cut with an even pressure so you don't squash the bread down trying to cut through the top crust.

Bread knives: A long (10 inches or longer), stiff, serrated knife is best for slicing.

247

The teeth, or serration, of the knife will cut through both the crust and tender crumb without your having to apply so much pressure that you squash the bread as you slice it.

About storing breads: After the loaf has cooled completely, wrap it in foil or toss it into a plastic bag and store it at room temperature if you are going to eat it within a day or so; refrigerate it if you plan to eat it within the next 2 or 3 days; or seal it airtight in plastic and freeze it.

Making Your First Loaf into Rolls

The best way to learn about bread making is to make this recipe in its loaf form a couple of times, until you are comfortable with the basic principles and techniques. If you feel like playing with this recipe, rather than changing the ingredients, I suggest you try making the dough into clover leaf rolls rather than a loaf. This will give you a better sense for the "feel" of a bread dough.

CLOVER LEAF ROLLS

Clover leaf rolls are made by placing 3 small balls of dough in each section of a muffin pan so that the rolls, after baking, resemble a three-leaf clover. When I make these with children, or when I'm feeling silly, I make one or two of the rolls with 4 slightly small balls into lucky four-leaf clovers.

For a dozen clover leaf rolls, you'll need a standard muffin pan, each section having a 5- or 6-ounce capacity.

After the second rising, punch down the dough. Roll it under the palms of your hands, pressing firmly and evenly and stretching the dough as you roll, to form a long strand about ¹/₂ inch in diameter.

Divide the dough strand into 12 pieces. I do this by cutting it in half, then I cut each of the halves into thirds, making 6 pieces; and finally, each of those 6 pieces is cut in half to make 12 pieces. Drape loosely with a clean kitchen towel or some plastic wrap.

Spray the muffin pan with vegetable oil spray.

Cut 1 piece of dough into thirds. Roll each third into a ball under the palm of one hand, swiftly moving your hand around in a circle as you press the dough hard against a clean work surface. Roll, circling and pressing, for 8 to 10 seconds to form a smooth ball, then gradually lessen the pressure, cup your hand slightly, and release the dough. It should be a smooth ball. If not, practice again, using more pressure and narrower, more circular motions. Or roll between the palms of your hands, pressing hard enough on the dough to eliminate any cracks or seams.

Place the 3 balls of dough in a section of the prepared muffin pan, then repeat with the remaining dough until all 12 sections are filled. Drape loosely with plastic wrap and set aside to rise until the balls have doubled in size, puffily pressing against themselves, about 45 minutes.

Heat the oven: About 20 minutes before the rolls have finished rising, heat the oven to 425 degrees F.

When rolls have finished rising in the pan, spray the tops of each lightly with vegetable oil spray and place in the center of the oven. Do not glaze. Bake until an even, light brown color appears on the tops of the rolls, about 18 minutes.

Remove from the oven and allow to cool in the pan for 2 or 3 minutes, then turn out of the pan and cool on a rack.

If you would like the rolls to have a soft outer crust, cool them on the counter, not a rack, draped with a clean kitchen towel.

Cool for 10 to 15 minutes before serving.

EVERYDAY WHOLE WHEAT BREAD

Makes 1 large loaf

This is a soft-textured, slightly crusty, nutty-flavored, basic whole wheat loaf. It is an excellent sandwich bread, it toasts particularly well for breakfast, and it makes fine light rolls.

A half-cup of wheat germ, cooked brown or white rice, oat bran, corn bran, or bulgur can be mixed with the whole wheat flour to give the bread additional texture and fiber.

2 cups lukewarm water
2 packages dry yeast
1 1/2 cups whole wheat flour
1/2 teaspoon salt
2 tablespoons canola or safflower oil
About 5 cups bread flour
Vegetable oil spray

Place the water in a very large bowl that has been warmed a bit. Sprinkle the yeast over the top and allow to soften. Mix the whole wheat flour and the salt together, then stir into the yeast mixture. Stir in the oil, then 4 cups of the bread flour. When a single mass of dough forms, dump onto a generously floured work surface and begin kneading.

Knead in enough additional flour to make the dough firm and resilient. It should feel soft and only slightly moist. Continue kneading for 8 to 10 minutes to develop a bouncy elasticity in the dough.

Lightly mist the inside of a very large bowl with vegetable oil spray. Press the dough onto the bottom of the bowl and cover tightly with plastic wrap. Set aside in a warm place to rise until doubled in volume, about 1 hour.

Press the dough flat to deflate it, then shape into a loaf. Spray the inside and top edge of a standard loaf pan and press the dough into place. Drape loosely with plastic wrap and set aside in a warm place until the center of the loaf has risen about 2½ to 3 inches above the edge of the loaf pan, about 1 hour. Letting the bread rise above the pan in this way produces a mushroom-shaped loaf.

After the dough has risen for about 25 minutes, heat the oven to 375 degrees F.

Spray the top of the loaf lightly with vegetable oil spray and slip into the oven. Bake for 35 minutes. To soften the hard crust, turn the bread out of the pan, spray all sides lightly with oil, place on a counter, and cover loosely with a clean kitchen towel.

Cool for at least 30 minutes before slicing.

MIXED-GRAIN FARMHOUSE LOAF

Makes 2 loaves

As the 3 flours in this loaf are added to the yeasty water, the dough develops a mild aroma reminiscent of recently mown hay, the kind of fragrance that would permeate the air around a farmhouse during harvest.

The dough, when baked, has a gentle, fresh grain flavor, with a thin, crisp crust and a soft crumb.

Soy and millet flours are available in health food stores.

This recipe can be cut in half to make 1 loaf, or the second loaf can be wrapped in several layers of plastic film, then placed in an airtight freezer bag and frozen for up to 2 months.

2 cups warm water
2 tablespoons sugar
1 package active dry yeast
2 tablespoons bland-tasting oil, such as canola or safflower
3/4 cup soy flour
3/4 cup millet flour
1/4 teaspoon salt
About 6 cups bread flour
1 cup cooked bulgur wheat, or wheat germ, or cooked brown rice
Vegetable oil spray

Stir the water and sugar together in a very large bowl. Sprinkle the yeast over the top and allow to soften. Add the oil, soy flour, millet, and salt and mix well. Add 4 cups of the bread flour and the bulgur, wheat germ, or brown rice. Stir to form a thick sticky dough. Add another cup of flour and mix until too stiff to stir, then dump onto a generously floured work surface and begin kneading.

Knead in enough additional flour to make the dough firm and resilient, and only the slightest bit moist. Continue kneading for 8 to 10 minutes to develop a bouncy elasticity in the dough.

Lightly mist the inside of a very large bowl with vegetable oil spray. Press the dough into the bottom of the bowl and cover tightly with plastic wrap. Set aside in a warm place to rise until doubled in volume, about 2 hours.

Press the dough flat to deflate it, then divide in half and shape into 2 loaves. Lightly spray the inside of 2 standard loaf pans and press the dough into place. Drape loosely with plastic wrap and set aside in a warm place until generously doubled in volume, about 1 hour.

After the dough has risen for about 40 minutes, heat the oven to 350 degrees F.

Spray the tops of the loaves lightly with vegetable oil spray and slip into the oven. Bake for 35 minutes. Turn out of the pans onto a clean counter, and to keep the crust soft, very lightly mist the bread all around with oil. Drape with a clean kitchen towel and allow to cool completely before cutting.

OLD-FASHIONED WHITE BREAD

Makes 1 large or 2 medium-sized loaves

A big, crusty loaf with a chewy, pale straw–colored crumb, this bread is made, in the way most of the great breads of Europe are made, with a sponge. A sponge is a small amount of yeast mixed with some flour and water that is then allowed to grow, attracting some of the yeast naturally present in the air, for a day or more, and is then used as the "starter." The starter is then mixed with the remaining flour and other ingredients to make the bread dough.

Breads made with sponges have the thick, crumbly crusts and chewy texture that bread aficionados believe are essential to a great bread.

For the sponge:

1 cup warm water
1 teaspoon (about ⅓ package) dry yeast
1 cup bread flour

To make the bread:

1½ cups cold tap water
2 teaspoons salt
About 6 cups bread flour
Vegetable oil spray
2 tablespoons cornmeal (preferably white)

Prepare the sponge: Pour the warm water into a very large mixing bowl and sprinkle the yeast evenly across the top of the water. In a few seconds, the yeast will soften, losing its granular shape and becoming wet. When this happens, dump in the cup of bread flour and stir to make a thick sponge. Stir hard until no lumps of unmoistened flour can be seen.

Cover loosely with plastic film and set aside at room temperature for 24 hours to allow the yeast to develop and the sponge to mature.

With a heavy spoon, stir the cold tap water into the sponge until well blended. Mix the salt into 5 cups of the flour and stir (you may want to use your hands for this) into the sponge to form a single mass of dough.

Dump onto a floured counter and knead, adding more flour as required, to form a very resilient, bouncy dough, about 16 to 18 minutes.

Lightly mist the inside of a very large bowl with cooking oil spray. Press the dough into the bottom of the bowl, cover tightly with plastic film, and set aside in a cool place to rise until tripled in volume, about 3 hours.

Sprinkle the center of a heavy baking sheet with the cornmeal, or lightly oil 2 standard loaf pans.

Press the dough down into the bowl to deflate completely. Lift the dough up into the air and gather it under itself so that it forms a big smooth ball. Continue pulling down until the top is well shaped and smooth, pinching the bottom very hard so it seals together. Alternatively, divide the dough in half and shape each piece to fit a loaf pan.

Place on the cornmeal (or in the loaf pans) and drape loosely with plastic wrap. Set aside in a cool place to rise until doubled in bulk, about 1 hour.

After 30 minutes, preheat the oven to 375 degrees F.

With a very sharp paring knife or a single-edged razor, gash the top of the loaf in the shape of an X, cutting about $1/2$ inch deep. Do not push or press on the dough in any way that will misshape it or cause it to deflate. Place a teaspoon of flour in a small fine sieve or strainer. Hold about 18 inches above the center of the loaf and shake gently so that the top is dusted with flour.

Bake in the center of the oven for 45 minutes.

Remove and transfer to a rack to cool.

MIXED-GRAIN BREAD

Makes 1 large or 2 medium-sized loaves

With mild sourdough overtones and a sweet, mixed-grain flavor, this extraordinary bread is worth waiting 3 days for the sponge to develop. As with other sponge doughs, this recipe produces a chewy, very evenly textured loaf with a crumbly, thick crust.

Graham, whole wheat, rye, and oat flours are available in most health food stores. If you want to make a milder version of this bread, reduce each of the specialty flours by half, increasing the bread flour accordingly.

For the sponge:

1 cup warm water
$^{1}/_{2}$ teaspoon ($^{1}/_{6}$ package) dry yeast
1 cup bread flour

To make the bread:

2 cups cold tap water
1 tablespoon salt
$^{2}/_{3}$ cup graham flour
$^{1}/_{2}$ cup whole wheat flour
$^{1}/_{2}$ cup rye flour
$^{1}/_{2}$ cup oat flour
About 7 cups bread flour
Vegetable oil spray

Prepare the sponge: Pour the warm water into a very large mixing bowl and sprinkle the yeast evenly across the top of the water. In a few seconds, the yeast will soften, losing its granular shape and becoming wet. When this happens, dump in the cup of bread flour and stir to make a thick sponge. Stir hard until no lumps of unmoistened flour can be seen.

Cover loosely with plastic film and set aside at room temperature for 3 days to allow the yeast to develop and the sponge to mature.

With a whisk, blend the 2 cups cold water into the sponge. In a very large bowl, mix the salt, graham flour, whole wheat flour, rye flour, oat flour, and 5½ cups of the bread flour. Pour the yeast mixture over the flours and stir with a heavy spoon to form a single mass of dough.

Dump onto a floured counter and knead, adding more bread flour as required, to form a resilient though slightly moist-feeling dough, about 15 minutes.

Lightly mist the inside of a very large bowl with vegetable oil spray. Press the dough into the bottom of the bowl, cover tightly with plastic film, and set aside in a cool place to rise until tripled in volume, about 3 hours.

Press the dough down into the bowl to deflate completely. Lift the dough up into the air and gather it under itself so that it forms a big smooth ball with some seams on the bottom. Continue pulling down so the top is well shaped and smooth, pinching the bottom very hard so it seals together. Press down on the ball of dough to flatten slightly, making it more a disk than a ball.

Alternatively, shape into 2 loaves and place in lightly oiled loaf pans.

Place on a heavy baking sheet and drape loosely with plastic wrap. Set aside in a cool place to rise until it appears twice its size, about 1 hour.

After 30 minutes, preheat the oven to 375 degrees F.

With a very sharp paring knife or a single-edged razor, slash the top of the loaf in the shape of a checkerboard, cutting about ¼ inch deep. Do not push or press on the dough in any way that will misshape it or cause it to deflate. Place a teaspoon of flour in a small fine sieve or strainer. Hold about 18 inches above the center of the loaf and shake gently so that the top is dusted with flour.

Bake in the center of the oven for 50 minutes.

Remove and transfer to a rack to cool.

WHOLE WHEAT FIG BREAD

Makes 1 large loaf

Although I have served fig breads for breakfast, with summer salads for lunch, and with dinners, not until recently did I begin to think of this as a dessert bread to be served with fresh fruit, such as a pear or a bowl of fresh berries.

The figs add texture and sweetness to this nutty whole wheat loaf, with its tender crumb that contrasts with the thin but hard crust.

The walnut version is not simply a variation, it is a very different bread. It will taste saltier, nuttier, and will feel lighter and softer.

I have sometimes made a full batch of dough from this recipe, added half the walnuts to half the dough, and half the figs to the other piece of dough, then formed them separately but baked them next to each other in the same loaf pan.

The yeast flavors, having developed for a day, are warm and inviting, soft and gentle, and complex and natural tasting, thanks to the time and the use of the sponge.

For the sponge:

1 cup warm water
1 teaspoon (¹/₃ package) dry yeast
¹/₂ cup bread flour
¹/₂ cup whole wheat flour

To make the bread:

1 cup cold tap water
1 teaspoon salt
¹/₄ cup whole wheat flour
About 4 cups bread flour
Vegetable oil spray
8 ounces moist mission figs, stems removed, cut into ¹/₄-inch slices

Prepare the sponge: Pour the warm water into a very large mixing bowl and sprinkle the yeast evenly across the top of the water. In a few seconds the yeast will soften, losing its granular shape and becoming wet. When this happens, dump in the ½ cup each of bread flour and whole wheat flour and stir to make a thick sponge. Stir hard until no lumps of unmoistened flour can be seen. With a rubber spatula, scrape down the sides of the bowl so all the dough is together in one sticky mass.

Cover loosely with aluminum foil or plastic film and set aside at room temperature for 3 days to allow the yeast to develop and the sponge to mature.

With a heavy spoon, stir the cup of cold water into the sponge until well blended. Mix the salt with the additional whole wheat flour and stir into the sponge. Add 3 cups of the additional bread flour and stir (you may want to use your hands for this after the dough has become a mass) into the sponge to form a single blob of dough.

Dump onto a floured counter and knead, adding more flour as required, to form a very resilient, bouncy dough, about 16 to 18 minutes.

Lightly mist the inside of a large bowl with vegetable oil spray. Press the dough into the bottom of the bowl, cover tightly with plastic film, and set aside in a warm place to rise until tripled in volume, about 1½ hours.

Spray the inside of a standard 9 × 5 × 3-inch bread pan lightly with oil and set aside.

Press the dough flat to deflate completely, then sprinkle with the figs. Fold the dough up so that the figs are inside, then slowly knead until the figs are well distributed.

Shape into a loaf and gently slide into the prepared pan. Drape (do not wrap securely) with a piece of plastic film and place in a warm spot to rise until doubled in volume, about 45 minutes.

After 30 minutes of rising in the pan, preheat the oven to 375 degrees F.

Bake in the center of the oven for 40 minutes.

Remove and turn out of the pan. Cool on a rack.

Whole Wheat Walnut Bread

Substitute 1 cup very coarsely chopped walnuts for the figs.

Whole Wheat Walnut Currant Bread

Substitute 1 cup very coarsely chopped walnuts and ½ cup currants for the figs.

OLIVE BREAD

Makes 1 loaf

With a strong crust and a rich Mediterranean character, this intensely olive-flavored bread will add a bold moment to a meal. The bread can be cut into slices or into 2-inch squares, using a very sharp serrated knife.

Kalamata olives are available in most supermarkets, Nice olives in premium supermarkets and specialty food stores.

If you like, you can make a basic rye bread simply by replacing the olives with $1^1/_2$ tablespoons caraway or fennel seeds.

For the sponge:

1 cup warm water
1 teaspoon dry yeast
1 cup bread flour
1 cup rye flour

For the bread:

1 teaspoon salt
About $2^1/_2$ cups bread flour
$1^1/_2$ cups pitted, coarsely chopped Kalamata or Nice olives, patted dry

Prepare the sponge: Pour the warm water into a large mixing bowl and sprinkle the yeast evenly across the top of the water. In a few seconds the yeast will soften, losing its granular shape and becoming wet. When this happens, dump in the 1 cup each of bread flour and rye flour. Stir to make a thick, lump-free sponge. With a rubber spatula, scrape down the sides of the bowl so all the dough is together in one sticky mass.

Cover loosely with aluminum foil or plastic film and set aside at room temperature for 2 days to allow the yeast to develop and the sponge to mature.

Mix the salt with 1 cup of the bread flour and stir into the sponge to make a very thick, sticky mass. Add another cup of bread flour and stir (you may want to use your hands for this after the dough has become a mass) to form a single blob of dough.

Dump onto a floured counter and knead, adding more flour as required, to form a very resilient, bouncy, but slightly moist-feeling dough, about 16 to 18 minutes.

Lightly mist the inside of a large bowl with vegetable oil spray. Press the dough into the bottom of the bowl, cover tightly with plastic film, and set aside in a warm place to rise until tripled in volume, about 1½ hours.

On a counter, press the dough into a rectangle about ½ inch thick. Sprinkle the olives evenly over the dough, then roll up tightly. This helps to ensure that the olives are evenly distributed throughout the loaf. Knead the dough for about 2 minutes, adding a little more flour if needed to work the olive pieces evenly throughout the dough.

Spray the inside of a standard 9 × 5 × 3-inch bread pan lightly with oil and set aside.

Shape dough into a loaf and slide into the prepared pan. Drape (do not wrap securely) with a piece of plastic film and place in a warm spot to rise until doubled in volume, about 1 hour.

After 45 minutes of rising in the pan, preheat the oven to 375 degrees F.

Bake for 40 minutes. Turn out of the loaf pan and cool on a rack.

WHOLE WHEAT PIZZA DOUGH

Makes enough dough for 1 large (14-inch) round pizza, 6 small (6-inch) pizzas,
or a 10- × 16-inch rectangular pizza

This is a tasty whole wheat dough. When baked, rather than becoming soft or wet under
the toppings, it quickly forms a hard crust.

For the sponge:

¹/₄ cup warm water
2 teaspoons (²/₃ package) dry yeast
¹/₄ cup bread flour

To make the pizza dough:

¹/₂ cup whole milk
¹/₄ teaspoon salt
¹/₂ cup whole wheat flour
About 1¹/₂ cups bread flour
Olive oil spray

Prepare the sponge: Pour the warm water into a large mixing bowl and sprinkle the yeast evenly across the top of the water. In a few seconds the yeast will soften, losing its granular shape and becoming wet. When this happens, dump in the ¹/₄ cup of bread flour and stir hard to make a thick sponge. Stir until well blended, scraping down the sides of the bowl.

Cover loosely with aluminum foil or plastic film and set aside at room temperature for 40 minutes.

Stir the milk into the sponge until it is absorbed. Mix the salt, whole wheat flour, and 1¹/₄ cups of the bread flour together and add to the sponge. Stir to form a single mass of slightly sticky dough.

Knead the dough until it becomes elastic and resilient, about 10 to 12 minutes, on a very lightly floured work surface. Incorporate as little extra flour as necessary; the dough should feel slightly softer (and consequently more moist) than traditional bread doughs.

Lightly mist the inside of a bowl with olive oil spray. Gently press the dough into the bottom of the bowl, mist the top, and cover with plastic film. Set aside to rise until generously doubled in volume, about 45 to 60 minutes.

Preheat the oven to 500 degrees F.

Punch down and roll into a circle about 14 inches in diameter, or divide into 6 pieces and roll each into a circle about 6 inches in diameter, or roll to fit a rectangular baking pan 10 × 16 inches. The dough will be soft and will roll out easily without sticking, even on an unfloured surface.

Arrange topping on the dough and bake at 500 degrees F for 10 minutes.

Whole Wheat Chive or Basil Pizza Dough

Knead ¼ cup roughly chopped chives or basil into the dough after the hour of rising, return to the bowl, cover, and let rise again for 30 minutes, then proceed with shaping and baking.

Honey Whole Wheat Pizza Dough

Stir a generous tablespoon of honey into the milk.

Traditional Pizza Dough

Replace the whole wheat flour with white bread flour.

Traditional Pizza Dough with Herbs

Replace the whole wheat flour with white bread flour. Knead ¼ cup roughly chopped chives or basil into the dough after the hour of rising, return to the bowl, cover, and let rise again for 30 minutes, then proceed with shaping and baking.

WHITE PIZZA BREAD

Makes 6 small appetizer-size (6-inch) pizzas

This unusually simple white pizza is meant to be served as a bread, not a meal. Its simplicity, however, demands that it be made with a very fine, very fruity olive oil and imported Parmesan, grated while the dough is baking.

The dough can also be shaped into a large (14-inch) round pizza, or a 10- × 16-inch rectangular pizza.

1 recipe Traditional Pizza Dough with Herbs (using chives, page 265)
3 tablespoons virgin or extra virgin olive oil
2 tablespoons freshly grated Parmesan cheese
Freshly ground black pepper

Preheat the oven to 500 degrees F.

On a clean work surface, divide the dough into 6 pieces and roll each into a circle about 6 inches in diameter. Place on a baking sheet and brush each pizza with about a teaspoon of the oil.

Bake until puffy and just beginning to become golden brown, about 8 minutes.

Remove from the oven, and quickly brush each pizza with 1/2 teaspoon of the remaining olive oil, then sprinkle each with a teaspoon of cheese and a little pepper. This must be done quickly enough for the cheese to melt on contact with the dough. If not, return to the oven for another minute to melt the cheese.

Cut each pizza into 2, 3, or 4 pieces and serve.

A MICROWAVE-BAKED ENGLISH MUFFIN BREAD

Makes 1 loaf

This loaf has the traditional holey texture and chewiness of an English muffin, and slices of this bread, like English muffins or their sister bread, crumpets, must be toasted. You can make a whole wheat version by substituting ½ cup of whole wheat flour for ½ cup of the all-purpose flour.

This is a good loaf for baking with children on a cold or rainy afternoon, because it requires no kneading, and though it does take about 1½ hours for its 2 risings, it bakes, to everyone's astonishment, in just 4 minutes.

Thickly sliced and toasted, this is a great breakfast bread, but it is even more exciting when used as the base for open-faced sandwiches, or croustades, which are to be eaten with a knife and fork (the holes make it less than ideal as finger food).

2 cups all-purpose flour
1 package (1 tablespoon) dry yeast
2 teaspoons sugar
½ teaspoon salt
1 cup skim milk
Vegetable oil spray
¼ teaspoon baking soda
1 tablespoon cold water

In a large bowl, mix together the flour, yeast, sugar, and salt.

Heat the milk, either in a small saucepan or in the microwave (about 1 minute 30 seconds on high), until it is lukewarm to the touch (about 110 degrees F).

Pour the milk onto the dry ingredients and, with a sturdy spoon, stir together to form a very thick batter, then beat vigorously for 15 to 20 seconds. The batter will become stretchy as you beat.

Cover with plastic wrap and set in a warm place to rise for 45 minutes. The batter will appear to have doubled or tripled in volume.

With vegetable oil spray mist the inside of a glass baking dish (my mother used to call this her "meatloaf pan"), about $8\frac{1}{2} \times 4\frac{1}{2} \times 2\frac{1}{2}$ inches, or a 6-cup microwave-safe soufflé dish.

Blend the baking soda and water together, then beat into the bread batter, beating until the batter becomes stretchy again. Scrape the batter into the prepared dish, drape loosely with plastic wrap, and return to the warm place to rise again until doubled in volume, until it fills the pan about $\frac{2}{3}$ to $\frac{3}{4}$, about 30 minutes.

Microwave on high, uncovered, for 4 minutes, or until no doughy spots can be seen on top of the loaf.

Cool the bread in the pan for 10 minutes, then gently but firmly pull back on the sides of the loaf to release from the pan. Unmold and cool completely on a rack.

9

Animal Protein

FISH

Spicy Salmon Fillets
Maryland Crabcakes
Fresh Tuna and White Bean Ceviche, Italian-style
Seared Halibut with Chermoula Sauce

RED MEATS

Marinated Flank Steak
Roasted Marinated Leg of Lamb for a Party
Chinese-style Sweet-and-Sour Pork Tenderloins

POULTRY

Thai Chicken Salad
Chicken Breasts with Curry Yogurt Marinade
Rosemary Lemon Chicken

Introduction

In a healthy, ecologically aware style of cooking, meat cannot be the main event in a meal; rather it is a condiment to a meal full of vegetables, cereals, and grains.

Unlike the counterculture of the late 1960s, which promoted vegetarianism because it was different, because it was what mainstream eating was not, we now know that reducing our animal protein consumption to about one 3- to 4-ounce serving a day is the single most important step most Americans can take to live a longer, healthier life.

About $\frac{1}{3}$ of the total fat and over $\frac{1}{3}$ of the saturated fat and cholesterol in the American diet comes from eating oversized portions of animal protein. Just cutting down to one modest portion a day will, for most Americans, solve the whole problem of too much fat in the diet.

Traditionally, the meat chapters in cookbooks are the largest and most important. Here, because of the diminished importance of cooking meat in a healthy diet, the chapter has shrunk dramatically and has been moved toward the back of the book in accordance with Culinary Guidelines for a New Earth (chapter 2).

Fish

SPICY SALMON FILLETS

Makes 6 servings

These succulent, moist, perfectly cooked salmon fillets are coated with homemade chili powder that produces a bold, spicy coating to balance the rich sweet flavor of the salmon. These are small, highly seasoned portions, emphasizing the use of animal protein as an accent, rather than central character, in the meal.

Serve hot with brown rice (see chapter 7), Emerald Spinach with Hidden Herbs (page 180), and Sweet Red Pepper Ragout (page 177), or cold, as part of a summer buffet.

To serve as an appetizer, cube the salmon, or cut it into strips. Cod, halibut, and red snapper can be substituted for the salmon.

1/4 **cup hot or sweet chili powder (pages 191 and 192)**
1/4 **teaspoon salt**
A 1-pound skinless fresh salmon fillet, cut into 6 equal pieces

Preheat the oven to 450 degrees F.

Pour the chili powder and salt into a bowl. Add the salmon pieces, one at a time, rolling the fillets in the spice mixture and pressing gently on the fish so that the fillets are evenly coated on all sides.

Arrange the salmon in a large baking dish so that none of the pieces are touching. Bake, uncovered, for 10 minutes.

Serve immediately; or, to serve cold, transfer to a cold plate or dish, cover, and refrigerate until needed.

MARYLAND CRABCAKES

Makes 6 servings

Warm, soft, rich, and creamy, this is the ultimate crabcake. Here fresh crabmeat is bound together with a minimal amount of white breadcrumbs, moistened with a velvety reduction of fish broth and cream, and flavored with just enough fresh herbs to bring out its sweetness. The crabcakes are then sautéed until a paper-thin auburn-colored crust forms, and served with only a wedge of lemon; this is Chesapeake Bay at its best.

Buy only the freshest white, large-lumped, sweet-smelling crab, usually found packed in plastic containers. Open the container before purchasing to check for color and fragrance; the crabmeat should not have a fishy smell.

Lemon thyme, as its name suggests, is a lightly lemon-scented variety of thyme. It is frequently available in the fresh herb section of premium food markets. Fresh tarragon can be used if lemon thyme is not available. Fish stock can be prepared from the recipe on page 118, or it can be purchased at some fish markets and specialty food stores.

Serve as an accent to a formal dinner, accompanied by Haricots Verts with Chanterelles (page 166) and Wild Mushroom Risotto with Sun-dried Tomatoes (page 200).

1 cup fish stock
About 2 tablespoons heavy cream
1 pound fresh lump crabmeat
5 slices soft white bread, crusts removed and each slice torn into 4 or
    5 pieces
3 tablespoons finely chopped fresh chives
1^1/$_2$ tablespoons finely chopped fresh lemon thyme
Salt
Freshly ground black pepper
Olive oil spray

For garnish:

4 lemon wedges

Pour the stock into a medium-sized saucepan set over moderately high heat. Bring to a boil, then lower the heat slightly and reduce the stock to ⅓ cup. Pour into a measuring cup and add enough cream to make ½ cup.

Meanwhile, pick over the crabmeat and remove any fragments of broken shell or small pieces of white cartilage. Try not to break up the large, splendid lumps of crab as you do this. Place the cleaned crab in a large mixing bowl.

Toss the bread into a food processor and process, pulsing as needed, until fine breadcrumbs form. Measure 1½ cups of the crumbs and sprinkle them over the crabmeat along with the herbs. Season very lightly with salt and pepper. Toss together with your hands, fingers spread widely apart, so that the ingredients are reasonably well mixed with only the minimum amount of damage to the lumps of crab.

In a thin stream, pour about ¾ of the reduced stock and cream mixture over the crab and toss, again with fingers outspread.

Test to see if the mixture is moist enough by wadding a couple of tablespoons of it together in your hand. It should hold together easily, and feel moist and just a little sticky. If it feels dry or breaks apart when handled, add a little more of the reduced stock and test again.

Shape into 16 patties, each about ¾ inch thick. Don't squeeze or squash, but gently pat the crabmeat into shape, using as little pressure as possible to form the patties.

Place a large nonstick skillet over medium heat and spray with olive oil. When it is hot, arrange the crabcakes in the pan without allowing them to touch. Reduce the heat slightly and cook until a deep auburn color forms on the bottom of each crabcake. Carefully flip the crabcakes and reduce the heat to medium low. Cook until the second side is golden brown; at this point the center of the crabcakes should be warm, the ideal temperature for a great crabcake.

Serve immediately, with a wedge of lemon next to each crabcake.

FRESH TUNA AND WHITE BEAN
CEVICHE, ITALIAN-STYLE

Makes 6 to 8 servings

Leaping continents in a single bound, this recipe combines the idea of the South American ceviche (fish that "cooks" in a highly acidic marinade) with the classic Italian tuna salad (usually made with canned tuna).

The result is a spectacular salad, perfect for an elegant lunch or an appetizer for adventurous culinarians.

12 ounces skinless, very fresh tuna, cut into 1/2-inch dice
2 cups home-cooked small white navy beans
1/2 small red onion, peeled and thinly sliced
5 thin scallions, white part and a little of the green tops, thinly sliced
1/2 cup chopped fresh parsley, preferably Italian flat-leafed parsley
1/2 cup chopped fresh basil
6 to 8 canned anchovy fillets, rinsed under running cold water if bony
    or salty, coarsely chopped
2 tablespoons capers, rinsed and coarsely chopped
3 tablespoons virgin or extra virgin olive oil
2 tablespoons red wine vinegar
Juice of 1 large lemon
1 large garlic clove, peeled and very finely chopped
A little freshly ground black pepper

In a large nonaluminum bowl, gently mix together all the ingredients. Cover and refrigerate overnight, to allow the tuna to "cook" in the vinegar and lemon juice, and to allow the flavors to mellow.

Taste and add more pepper if desired.

Serve cold, or at room temperature.

274

SEARED HALIBUT WITH
CHERMOULA SAUCE

Makes 6 servings

When fish is seared, it develops a crust with a deep mahogany color. The crust not only seals in the natural flavors and juices, making the fish tender and moist, but adds sweetness as well.

Firm white fish, like halibut, grouper, mahimahi, and red snapper, with their mild flavor, sear exceptionally well. Here, halibut is seared and served with spicy North African sauce. In the variations following, salmon and tilefish are seared and served with different sauces.

1 pound fresh halibut in a 1-inch thick fillet, quartered
Olive oil spray
1 recipe Chermoula Sauce (page 164)

Pat the halibut very dry so it will sear well.

Place a large nonstick sauté pan over medium heat. When it is hot, coat the bottom lightly with olive oil spray. Add the halibut and reduce the heat to medium low. Cook until golden brown on the bottom, 4 or 5 minutes, without moving the fish. The halibut should be a deep golden mahogany color, but not blackened or burned. Adjust the heat, if necessary, to achieve this color in the time specified. With tongs, carefully turn the fish and cook the other side until golden, about 4 more minutes.

While the halibut is cooking, warm the sauce, either in a microwave oven or in a saucepan on the stovetop.

Spoon chermoula sauce onto the plates, and top with the seared halibut.

Serve immediately.

Seared Fresh Salmon
with Jean-Louis Palladin's Versatile Onion Sauce

Substitute salmon for the halibut, and Jean-Louis Palladin's Versatile Onion Sauce (page 161) for the chermoula.

Seared Tilefish with Sun-dried Tomato Sauce

Substitute tilefish for the halibut, and Sun-dried Tomato Sauce (page 156) for the onion sauce.

Red Meats

MARINATED FLANK STEAK

Makes 6 servings

This marinade adds a mahogany color and a complex Madeira flavor with bursts of garlic and ginger to the flank steak. A few slices of this steak will enliven any family meal or a company dinner. In warm weather, leftovers can be refrigerated and served cold in sandwiches later in the week. Pork tenderloin takes well to this Madeira marinade, and is cooked in exactly the same manner.

3/4 cup Madeira
1/4 cup soy sauce
2 shallots, peeled
A 1/2-inch chunk fresh gingerroot
3 garlic cloves, peeled
Juice of 1/2 lemon
1/2 teaspoon coarsely ground black pepper
1 pound flank steak, trimmed of all excess fat

In a food processor, combine the Madeira, soy sauce, shallots, ginger, garlic, lemon juice, and pepper and process, pulsing frequently, until the shallots, ginger, and garlic are finely chopped. Pour into a shallow glass dish large enough to hold the flank steak in a single layer.

Place the flank steak in the dish and rub it all over with the marinade. Marinate overnight in the refrigerator for 48 hours, turning occasionally and rubbing each time so the marinade evenly coats the meat. The longer the steak marinates, the more deeply the marinade will penetrate.

Heat the broiler.

Lift the steak over the dish and scrape off the marinade. Pat dry. Place on an aluminum foil–lined roasting pan and slide under the broiler. Broil until medium rare, about 4 minutes on each side. To test for doneness, with the tip of a sharp paring knife make a small slit in the meat. It should be very pink, but not rare red.

Transfer the steak to a cutting board and allow to rest for 5 minutes before carving. Carve into thin slices on the bias across the grain. (Carving the meat this way will make it more tender.)

ROASTED MARINATED LEG OF
LAMB FOR A PARTY

Makes about 10 to 12 servings

This is a grand roast for large parties or buffets, with a special cooking process that gives it a richly colored surface. The lamb is marinated to give it additional flavor and to tenderize it in a mixture of oil and soy sauce flavored with lemon, garlic, onions, and herbs. A honey glaze flavored with anise is brushed onto the lamb, and then it is roasted to produce a succulent medium rare interior and a dark, sweet, fragrant crust.

Special note: This recipe requires 2 days of marinating and considerable attention during cooking. Serve this as part of a formal dinner, with Brown Rice Risotto with Azuki Beans (page 201) or Baked Jasmine Rice with Coconut (page 206), Fluffy Whipped Potatoes (page 178) or Mixed Winter Root Vegetables (page 193), and Sweet Red Pepper Ragout (page 177).

Half a lemon
1 medium-sized onion, peeled and quartered
2 shallots, peeled
4 large garlic cloves, peeled
2 bay leaves, crumbled
1 tablespoon dried rosemary
1/4 cup peanut oil
1 cup soy sauce
1/2 cup honey
1 tablespoon anise seeds
1/2 teaspoon freshly ground black pepper
One 6- to 7-pound leg of lamb, trimmed of excess fat and fell, and
    pelvic bone removed

In a food processor, combine the lemon, onion, shallots, garlic, bay leaves, and rosemary, and pulse until everything is coarsely chopped. Do not overprocess.

Pour the oil and soy sauce into a nonaluminum pan or baking dish large enough to hold the lamb leg, add the chopped vegetables, and mix together.

Slip the lamb into the marinade, turning it until it is well coated, then scatter some of the vegetables over the top. Cover and refrigerate for 2 days, turning several times each day to ensure that the leg marinates evenly. Remove from the refrigerator 3 to 4 hours before cooking to allow the lamb to come to room temperature.

Preheat the oven to 500 degrees F.

Lift the lamb out of the marinade and scrape the vegetables off the meat. Pat the lamb dry. With a piece of kitchen string, tie the flappy top of the leg (the sirloin end) neatly together and place the lamb on a rack in a large roasting pan. Strain the marinade and discard the vegetables. Pour 1 cup of the marinade into a bowl and add the honey. Grind the anise seeds finely in a spice mill or electric coffee grinder, or crush well in a mortar. Add the anise and the pepper to the cup of marinade. Beat lightly with a whisk, and pour slowly and evenly over the leg of lamb.

Place the lamb in the center of the oven and roast for 10 minutes. Remove from the oven, turn the lamb over, and quickly baste all round with the marinade from the pan. Slip the lamb back into the oven, reduce the heat to 450 degrees F and roast for 10 minutes. Turn and baste again, then reduce the heat to 400 degrees F and roast for 10 minutes. Turn and baste. Return the lamb to the oven, reduce the heat to 350 degrees F and roast for 10 minutes. Turn and baste again (the basting liquid will have thickened considerably by now), return to the oven, and reduce the heat to 300 degrees F. Roast until done, turning and basting every 10 minutes. The total cooking time for medium rare meat will be about 12 minutes per pound; for medium, about 14 minutes per pound.

If you do not have an instant-read thermometer, use these minute-per-pound figures to determine when the roast is done.

If you do have an instantly registering thermometer, about 10 to 15 minutes before you estimate the roast will be done, insert it into the thickest part of the leg without touching the bone. For medium rare, it should register 130 to 135 degrees F when the lamb is done; for medium, 150 degrees F.

At this point in the roasting, the internal temperature of the lamb will rise about 1 degree every 1½ minutes, so for the temperature of the roast to increase by 10 degrees will take 15 minutes.

By the time the lamb is done, the kitchen will be perfumed with its fragrance. Remove the lamb from the oven, lift out of the roasting pan, and place on a cutting board, where it should rest for 15 minutes so the juices can settle back into the meat.

Just before carving, remove the string. Slice and serve without a sauce.

CHINESE-STYLE SWEET-AND-SOUR PORK TENDERLOINS

Makes 8 servings

This is a light version of the glaze often used for sweet-and-sour Chinese spareribs. It can also be used to marinate and baste grilled or broiled chicken, turkey, or beef.

Chinese black vinegars are available in Chinese and some other Asian markets. The best have a rich fragrance and a complex, mildly smoky flavor that is rounder and more gentle than Italian vinegars. Once you start to play with black vinegar, you'll find it can be used in almost all the ways balsamic vinegar can, but with more subtlety.

Most American-made soy sauces are salty, thin, and characterless. Chinese dark soy sauces, on the other hand, are rich in color, character, and texture. The best are smooth and velvety, with a complex grainy, woody, salty flavor. Mushroom soy is a variety of dark soy sauce.

²/₃ cup Chinese black vinegar
²/₃ cup brown sugar
3 tablespoons Chinese dark soy sauce
2 pork tenderloins (together weighing about 1¹/₂ pounds), trimmed of
   fat and silver-colored surface membranes
Vegetable oil spray
Freshly ground black pepper

In a shallow dish just large enough to hold the pork, stir together the vinegar, brown sugar, and soy sauce. Turn the pork until lightly coated, then cover and marinate overnight in the refrigerator, turning once or twice to ensure even marination.

Preheat a charcoal grill to moderately hot, or adjust the grate so that the pork is raised sufficiently to moderate the heat. If it is too hot, the pork will become dry.

While the grill is heating, pat the pork dry and set aside. Pour the marinade into a saucepan and set over medium high heat. Stir once or twice, then just let the marinade boil until it is reduced to $1/3$ cup of syrupy glaze. Remove from the heat.

Mist the pork lightly with vegetable oil spray to prevent it from sticking to the grill, and season a little more heavily than you usually would with pepper. Grill the pork, turning 3 or 4 times to ensure even cooking, until the center of the meat is no longer pink, about 8 minutes in total or until an instantly registering thermometer inserted into the thickest part reads 145 degrees F. When the pork is removed from the grill, brush it with the reduced marinade.

Allow the tenderloins to rest for 10 minutes so the juices can settle back into the meat, brushing them occasionally with any remaining marinade, then slice on the bias and serve. Any extra marinade can be spooned over the pork.

Poultry

THAI CHICKEN SALAD

Makes 4 servings

This salad is full of flavor and texture; it can brighten up a scorchingly hot day or a dull rainy summer day. It is at once sweet, hot, and sour; soft and crisp, moist and crunchy. For a different taste, substitute a poached or grilled duck breast for the chicken.

Fish sauce, a thin, brown, salty and fishy liquid, is as essential to Southeast Asian cooking as soy sauce is to Japanese and Chinese cooking. Thai fish sauce, called nam pla, *and Vietnamese fish sauce, called* nuoc nam, *are the two most commonly available in the United States, and can be found in supermarkets, specialty stores, and Asian groceries.*

1 whole boneless, skinless chicken breast (about 8 ounces), cut in half lengthwise
2 celery ribs, julienned into 1-inch-long matchsticks
1 large cucumber, peeled, seeded, and julienned into 1-inch-long matchsticks
1/2 red onion, peeled, cut in half lengthwise, and thinly sliced
A 1 1/2-inch-long chunk of fresh gingerroot, peeled and finely chopped
1 small bunch cilantro, very coarsely chopped to make about 1/2 cup
2 garlic cloves, peeled and finely chopped
1/2 small jalapeño pepper, seeded and julienned into 1/2-inch-long matchsticks
2 tablespoons fish sauce (see above)
Juice of 2 large limes

Fill a medium-sized pot 1/4 full with hot tap water. Place over a burner set on high and bring to a boil. Add the chicken, reduce the heat, and simmer for 3 minutes. Turn off the heat and allow the chicken to finish cooking as the water cools, about 20 minutes.

When chicken is cool, either tear into shreds with a fork or cut into thin strips. Toss the chicken with the remaining ingredients.

Serve at room temperature or slightly chilled, but not refrigerator cold.

CHICKEN BREASTS WITH
CURRY YOGURT MARINADE

Makes 6 servings

Although the marinade will taste very spicy, the chicken will be barely curried, though well tenderized from the natural enzymes in the yogurt. Or use chili powder instead of curry powder for flavoring.

Serve with Zucchini Sauté (page 184) and Baked Jasmine Rice with Coconut (page 206).

$^1/_2$ small onion, peeled
1 large garlic clove, peeled
A $^3/_4$-inch piece fresh gingerroot
1 cup plain (unflavored) nonfat yogurt
1 tablespoon curry powder
$^1/_8$ teaspoon freshly ground black pepper
$1^1/_4$ pounds boneless, skinless chicken breasts, cut into 6 equal pieces
Vegetable oil spray

In a food processor, combine the onion, garlic, ginger, yogurt, curry powder, and pepper. Process until onion has been chopped smooth. Pour into a nonreactive bowl and submerge the chicken in the yogurt marinade. Marinate for 1 to 2 days in the refrigerator.

Preheat the broiler, removing the broiling pan. Mist the pan with vegetable oil spray.

Remove the chicken from the marinade, gently pulling the chicken through your fingers to remove as much of the marinade as possible. Pat the chicken dry, then arrange on the pan.

Broil until the breasts are cooked through, about 5 minutes on each side.

Serve immediately.

ROSEMARY LEMON CHICKEN

Makes 6 servings

Elegant, light, and lemony with a gentle scent of rosemary, this simple dish is excellent for outdoor grilling.

1 small onion, peeled and halved
Leaves from 5 large stems of rosemary, or 1 heaping tablespoon dried
   rosemary
2 garlic cloves, peeled
Juice of 1 large lemon
1/3 cup chicken stock
1¼ pounds boneless, skinless chicken breasts
Olive oil spray

In a food processor, purée the onion, rosemary, garlic, lemon juice, and chicken stock to make a thick, somewhat sloshy marinade. Transfer to a nonreactive bowl, add the chicken, and rub and toss so the chicken is evenly coated with the marinade. Marinate for 2 to 4 hours.

Preheat a grill or broiler.

Remove the chicken from the marinade and pat dry. Spray lightly with olive oil spray to prevent the chicken from sticking. Grill or broil until the chicken is cooked through, about 4 or 5 minutes on each side.

Cut into portions and serve immediately.

10

Desserts

Grand Marnier Soufflé
James Beard's Mother's Chocolate Christmas Fruitcake
Amaretto Rice Pudding
Chocolate Pudding
The Perfect Custard
Fresh Raspberry Yogurt Cheesecake
Alice's Date Truffles

SORBETS

Pink Cranshaw Sorbet with Vodka
Blackberry, Pineapple, and Peach Sorbet
Kiwi Sorbet

Introduction

Big squares of heavy, dense carrot and zucchini cakes (made with whole wheat flour, honey—never sugar—and with wheat germ and soy pulp added on principle) were dessert specialties in counterculture communes and group houses in the 1970s. It was believed that these cakes were healthy because they were made with so many politically correct ingredients. Unfortunately, the counterculture chose the wrong culprit, even with its seemingly politically correct reasoning.

Nutritional science has proven beyond any doubt that the real villain in the dessert world is fat, or a combination of fat and sugar in certain exact ratios, not sugar. The sugar versus honey issue, though still raging in some circles, has all but been dismissed, for we now know that the body cannot tell the difference between them.

During the 1980s, recipes began appearing for "light" desserts. Editors searched without a great deal of success for cakes without flour and cookies without sugar (oops, wrong direction), and cakes, pie crusts, and cookies made without butter (right direction, but barely edible).

Now these are no longer of prime importance, because when today's healthy gourmet eats three full, high-carbohydrate meals a day, the physiological yearnings for sugar and fat disappear and any desire for sweet, lipid-laden dessert is minimal.

The best desserts are as simple as a truly ripe fresh fruit, or a fruit salad, or a fruit sorbet. In this chapter are a handful of desserts like a gloriously light-as-air soufflé that has been dramatically reduced in fat without losing any of its magic. Here are James Beard's mother's chocolate fruitcake, miraculously low in fat, which I believe belongs at every Christmas dinner; a rice pudding flavored with Amaretto; and an extraordinary, utterly simple baked custard; as well as a cheesecake and a chocolate pudding. There is also an Alice B. Toklas recipe for a confection best served with coffee after dinner.

And finally, here are a handful of sorbet recipes. Poached fruit, fruit salad, and a bread pudding recipe, all of which can be used for dessert, are in the breakfast chapter.

GRAND MARNIER SOUFFLÉ

Makes 4 servings

Forget everything you've ever heard about soufflés being difficult to make. They are easy to make, as this recipe will prove to you.

This light soufflé will dissolve in your mouth like a puff of air as you swallow. And it only takes about 15 minutes to make!

A soufflé should be prepared in the last seconds before you sit down to dinner. Cover the soufflé dish and leave it on the kitchen counter, undisturbed, until you have served the entrée, then simply slip the soufflé into the oven. In 16 minutes, it will be done. It will not hold once it is baked, so it must be taken directly from oven to table. If you have planned a long leisurely meal, then wait until the entrée has been cleared from the table before baking the soufflé.

For the soufflé dish:

Vegetable oil spray
1 tablespoon sugar

For the soufflé:

5 egg whites
¹/₂ cup sugar
3 egg yolks
3 tablespoons Grand Marnier

Spray the inside of a 6-cup soufflé dish with vegetable oil spray. Add the sugar and tilt and roll the dish until the sides and bottom of the bowl are coated. Shake out any excess sugar.

In the bowl of an electric mixer, beat the egg whites until frothy and just about doubled in volume, then add ¹/₄ cup of the sugar and beat until a shiny meringue forms that will just hold a stiff peak, about 3 minutes. Gently transfer to a very large bowl and set aside.

In a clean bowl with clean beaters, beat the egg yolks with the remaining 1/4 cup sugar until very pale in color and as thick as sour cream, about 3 minutes. Add the Grand Marnier and beat just until blended.

Pour the Grand Marnier mixture over the egg whites and gently fold together with a large spatula. The two mixtures should be just blended, with no streaks, or virtually no streaks. Do not overfold; overfolding will deflate the egg whites and the soufflé will not rise elegantly above the top of the dish. Preheat the oven to 375 degrees F about 20 minutes before you plan to bake the soufflé.

Pour the mixture into the prepared soufflé dish. Cover and set aside, undisturbed, for up to 30 minutes before baking (see the headnote to this recipe). Remove cover before baking.

Bake in the center of the oven for 16 to 18 minutes. The soufflé will rise high above the dish; the top will be darkly browned. In 16 minutes, when it is touched on top, the edges of the soufflé will be firm but the center will still be slightly moist. In 18 minutes, the center will be firm as well. Soufflés have a lighter, airier, smoother feel in the mouth if they are still moist in the center.

Carefully remove from the oven and slip the soufflé dish onto a large plate so the soufflé can be carried to the table for presentation. Use 2 large spoons to scoop the soufflé onto serving plates, scooping some of the top, some of the firm outer edge, and some of the soft center onto each plate.

Coffee–Hazelnut Liqueur Soufflé

Substitute 4 tablespoons Kahlúa and 1 tablespoon Frangelico for the Grand Marnier.

Lemon Soufflé

Substitute the grated zest of 1 small lemon and 1/4 cup freshly squeezed lemon juice for the Grand Marnier.

JAMES BEARD'S MOTHER'S
CHOCOLATE CHRISTMAS FRUITCAKE

Makes 30 servings

This is the other fruitcake. It is moist and tender, and laden with glazed fruits that have been drowned for a week in fine bourbon before being bound in a casing of chocolate batter.

This recipe, which is an adaptation of James Beard's mother's chocolate fruitcake, will generously serve 30. If you aren't planning that large a Christmas dinner, consider baking some of the batter in individual loaf pans and giving them as Christmas presents.

To serve this fruitcake for Christmas, start the preparation by mid-December. The fruit needs a week to soak, and the cake should have a week or two to mature after it comes from the oven.

You can cut this recipe in half, if you wish, but I find that with gift-giving and children (and me) nibbling, this cake will stretch the Christmas season into mid-January before all the cake is eaten.

There are 3 types of dried fruits: the common variety, which are simply dried, like the apricots or prunes found in supermarkets; candied dried fruits that have been coated with granulated sugar, like crystallized ginger and sometimes candied orange peel; and glazed fruits, which have been cooked in syrup and then partially dried. Glazed fruits should glisten, and should be tender but not soft. Avoid any that are hard and dry, or that appear to be coated with a dried white powder.

Glazed fruits are expensive, and are only available from about Thanksgiving to Christmas in specialty food shops. If you are planning to make this fruitcake for Christmas, do some telephone shopping in search of glazed fruits about mid-November. And read the paragraph in the procedure about the number and size of the cake pans needed for baking.

12 ounces glazed pears, diced
8 ounces glazed pineapple, diced
6 ounces glazed lemon peel, diced
6 ounces glazed orange peel, diced
8 ounces glazed citron, diced
16 ounces large seeded raisins
8 ounces sultanas (dried Thomson grapes)
8 ounces currants
1 quart fine-quality bourbon
8 ounces walnut or pecan meats, in large broken pieces
8 tablespoons (1 stick) unsalted butter
2 cups sugar
$1/4$ teaspoon ground cinnamon
$1/4$ teaspoon ground nutmeg
$1/8$ teaspoon ground cloves
3 ounces (3 squares) bitter (unsweetened) chocolate, grated
6 eggs, beaten together with a fork
$1 1/2$ cups all-purpose flour
$1/2$ teaspoon baking soda
Vegetable oil spray and baker's parchment paper for the pans
About $3/4$ cup fine-quality Cognac or very dark rum (optional)

In a very large nonaluminum bowl, combine pears, pineapple, lemon peel, orange peel, citron, raisins, sultanas, and currants, and mix well. Stir in the bourbon. Cover with plastic wrap and set aside in a cool spot for a week, turning the fruit in the juices every other day. In the course of the week, the fruit will absorb most of the liquor.

Heat the oven to 275 degrees F.

Mix the nuts into the fruit.

Beat the butter with an electric mixer until very light and fluffy, then gradually add the sugar and continue beating for 1 minute. Add the spices, chocolate, and beaten eggs, and beat until well blended, scraping down the sides of the bowl once or twice.

In a separate bowl, sift together the flour and baking soda. Remove $1/2$ cup of the flour mixture and set aside. Combine the remaining flour with the butter mixture and fold together with a large spatula to form a thick batter.

There will be just enough batter to bind the fruits together, though it will seem like very little batter compared to most fruitcakes.

Drain the fruits in a large colander, then firmly press, but don't crush, to remove most of the liquid clinging to them. Combine the fruits with the reserved ½ cup of flour mixture and toss to coat. This will prevent the fruits from settling to the bottom of the pan during baking. Mix the fruits into the chocolate batter, tossing with your hands until well combined.

The cake pans:

These fruitcakes can be baked in almost any assortment of baking pans, from 1 very large pan to a dozen or so individual-size bread pans. My preference is for 3 standard loaf pans (8 to 9 inches long). Spray the pans with vegetable oil and line with baker's parchment. You can also use 2 smaller bread pans and a large round or square baking pan or individual loaf pans, for part of the batter. Ultimately, the size of the pans is irrelevant, but it is essential that they be lined with parchment, and they should be filled ¾ full with the cake batter.

Bake until a toothpick inserted into the center comes out clean.

Cakes in small pans will need about 1½ to 2 hours; cakes in large pans as much as 3 to 4 hours.

Cool the cakes in their pans until they feel just warm to the touch. Insert a toothpick deeply into the cake every 2 or 3 inches, then brush generously with Cognac or rum, allowing the liquor to seep into the cake through the toothpick holes.

If you are planning to serve the cake to children, you may want to reserve 1 loaf unbathed in liquor.

For the best flavor, allow the cakes to mellow for a week or so before serving.

AMARETTO RICE PUDDING

Makes 6 servings

This rice pudding, flavored with Amaretto liqueur and currants, is worthy fare for a company dinner. The variation below is for a family version of this old-fashioned classic.

Currants are sometimes available in supermarkets, and usually available in premium food shops and health food stores.

1/2 **cup currants (or raisins if currants are not available)**
1/4 **cup Amaretto**
1 quart skim milk
2/3 **cup uncooked long-grain white rice (not parboiled or converted)**
6 tablespoons sugar
1 vanilla bean, cut in half lengthwise, then cut into pieces about 2 inches long
3 eggs
Vegetable oil spray

Place the currants and Amaretto in a small nonaluminum saucepan and set over medium heat. (Do not use high heat as it might cause the Amaretto to ignite.) Cook just until you see a little steam rising from the surface as the Amaretto gets close to boiling. Immediately remove from the heat and set aside to cool.

In a heavy-bottomed saucepan that has a tight-fitting cover, combine 3 cups of the milk, the rice, 3 tablespoons of the sugar, and the vanilla bean lengths. Bring to a boil over medium high heat, uncovered, then reduce the heat to low, cover, and allow to simmer until the milk is absorbed and the texture is creamy, about 55 minutes, stirring every 10 to 15 minutes.

When the rice has cooked for 40 minutes, preheat the oven to 375 degrees F.

Put an inch or so of hot tap water in the bottom of a double boiler and set over medium heat. Pour the remaining cup of milk into the top (the saucepan part) of the double boiler and cook directly over medium heat until steaming hot but not boiling. Meanwhile, combine the eggs and the remaining 3 tablespoons of sugar in the bowl of an electric mixer and beat at high speed until pale in color and thick and ribbony in texture, about 3 minutes.

Slowly pour about ⅓ of the hot milk into the egg mixture, beating the whole time; then reverse the process and beat the egg and milk mixture into the milk remaining in the top of the double boiler. Adjust the heat under the bottom of the double boiler so the water simmers, then insert the top of the double boiler and cook the egg and milk mixture until it thickens enough to generously coat the back of a spoon and the first signs of steam rise from the surface. Do not overcook or the eggs will curdle. Immediately pour into a bowl, cover, and set aside until the rice has finished cooking.

When the rice is ready, remove from the heat. With tongs, lift out the vanilla beans, which will be very hot. Carefully hold the beans over the rice and squeeze them so the little black specks fall into the rice. Stir in the Amaretto and currants.

Lightly spray the inside of a 6-cup baking dish with the vegetable oil spray. Stir together the custard (the cooked egg and milk mixture) and the rice and currants and pour into the dish.

Bake for 45 minutes, then drape a sheet of aluminum foil loosely across the top of the pudding to prevent it from browning too much on top. Continue baking until a toothpick inserted into the center comes out clean, about 15 minutes longer.

Serve warm, or, if made ahead, cool to room temperature, cover, and refrigerate, then remove from the refrigerator about 2 hours before serving so the pudding can warm to room temperature.

Old-fashioned Family-style Rice Pudding

Substitute raisins for the currants, apple juice for the Amaretto, and eliminate the vanilla bean, stirring 2 teaspoons of vanilla extract into the rice when the raisins are added.

CHOCOLATE PUDDING

Makes 4 servings

Here is a healthy, reduced-fat chocolate pudding that has a real chocolate flavor (unlike boxed chocolate puddings) and a thick, smooth texture. It is the ultimate chocolate comfort food.

Even chocoholics used to the rich, dark chocolate mousses and terrines of the 1980s will find a bowl of this pudding satisfying. And it takes only about 15 minutes to make.

2 ounces (¹/₃ cup) semisweet chocolate, very coarsely chopped
1 ounce (1 square) unsweetened chocolate, very coarsely chopped
3 tablespoons cornstarch
¹/₃ cup sugar
3 cups skim milk
1¹/₂ teaspoons vanilla extract

In a food processor, combine the semisweet chocolate, unsweetened chocolate, cornstarch, and sugar. Process to form a finely granulated texture with no bits or chunks of chocolate. Add the milk and vanilla and process until well blended with only some fine specks of chocolate visible.

Pour into a heavy-bottomed saucepan and cook over medium heat until the mixture comes to a boil, stirring frequently to prevent scorching. Reduce the heat and simmer for 2 minutes, stirring constantly. Whisk hard to ensure that there are no lumps, then pour into 4 individual custard cups or a bowl. Cover tightly with plastic wrap and refrigerate until cold.

THE PERFECT CUSTARD

Makes 6 servings

This baked custard takes only a few minutes to make, though it bakes for nearly 3 hours. It has a silky satin texture with a delicate, refined flavor.

5 large eggs
1 quart skim milk
2 teaspoons pure (not imitation) vanilla extract
1/3 cup sugar, preferably superfine
Vegetable oil spray

In a large bowl, gently beat the eggs with a fork until just blended, trying not to let a froth form on the surface. Add the milk, vanilla, and sugar and stir with a large spoon until the sugar is dissolved, again trying not to let a froth form. If a froth does form, skim it off with the spoon or it will leave the surface of the custard rough and pockmarked when it is baked.

Lightly mist the inside of a 6-cup baking dish with vegetable oil spray. Pour the egg and milk mixture through a strainer into the baking dish. Cover securely with aluminum foil.

Place a rack (such as a small cake rack) on the bottom of a deep pan (like a roasting pan) that is high-sided enough to be at least as high as the top of the baking dish when it is placed on the rack. Place the baking dish on the rack.

Carefully pour enough cold water into the pan so that the water level reaches almost to the top of the baking dish.

Place in the center of a cold oven. Set the thermostat to 275 degrees F and turn the oven on to bake (do not preheat).

Cook until a toothpick inserted into the center of the custard comes out clean, about 2 1/2 to 3 hours. Be careful not to burn yourself when lifting the foil to insert the toothpick; the water will be nearly boiling and both the baking dish and pan will be very hot.

Starting the custard in a cold water bath in a cold oven and baking it very slowly produces its incredible texture.

Ideally, this custard should be served warm from the oven. However, if made ahead, cool it at room temperature, cover, and refrigerate, then remove from the refrigerator about 2 hours before serving so the pudding can warm to room temperature.

FRESH RASPBERRY
YOGURT CHEESECAKE

Makes 6 servings

This is a rich lowfat cheesecake covered with fresh raspberries. Although the yogurt needs to drain for several hours, there is no crust to make, and the batter can be beaten together in a couple of minutes, so this is a simple cake to prepare.

32 ounces plain (unflavored) nonfat yogurt
4 ounces light (reduced fat) cream cheese
1/2 cup sugar
3 eggs
1 teaspoon vanilla
1/4 cup graham cracker crumbs (about 4 graham crackers)
Vegetable oil spray
1 pint fresh raspberries

Line a large strainer with paper toweling or a clean, lightly dampened kitchen towel. Pour the yogurt into the strainer and set over a bowl. Cover the top of the yogurt with plastic film. Set aside until about 1 1/2 cups of the whey (the clear liquid) drips from the yogurt, leaving a soft cheese in the strainer, about 4 hours at room temperature or about 10 hours in the refrigerator. Discard the whey.

Preheat the oven to 300 degrees F.

With an electric mixer, beat the yogurt cheese and cream cheese until well blended. Add the sugar and mix well. Add the eggs and beat until blended. Beat in the vanilla.

Spray the inside of an 8-inch nonstick pie plate with the vegetable oil spray. Add the graham crumbs and shake and swirl so that the bottom and sides of the pie plate are evenly coated.

Pour the cheese mixture into the crumb-coated pan and slide into the middle of the oven. Bake until the center of the cake is puffy (it won't puff as high around the edge) and a toothpick inserted into the center comes out clean, about 1 hour 15 minutes. Cool completely (the puffy part of the cake will collapse as it cools). Cover and refrigerate.

Two to 3 hours before serving, arrange the berries in concentric circles to cover the top of the cake and return to the refrigerator, uncovered.

To serve, cut with a serrated knife and lift out of the pie plate with a cake server.

ALICE'S DATE TRUFFLES

Makes 36 truffles

The idea for these dried fruit truffles comes from the recipe for "Haschich Fudge" in the original British edition of The Alice B. Toklas Cookbook. *The recipe was not included in the first American edition of the book. So, never having seen the recipe, members of the counterculture mistakenly called the fudge "Alice B. Toklas's Marijuana Brownies," and made Toklas into a minor folk hero.*

The infamous fudge wasn't a fudge at all, but a North African–inspired confection made of dates and figs, almonds and peanuts, all ground together, then moistened with butter and flavored with spices. Using Toklas's recipe as a point of departure, and eliminating the heaping tablespoon of ground marijuana that was in the original recipe, I created these innocent little confections.

Whether the flavors used to spice these moist, nutty little truffles remind you of the casbahs of North Africa or the gingerbread men of a New England Christmas, 2 or 3 on a plate next to a cup of strong coffee make a healthy, stylish way to end a dinner.

$^1/_2$ cup moist pitted dates (about 4 ounces unpitted)
$^1/_2$ cup pecan pieces (about 1$^1/_2$ ounces)
$^1/_4$ cup moist black mission figs (about 2 ounces)
1$^1/_2$ tablespoons melted butter
2 tablespoons powdered sugar
$^3/_4$ teaspoon ground coriander
$^1/_2$ teaspoon ground cinnamon
$^1/_2$ teaspoon ground nutmeg
$^1/_4$ teaspoon ground ginger
$^1/_4$ teaspoon ground black pepper

Combine all the ingredients in a food processor. Pulse quickly and repeat, allowing the mixture to settle down each time, until everything is finely chopped.

The fruit and nuts will look like fine gravel. Test to see if a small amount will roll together into a ball between your fingers.

Remove the blade and shape, a teaspoon at a time, into balls.

Place in a container, cover airtight, and refrigerate until needed. Serve at room temperature.

Peach Truffles

Substitute moist dried peaches, or a combination of peaches and apricots, for the dates; use almonds instead of pecans.

Sorbets

PINK CRANSHAW SORBET
WITH VODKA

Makes 6 to 8 servings, about 4 cups

This soft, delicately flavored sorbet makes an elegant light finish to a late summer meal. There is enough vodka in the recipe not only to add balance to the flavors of the fruits, but also to make this an adult dessert. You can, of course, use sliced fresh strawberries instead of the raspberries. Eaux-de-vie are flavored white brandies. Inexpensive white brandies taste like chemically scented gasoline, but the fine, expensive eaux-de-vie have the fragrance of a field of fresh fruit, the texture of the fruit as you swallow, and a burst of alcohol in the back of your throat. Rare as they are, eaux-de-vie are worth exploring. They are not like flavored vodkas.

1 large (about 4 pounds) ripe cranshaw melon, peeled, seeded, and cut
    into 2- to 3-inch chunks
1/3 cup fresh raspberries
1/2 cup vodka or framboise eau-de-vie
1 or 2 teaspoons sugar

Toss the melon into a blender or food processor and process to form a thick, chunky liquid. Pour the liquid into a separate bowl. Drop the raspberries into the blender or processor and add about half the liquefied melon. Blend until smooth. Pour through a strainer, and repeat with the remaining melon so that you have a light pink mixture, melony tasting with just a hint of raspberry. Stir in the vodka or a framboise eau-de-vie and a teaspoon or so of sugar, if necessary, to make the liquid just a touch on the sweet side, as freezing it will make it taste less sweet.

Freeze in an ice cream freezer according to the manufacturer's directions. If not serving immediately, transfer to a microwave-safe freezer container and store in the freezer. The sorbet will become very hard. To soften before serving, microwave on high for 1 minute 15 seconds to 1 minute 30 seconds.

BLACKBERRY, PINEAPPLE,
AND PEACH SORBET

Makes 8 servings, about 4 cups

This is a thick, chewy sorbet with a flavor evenly balanced among the 3 fruits. It screams with the flavors of summer. Raspberries or blueberries (use only 1/4 cup) are good substitutes for the blackberries.

If you have a juice extractor, you can make a cup of your own peach nectar (juice) by extracting 3 large, lusciously ripe peaches. Otherwise, it can be purchased canned in premium supermarkets.

1/2 cup fresh washed ripe blackberries, or frozen blackberries
1 small ripe pineapple, peeled, cored, and cut into 1- to 2-inch chunks
1 cup peach nectar
About 3 to 4 tablespoons sugar

In 2 or 3 batches, purée the blackberries, pineapple, and peach nectar in a blender. Strain, gently shaking or rapping the strainer against the bowl, and discard any pulp that remains.

Taste the purée. It will usually need at least 2, sometimes 3 or 4 tablespoons of sugar to bring out the flavors. The purée, though a little acidic, needs to be just slightly sweet, as freezing will dull the sweetness.

Freeze in an ice cream maker according to the manufacturer's directions. If not serving immediately, transfer to a microwave-safe freezer container and store in the freezer. The sorbet will become very hard. To soften before serving, microwave on high (100%) for 1 minute 15 seconds to 1 minute 30 seconds.

KIWI SORBET

Makes 8 servings, about 4 cups

With its fuzzy brown skin, its soft green flesh, its sweet flavor, and its jet-black-speckled interior, this once quite exotic fruit makes a beautiful sorbet.

3 pounds (about 18) ripe kiwis, peeled
Juice of ½ lime
1 or 2 tablespoons sugar

Cut the kiwis into chunks and toss into a food processor. Add the lime juice and process until smooth. Taste and add enough sugar to give the purée a slightly sweet flavor.

Freeze in an ice cream maker according to the manufacturer's directions. If not serving immediately, transfer to a microwave-safe freezer container and store in the freezer. The sorbet will become very hard. To soften before serving, microwave on high (100%) for 1 minute 15 seconds to 1 minute 30 seconds.

11

Canning and Preserving

Sweet-and-Sour Corn Relish
Onion and Fennel Relish
Dilled Green Beans
Lebanese Pink Pickled Turnips
Homemade Ketchup
Brandied Cherries

Introduction

Canning is safe, easy, and enormously satisfying. Unfortunately, most canning recipes are so laden with warnings and cautions that many a would-be canner is scared off before beginning. The process is time-consuming and a bit messy, but it is simple, and everything you need to know to can successfully is clearly explained here and in the recipe for Sweet-and-Sour Corn Relish, page 313.

Although canning was once the method of choice for jams, jellies, and preserves, I now freeze these and can only pickles and relishes.

Canning is more than just a way of preserving foods. It is a way of getting closer to our food, of sharing essential elements of our lives with our friends and neighbors, either in the process of canning, or in the giving of our home-canned foods as gifts.

The Basics of Canning

What to Expect (and Not Expect) from Your First Day at Canning

Expect much of the kitchen to be splattered or dripped upon. There is just no way to keep the kitchen clean, much less immaculate, while canning.

Expect the canning to take longer than you planned. Canning is not something you can rush.

Expect to get burned at least once, though not seriously. You'll be amazed at how far boiling liquid can spatter and spurt, so wear long sleeves, jeans or long pants (no shorts or skirts), and socks with an old pair of shoes.

Don't expect to produce a whole cupboard of canned goods on your first day. Start out slowly. Never double a recipe. Recipes that produce about 8 pints are just right for home canning. More than that and you probably won't have enough burners for the cooking or enough arms for the stirring. And remember, an overly ambitious first day might just end your desire ever to can again.

Expect to produce only 2 recipes in a day, each yielding 6 to 8 jars.

Essential Equipment

The most important piece of equipment is a canning kettle fitted with a 7-compartment rack capable of holding quart jars (about $40). While any large pot and a cake rack could be used, a jury-rigged setup is neither safe nor satisfying to use. Two other essentials are a canning funnel (about $5), which has a wide mouth and is designed to fit securely inside the mouth of the jar, making filling the jars quick and easy, and a jar-lifter (about $5), which is a specially shaped set of tongs used to lift the jars out of the boiling waterbath.

Canning Jars

Have a sufficient supply of Mason or Ball jars, with their lids and bands, on hand before beginning to can. Wide-mouthed jars are easier to fill and handle than the traditional narrow-mouthed jars.

In canning, the jars are sealed with dome lids (flat metal disks with a sealing compound on the perimeter of one side) that are held in place by threaded ring bands. After being filled and covered, the jars are submerged in a boiling waterbath, then cooled. After the seal on the lids has been checked, some people remove the bands and store them for future use. I leave the bands in place for added security, and for ease of use when the jar is opened, saving those bands after the jar has been emptied. The jars and bands, if undamaged, can be reused, but always use new lids.

While there are several other types of canning jars available, with other types of sealing mechanisms, these are the most widely available and the safest and easiest to use. Regardless of the type of jars you use, can only in jars made for canning, and never use a jar or lid that is cracked, rusted, or damaged in any way.

Wooden Spoons for Stirring

Although any long-handled nonaluminum (nonreactive) spoon will do for canning, wooden spoons are not only nonreactive but they act as insulators, preventing the spoon from getting so hot that it accidentally burns your hand.

311

Unbreakable Rules

Never can alone; canning is a communal activity. On the other hand, don't invite half the neighborhood to come by. One friend to help, and to talk to, is all that is necessary or useful.

Plan to spend the whole day canning. Don't consider stopping until everything has been finished and the kitchen is clean and back to normal.

Don't buy more produce than needed for a single batch of a recipe. And don't let yourself get conned into buying a bushel of peaches just because it was only $2 more than half a bushel—you'll regret having that many peaches rot in your kitchen while you try to find the time to can again and everyone in the house grows to hate peaches because you have sliced them onto everything you have served for 3 days.

SWEET-AND-SOUR CORN RELISH

Master Recipe

Makes about 7 pints

This recipe, which produces an utterly American, colorful, sweet-and-sour corn relish, can be used as a guide to all canning and preserving, for once you've mastered the basic techniques, there is little difference between putting up brandied cherries and putting up dill pickles.

Add this relish to sandwiches, use as a garnish on plates of cold summer foods, or as a side dish on any summer or winter buffet.

20 ears sweet, tender corn, about ¼ bushel
2 cups coarsely chopped green bell peppers
2 cups coarsely chopped red bell peppers
2 cups coarsely chopped celery
2 cups coarsely chopped onions
2 cups sugar
1½ tablespoons pickling salt
1½ tablespoons mustard seeds
1½ tablespoons celery seeds
1 tablespoon dried dill weed
3¾ cups cider vinegar (5 percent acidity)

Checking the Jars, Lids, and Bands

Inspect the jars. Be certain that none is cracked or chipped. Check the rims carefully. Cracks will cause the jars to break when heated, and chips on the threading or rims will prevent proper sealing. Discard any damaged jars.

Examine the lids. These must be new, or at least never used. The lids should be flat. If they are bent from storage or mishandling, they will not seal properly. Also, inspect the sealing compound, the rings around the bottom of the lids. These should appear clean, showing no signs of rust or mold. Wash with soapy warm water, then rinse under running hot tap water and gently wipe dry. If lids are not absolutely clean and apparently in perfect condition, discard.

Examine the bands. Check to see that the threaded bands are clean and that none has been bent out of shape. These can be washed in hot water with some kitchen detergent, if dirty. If bent, discard because they will not fasten to the jars properly.

Preparing the Equipment for Canning

To ensure that no bacteria or fungus is accidentally introduced into canned foods, the jars must be sterilized, and all the other canning equipment must be thoroughly washed and kept clean throughout the canning process.

Sterilizing the jars: In the dishwasher, place the already inspected 7 pint-size jars, their bands (not the lids; the dishwasher would destroy the sealing compound), and a large ladle. Run the dishwasher fully through its longest cycle, including a heated drying. Use the manufacturer's recommended amount of dishwasher detergent, and pour 1/4 cup household bleach into the bottom of the dishwasher just before turning it on.

If you are not ready to use the jars or ladle when the dishwasher finishes its heated drying cycle, simply leave the dishwasher closed to keep the equipment sterile.

Wash out the canner kettle and its cover with lots of hot soapy water, rinse thoroughly, then fill it with enough hot tap water to reach 2 inches above the jars when they are inserted into the rack.

(After the first batch of jars have been filled and inserted in the kettle, make a note of how high the water level should be for future canning.)

Wash the funnel and a large clean bowl with lots of soapy water and then rinse for about 30 seconds under the hottest possible tap water. Shake the bowl dry, then fill it with the hottest water that flows from the sink, and place the funnel in hot water.

Place the lids in a small saucepan and fill with the hottest water that flows from the sink. Set aside.

Find the jar lifter and place it conveniently near the stovetop.

Preparing the Relish

When all the equipment is ready, prepare the relish.

Shuck the corn and remove all the silk adhering to the ears. Rinse under running cold water, then with a sharp paring knife (or with one of those special devices for removing corn from the cob that are sold in some housewares shops), stand the corn on its stalk end and, cutting downward, keeping the knife as close to the cob as possible, remove the kernels, tossing them into a very large non-aluminum bowl.

Add the green and red peppers, the celery, and the onions and mix well.

Combine the remaining ingredients in a very large nonaluminum kettle and bring to a boil over high heat, stirring once or twice to dissolve the sugar. Add the mixed vegetables to the boiling liquid and allow it to come back to a boil. Cover and set aside.

Filling the Jars

Place the saucepan containing the lids on a burner set over high heat and bring the water to just under a boil, until steam just begins to rise from the surface. Remove from the heat and set aside. This will soften the compound around the edge of the lids, ensuring that the lids adhere properly to the jars. Remove the jars and bands from the dishwasher, as well as the ladle.

Arrange the jars on the counter and place the kettle holding the relish close by. Remove the funnel from the water, shake dry, and insert into one of the jars. Stir the relish and ladle it through the funnel into the jar. Fill all the jars so that the relish comes to 1/4 inch below the top of the jar. This is known as leaving "1/4 inch headspace." The crease in the funnel is at exactly the same point as the top of the jar, so use it as a guide when filling the jars. By letting the top edge of the funnel touch the side of the kettle, you can ladle the jars full with very little dripping onto the counter. Remove the funnel. Wrap a clean kitchen towel around your index finger and dip it into hot water. Rub around the top edge of each jar to be sure that the surface is clean and free of any drippings.

Carefully lift the lids out of the water, shake dry, and place them, sealing compound side down, on the top of the jars. Screw a band very securely onto each jar. Do not tighten too hard, because the lid will have to give slightly during the processing so the air inside can escape.

Processing

Processing is a "cooking" of the jars in a waterbath. Processing serves 2 purposes. It sterilizes the food inside the jars, and vacuum-seals them at the same time. Always process for the time recommended in a recipe to ensure that the jars are safe for storage.

Lift the rack in the canner kettle up and hang it on the sides of the kettle. Place the first jar in the center well so that the rack will remain balanced as the jars are added, then add the remaining jars, remembering to keep the rack balanced by placing the jars on opposite sides of the rack.

Lower the rack to the bottom of the pot, then release the handles. Check to see that the water comes 2 inches above the tops of the jars. If not, add additional hot tap water. Cover and "process" for exactly 10 minutes from the time the water comes to a full rolling boil.

Cooling

After the full 10 minutes of processing, carefully lift the handles of the rack out of the water and secure them on the sides of the kettle again. Using the jar lifter, remove the relish, one jar at a time, and place them on a large cake rack or wooden surface, leaving plenty of space between the jars as they cool. (Do not place the jars in a draft or on a cold surface, which could cause cracking.) Do not tighten the bands after the jars are removed from the waterbath, as this can cause the seal to break. Some of the bands may be quite loose.

As you lift the jars out of the water, some may make a clicking sound, indicating that the seal is complete. Some will not make that clicking *pop* sound until the relish is considerably cooler.

In several hours, when the jars have cooled completely, check the seals. Do this by tapping on the tops of the lids. If the lids make no sound, or if there is a click and the lids stay down, the seals are complete. If the lids pop up and down when tapped, the seal is not complete.

Any jar that is not completely sealed, regardless of the reason, should be opened, the relish transferred to another container, and then stored in the refrigerator for current use.

Storing

Label the contents of the jars and date them. Place the labels on the sides of the jars if storing on open shelving; write (or paste on a label) directly onto the lids if storing in boxes.

Store the jars in a dark, cool place. Ideally, the temperature should be 50 to 60 degrees F. Light can cause some canned foods to discolor, as can temperatures that are too warm. But even under less than ideal storage conditions (I store most of my canned goods in cardboard boxes in the bottom of my coat closet), the relish can be kept for 2 or 3 years.

ONION AND FENNEL RELISH

Makes 6 half-pints

Onions and fennel combine here with tarragon and a hint of rosemary to make a sweet tarragon-flavored relish. The relish is easy to prepare and cooks in about half an hour, with very little mess in the kitchen.

Because fennel and onions are available most of the year, you can make this relish any time. Since most canning requires the summer's bounty, I usually make this recipe on a snowy winter Sunday.

Use this relish on hot or cold sandwiches, to accompany roasted meats or richly flavored fish, or stir some into leftover rice or vegetables to give them new life.

Important special note: Please read through the master recipe for canning on page 313, which explains the easiest and safest way to sterilize, fill, seal, waterbathe, cool, and store home-canned foods.

2 pounds large Spanish onions, peeled and cut into eighths

A 2-inch piece gingerroot, peeled

3 medium-sized fennel bulbs, trimmed, outer layer removed if discolored

1 teaspoon fennel seeds

1 teaspoon crushed dried rosemary

1/2 cup sugar

1/2 cup rice vinegar or white wine vinegar

1/2 cup water

1 tablespoon dried tarragon

In small batches, combine the onion, ginger, and fennel in a food processor and pulse rapidly until finely chopped. Transfer to a large nonaluminum pot, add the fennel seeds, rosemary, sugar, vinegar, and water, and bring to a boil over medium heat, stirring occasionally. Cover, reduce the heat, and simmer for 15 minutes.

Uncover, stir in the tarragon, and cook until most of the liquid has evaporated, about 15 to 20 minutes longer.

While the relish is cooking, ready 6 half-pint jars, plus their lids and bands for canning.

Fill each jar with relish, leaving ¼ inch of headspace. Rap the jars on the counter to remove any bubbles and to pack the relish down, then check the headspace. Add more relish, if necessary, to maintain ¼ inch of headspace. Cover, seal, and process for 10 minutes in a waterbath, as directed in the master recipe.

Cool, check seals, and store as directed in the master recipe.

DILLED GREEN BEANS

Makes 6 pints

Use these dilled beans to accompany plates of cold summer foods, main-course salads, or as a garnish for sandwiches and school lunches.

Use young, tender green beans. When picking them in the market, choose beans that are all the same diameter so that they will cook to the same degree of doneness during processing.

Important special note: Please read through the master recipe for canning on page 313, which explains the easiest and safest way to sterilize, fill, seal, waterbathe, cool, and store home-canned foods.

6 bushy stalks fresh dill, thoroughly rinsed under running cold water
12 big, fat garlic cloves, peeled
2 tablespoons dill seeds
2 tablespoons mustard seeds
2 tablespoons celery seeds
2 tablespoons dried oregano
3½ pounds tender young green beans, washed, snapped, and strung
3 cups water
3 cups cider vinegar (5 percent acidity)
6 tablespoons pickling salt

Ready 6 pint-size jars plus their lids and bands for canning.

Into each jar, place the top 3 to 4 inches of a single stem of fresh dill, 2 garlic cloves, and a scant ½ teaspoon each dill seeds, mustard seeds, celery seeds, and dried oregano.

Line the beans up neatly in small bundles, then pack them as tightly as you can into the jars, with the beans standing upright.

Bring the water, vinegar, and salt to a full boil and ladle over the beans, leaving

1/4 inch headspace. Rap the jars on the counter to remove any bubbles, then check the headspace. Add more liquid, if necessary. Cover, seal, and process as directed in the master recipe. Process very young, thin, tender beans for 10 minutes; medium-sized, still young but not quite so tender beans for 16 minutes.

Cool, check seals, and store as directed in the master recipe.

LEBANESE PINK PICKLED TURNIPS

Makes 4 quarts

My pickling partner, Bob Galano, says that this recipe for very gently spiced pickled turnips has been in his family for generations, his mother having learned it at her mother's knee more than 60 years ago. Around his house, Bob calls it Nana's pickled turnips, while his mother refers to it by the Arabic her mother used, ach-ar liffet.

Serve these as an accent to a meal of fresh summer vegetables, or heap in a bowl and serve as part of a large party buffet or picnic. In winter, these festive-looking turnips will spice up any holiday meal.

Allspice berries (so named because they are traditionally described as having the flavors of all these spices: cinnamon, nutmeg, and mace) are available in some supermarkets, most premium food markets, and specialty spice shops. Kosher salt is available in most supermarkets.

Important special note: Please read through the master recipe for canning on page 313, which explains the easiest and safest way to sterilize, fill, seal, waterbathe, cool, and store home-canned foods.

2 cups distilled white vinegar
2 cups water
¼ cup kosher salt (do not use table salt)
5 pounds medium-sized white turnips, root ends cut off, peeled, and quartered
1 large beet (about 4 ounces), root end cut off, peeled, and quartered
4 garlic cloves, peeled
1 teaspoon allspice berries

Bring a very large pot of water to a boil over high heat.

In a nonaluminum pot set over medium heat, combine the vinegar, water, and kosher salt. Cook, stirring occasionally, until the salt is dissolved and the liquid is very hot, but not boiling.

Add the turnips and beet to the boiling water and allow the water to return to a boil, then reduce the heat and simmer for 2 minutes. This is not meant to cook the turnips and beet, but only to make them very hot. Immediately drain and set aside to cool slightly.

When vegetables are just cool enough to handle, but still somewhat hot, place 1 piece of beet, 1 garlic clove, and ¼ teaspoon allspice berries in each of 4 sterile quart jars, then fill with turnips. Pour into each jar enough of the hot vinegar and water mixture to cover the turnips, leaving ½ inch headspace, then seal, process in the waterbath for 15 minutes, cool, and store.

HOMEMADE KETCHUP

Makes four ¹/₂-pint jars

Ketchup making isn't nearly as much fun as serving homemade ketchup, which invariably leads to questions like "Why would anyone in their right mind make ketchup?" and "Is it ketchup or catsup?" In response to the first question, I make ketchup because I find satisfaction in spending a few hours in the kitchen in late August playing around with gads and gads of luxuriously ripe plum tomatoes. For me, ketchup making is fun, even if it takes a lot of stirring and it makes a mess. To the second question, I answer, with no explanation, that it is "ketchup," not "catsup."

Homemade ketchup, unlike the plastic-bottled, over-sweetened, and under-flavored ketchups sold in supermarkets, has a deep tomato flavor full of character and dimension, with a spicy (but not hot) complex flavor, a slight sweetness, and a gentle tartness.

Important special note: Please read through the master recipe for canning on page 313, which explains the easiest and safest way to sterilize, fill, seal, waterbathe, cool, and store home-canned foods.

5 pounds ripe plum tomatoes, rinsed under running cold tap water,
   cored, and very coarsely chopped
1 large onion, peeled and coarsely chopped
1 large tart apple, quartered and cored
1 celery rib, cut into 1-inch pieces
Two 6-ounce cans tomato paste
3/4 cup dark brown sugar
1 1/4 cups balsamic or red wine vinegar
8 whole cloves
1/2 teaspoon celery seeds
2 tablespoons sweet Hungarian paprika
1 teaspoon cinnamon
1 teaspoon ground coriander seeds
1/2 teaspoon ground allspice
1 teaspoon fennel seeds
1/2 teaspoon anise seeds
1 teaspoon black peppercorns
2 teaspoons salt

Combine all the ingredients in a large nonaluminum kettle and bring to a boil over medium heat. Stir everything together, then reduce the heat and simmer, partially covered, for 1 hour.

In small batches, ladle the ketchup into a blender and purée. Hold the top securely in place to prevent the ketchup from spewing out of the blender. Pour into a fine strainer and, with the back of a spoon, press the ketchup through the strainer. Discard the fibrous material left in the strainer.

Rinse the pot and pour the strained ketchup back into it. Set over low heat and simmer, uncovered (it will now sputter, splatter, and seethe, so be careful), stirring occasionally, until it thickens to the texture you think ketchup should be, about 1 to 1 1/2 hours. After about 1 hour, taste the ketchup. Add a little more brown sugar, vinegar, or salt if necessary to balance the flavors.

To test the ketchup for thickness, stir it together, lift out a tablespoonful, and place it in the freezer. In about 5 minutes, this sample will be cold and will indicate the final texture of the ketchup. Simmer a little longer if you want it thicker. If it is too thick, add a cup of tomato juice, simmer for 10 to 15 minutes, then test again.

Ladle into sterile jars, seal, process in the waterbath for 10 minutes, cool, and store.

BRANDIED CHERRIES

Makes 10 pints

Eating large, dark, sweet Bing cherries, cold from the refrigerator, is one of the quiet little pleasures of summer. Canning them, especially with the intention of using them as house gifts and Christmas presents, is another one of summer's pleasures.

These cherries are made with 2 different kinds of brandy (a white brandy, called an eau de vie in French) and a Cognac. Both are expensive. Each pint of these cherries could cost as much as $7 to $8.

Important special note: Please read through the master recipe for canning on page 313, which explains the easiest and safest way to sterilize, fill, seal, waterbathe, cool, and store home-canned foods.

10 pounds plump Bing cherries
4 cups cold water
1½ cups fine-quality kirsch (white cherry brandy, see page 305)
2 cups granulated sugar
Thinly peeled zest of 1 lemon
About 1½ quarts fine-quality Cognac

Ready enough jars, lids, and bands for canning 10 pints or 5 quarts.

Pick over the cherries, discarding any that are bruised or damaged, and remove the stems. Place in a colander and rinse thoroughly under running cold water. Drain and set aside.

In a nonaluminum kettle large enough to hold all the cherries, stir together the water, kirsch, sugar, and lemon zest and bring to a boil over medium high heat. Lower the heat and boil gently for 5 minutes. Add the cherries, all at once, and raise the heat to high. As soon as the cooking liquid returns to a boil, quickly but carefully drain the cherries, saving the cooking liquid.

Spoon the cherries into sterile jars, rapping the jars on the counter just firmly enough for the cherries to settle down. Add enough cherries to fill each jar within about ³/₄ inch of the tops of the jars. Fill the jars halfway with Cognac, then add enough of the reserved cooking juices to just cover the cherries. There should be ¹/₂ inch of headspace.

Cover the jars, then process in a boiling waterbath, 15 minutes for pint jars, 20 minutes for quart jars. Cool, then check the seals.

Store in a cool, dark place for at least a month before serving.

Other Recipes for Canning

Although I generally freeze fruit sauces, preserves, and butters, they can all be canned and jarred, which, if you are giving them as gifts, is considerably more appealing than a soggy plastic bag.

To can the recipes listed below, read through the master recipe for canning on page 313, which explains the easiest and safest way to sterilize, fill, seal, waterbathe, cool, and store home-canned foods. Allow 10 minutes in the waterbath for ¹/₂ pint jars, and 15 minutes in the waterbath for pint jars.

Fresh Blueberry Sauce (page 55)
Blueberry Preserves (page 67)
Peach Butter (page 69)
Pear Butter (page 71)
Apple Butter (page 73)

Index

329

Index